ｊ

The Journeys series celebrates John Murray's history of publishing exceptional travel writing by rediscovering classic journeys from the past, introduced by today's most exciting writers.

We want the series to capture the wonder that comes from travelling, opening our imaginations to unfamiliar places and cultures, and allowing us to see familiar things through different eyes. These Journeys give fresh perspectives not only on the times and places in which they were originally published, but on the time and place we find ourselves in now.

As a traveller who has walked and written across much of Europe, the author of *Walking the Woods and the Water*, *Where the Wild Winds Are* (both finalists for the Stanford Dolman Travel Book of the Year), and most recently *Outlandish: Walking Europe's Unlikely Landscapes*, I am thrilled to have the role of seeking out these books. Hundreds of suggestions have come to me from the travel writing, nature writing and adventure communities, and also, appropriately enough, through serendipity – one of the titles on last year's list was dropped through my letterbox by a passing neighbour.

In this spirit of chance discovery, we invite your suggestions for books to republish in the future. We are looking for titles currently out of print in the UK, books that have been forgotten about, left to languish on dusty bookshop shelves, or that were unjustly ignored when they were first published – potentially including translated works by foreign language writers. If you have a suggestion, please get in touch with us on Twitter @johnmurrays or @underscrutiny. #JMJourneys

Nick Hunt, Series Editor

SYED MUJTABA ALI

A BENGALI IN AFGHANISTAN

In a Land Far from Home

INTRODUCED BY TARAN KHAN
TRANSLATED FROM THE BENGALI BY NAZES AFROZ

JOHN MURRAY

First published in Great Britain in 2022 by John Murray (Publishers)
An Hachette UK company

1

A CIP catalogue record for this title is available from the British Library

Paperback ISBN 978-1-399-80250-5
eBook ISBN 978-1-399-80251-2

Typeset in Hewer Text UK Ltd, Edinburgh
Printed and bound in Great Britain by Clays Ltd, Elcograf S.p.A.

John Murray policy is to use papers that are natural, renewable and
recyclable products and made from wood grown in sustainable forests.
The logging and manufacturing processes are expected to conform
to the environmental regulations of the country of origin.

John Murray (Publishers)
Carmelite House
50 Victoria Embankment
London EC4Y 0DZ

www.johnmurraypress.co.uk

To Moska Najib

*A dear Afghan friend whose persistence
made me take up this translation*

Contents

Introduction

In 1927, the young college graduate Syed Mujtaba Ali boarded a train in what was then called Calcutta on his way to his first job in Kabul. The journey spanned a vast physical distance, traversing the entire subcontinent. It was also a move from the idealistic, culturally erudite campus of Shantiniketan, the educational institution set up by renowned poet Rabindranath Tagore, to the unfamiliar terrain that lay beyond the Khyber Pass.

He arrived at a moment of transition in the city's life. The ruler, Amir Amanullah, was following the example of Mustafa Kemal in Turkey and Reza Shah in Iran, and pushing Afghanistan towards modernisation. In fact, Ali's own appointment as a teacher was part of this larger effort. It was in this 'land far from home' that Ali spent two years, living in a small village on the outskirts of the capital, wandering its bazaars, playing badminton with the king's brother, moving between ordinary Afghans, fellow Indians and the lively set of foreigners who inhabited the capital then. If anyone tried to achieve the impossible task of socialising across all the groups of Kabul's social life, he noted wryly, 'he would then be considered a spy'.

I walked through Kabul nearly eight tumultuous decades after Ali, in the period between 2006 and 2013. Despite the long years in between our journeys, reading his descriptions felt like encountering a memory from my own travels, or finding a friend to recall shared vistas with. Like the thrill I felt on encountering this portrait of the seasons shifting: 'Kabul showed the signs of middle-age spread at the end of autumn, its belly grew fatter and it seemed as though it was walking with a certain gravitas. The wheat and maize grains swelled, the apples were about to burst, even the leaves of the trees had become thick by sucking in air, sunlight and rain during the summer months.'

Passages like these are a testimony to Ali's skills as a writer, as well as an ode to the timeless city we both fell in love with.

For a place deeply inscribed in popular imagination by Western writers, Ali offers a unique perspective. These are the impressions of a precocious – only twenty-three-year-old – Bengali intellectual, with a keenly felt affinity to the city he is exploring. These are also the observations of an ardent nationalist and votary of India's struggle against British colonial rule – a perspective that makes him part envious, part admiring of Afghanistan's freedom. Listening to an Afghan border officer discuss the defeats inflicted on the British army in Egypt and Turkey, Ali writes: 'I almost jumped. Total sedition! No, not here. I had forgotten I was sitting in independent Afghanistan.'

It would be easy to describe this translation of *Deshe Bideshe* by Nazes Afroz as bringing an 'unknown' work into recognition. Except that Ali is one of the best-known figures in the illustrious pantheon of Bengali writers, and this memoir evokes instant recognition and near-universal affection from readers of the language. For generations of such readers, Ali's book has been an important literary connection to Afghanistan, one forged in part by his own teacher, Rabindranath Tagore, with his short story 'Kabuliwala', 'The Man from Kabul'. This translation places him in the company of the great travel writers of the world, a spot he richly deserves. It is also a reminder that travel, and writing on travel, comes from all directions.

It is possible to see the many sides of Ali's eclectic personality flitting through these pages. He was a statesman and diplomat; a polyglot who spoke around twelve languages, including Farsi and Pashto. The author of at least twenty-eight books, and a scholar educated at centres of learning as diverse as Bonn in Germany and Al-Azhar in Cairo – an education which deeply shaped how he saw the world. In fact, Ali embodied the kind of cosmopolitanism that is often assumed to be the domain, if not the invention, of Western writers, but has a long history spanning across Bengal to Iran, Egypt, Sudan and beyond.

But it is not only his unmistakable achievements that make this a remarkable book. It is not even Ali's skills as a raconteur, though from the first page onwards he keeps readers hooked with his witty portraits of characters, like the lonely Afghan border official reciting poetry to a river, or his faithful manservant Abdur Rahman's efforts to build up his diminutive employer's appetite to a healthy Afghan standard. 'A kilo of lamb qorma was swimming in a thick gravy of onion and ghee . . . while one outcast potato was trying to kill itself by drowning in one corner. There were eight jumbo-sized shami kebabs on a plate. A big serving dish was full of pulao with a roasted chicken sitting on top. Seeing me speechless, Abdur Rahman hurriedly said, "I have more in the kitchen."'

For me, the heart of this book is Ali's connection to Kabul. It is in the closely observed details he records with loving attention: the descriptions of its seasons and its people, of Abdur Rahman dreamily reciting the many kinds of snowflakes that fall in his native Panjshir, of Ali's homesickness evoked by the Kabul twilight, sparking the memory of his mother offering her night-time prayers in faraway Bengal. This is the Kabul that Ali illuminates for us; a place that, despite the book's title, feels close to home.

I came to Ali by way of the works of European travellers. For many of them, Afghanistan was a distant place, an empty canvas to be filled with their own urges and interpretations. Ali's book has no such ambitions, and is richer for it. With him, we spend long evenings in meandering conversations with friends, fuelled by endless cups of tea. His expeditions into the city come with a sense of affectionate intimacy, with tongue-in-cheek passages like this one:

If a lazy man ever wanted to make a trip but did not want to go through the troubles of sightseeing, then the best place for him to go to would be the narrow Kabul valley. Because, there was nothing worth seeing in Kabul . . . I was talking about ordinary tourists who had seen the shrines of Delhi, Agra or Secundra Bagh. There was nothing in Kabul to dazzle that lot. So you would not have to go on sightseeing tours after reaching Kabul. You would not have to walk barefoot on a hot stony terrace at midday for six furlongs; you would not have to climb steep spiral stairs through the stench of bat droppings . . . Hence Kabul was a beautiful city. And the best part was that you could see the city without much trouble. Some friend or the other would take you to one of the gardens to spend the whole day.

Alongside such interludes are insights into the complicated fallout of Amir Amanullah's modernisation measures. Ali reports seeing shops shut due to a sudden royal decree that business could no longer be carried out while seated on the floor, on traditional carpets. 'Every shop has to have chairs and tables like the way it is in the West.' By the stream in Paghman, the king's summer capital west of Kabul, he found members of Afghanistan's newly formed parliament uncomfortably kitted out in morning suits with silk top hats, walking through the woods barefoot. After watching the king talk to this ill-at-ease assembly the next day, he wrote, 'I did not know if they made any sense of Amanullah's speech – you could speak the same language yet you might not be able to communicate.'

By the winter of 1929, Afghanistan was caught up in a rebellion against Amir Amanullah. Ali's account captures the sense of tumultuous ending that unfolded. As the rebel troops took over the capital, he watched Amir Amanullah's pet white elephant – brought to Kabul from India – being ridden by the soldiers of the new king. Amanullah's impressive motor cars too were driven around until they ran out of fuel, and then abandoned.

There is another contemporary resonance at the end of this book that is particularly heartbreaking. As foreign nationals were airlifted to safety, Ali and his Indian friend found their names missing from the list of evacuees. 'Both of us agreed that the humiliation of a colonised country could not be felt fully until you went abroad,' he writes, in a pithy summary of powerlessness and the collapse of empires. The connection across the decades, to the images from Kabul airport after the Taliban's takeover in August 2021, is impossible to miss.

I have returned to this book repeatedly, and have thrust it on anyone who asks me what to read about Afghanistan. In Ali's Kabul, I found the city I began my own book by evoking. 'There it is, there it is not,' I wrote of this elusive place of beauty and history, a city that appeared and vanished, that seemed somehow known, yet new. 'Kabul appears where you don't expect to see it.'

This never felt truer than when I found a countryman, a writer for the world, wandering the streets of this city, waiting for listeners.

Taran N. Khan, April 2022

Translator's Note

As a teenager, when I picked up Syed Mujtaba Ali's *Deshe Bideshe*, literally meaning 'Home and Abroad', from the shelf of a library, little did I know that I had chosen a book that was to become a companion for life. The book stayed with me forever. I have read the book a couple of times a year since then and do so even now.

Deshe Bideshe was Syed Mujtaba Ali's debut book. First published in 1948 from Kolkata, it still continues to attract new readers in West Bengal, which remained his home for nearly five decades, and Bangladesh, which was his country of birth. There are hardly any discerning readers of Bengali literature who will not have read the book or appreciated it. Such is the cult attraction of the book.

Even though it was published in 1948, *Deshe Bideshe* was in the making for nearly twenty years. As a young man just out of college, Mujtaba Ali decided to take up a teaching job in Kabul in 1927. In those days not many young Bengali men would venture to a land like Afghanistan that was completely unknown to them. It was not a country one could travel to very easily in those days. The journey to Kabul from Kolkata was tough, in parts dangerous, but a gold mine for seekers of adventure and for gifted writers. When Mujtaba Ali made the journey in 1927 and spent the following year and a half in Kabul he was no writer of any description. He was then merely a young man of twenty-three, with a mercurial brain and an extremely inquisitive mind, who was ready to delve into the unknown. With these gifts, he picked up fascinating nuggets about Afghan lives and history, and kept on distilling them for almost twenty years as he grew in experience and knowledge, to eventually produce a classic like *Deshe Bideshe*.

Born on 13 September 1904 in Sylhet district in erstwhile East Bengal (now Bangladesh), in a well-known Pir family, Mujtaba Ali went to study at the Visva-Bharati University in Shantiniketan in 1923 when it was founded by the Nobel Laureate poet, philosopher and educationist Rabindranath Tagore. Shantiniketan was a great experiment in education by Tagore who wanted to create a seat of learning embedded in humanism, social awareness, creativity and internationalism. Under the direct tutelage of Tagore, Mujtaba Ali absorbed these values. So it was no wonder Mujtaba Ali wanted to explore the world and Afghanistan was his first stop. He would make many more journeys all through his life. After his sojourn in Kabul, Mujtaba Ali completed his Ph.D (on the origins of the Khojas and their religious life today) in comparative religion in Germany between 1929 and 1932 when he witnessed the rise of the Nazi party and Hitler, accounts of which made their way into his later writings. Finishing his degree in Germany he went on to do his post-doctoral studies at Al-Azhar University in Cairo (1934–5) before returning to India permanently. Upon returning to India, Mujtaba Ali got a job as the principal of the government college in the princely state of Baroda from 1936 to 1944. Following the death of the ruler of Baroda, he came back to Kolkata and did not take up any jobs for a few years when he travelled and started writing *Deshe*

Bideshe, which was to be serialised in the Bengali literary magazine *Desh* published from Kolkata, in 1948, before coming out in book form.

Following the partition of India and Bengal, he moved to his homeland, East Pakistan (now Bangladesh), briefly and joined a college in Bogura as its principal in 1949. But he returned to India in 1950, leaving his family behind, to become the first secretary of the newly formed Indian Council of Cultural Relations or the ICCR, a brainchild of India's first education minister, Maulana Abul Kalam Azad. He also edited the Arabic journal of the ICCR, *Thaqafat-ul-Hind*.

In 1952, Mujtaba Ali joined the All India Radio in New Delhi and later became its station director in Cuttack and Patna.

Finally, in 1956, he moved to his alma mater Visva-Bharati University, which had by then become a central university under the patronage of Prime Minister Jawaharlal Nehru and Abul Kalam Azad. He became a professor of the German language and later of Islamic Culture. Mujtaba Ali taught at Visva-Bharati until his retirement in 1969 after which he became a full-time writer and divided his time between Shantiniketan and Kolkata.

After the war of independence and the creation of Bangladesh in 1971, Mujtaba Ali spent considerable time in Dhaka with his family until his death on 11 February 1974.

Mujtaba Ali had the most amazing gift for learning languages. So no wonder he was a polyglot who mastered twelve languages – Bengali, English, Hindi, Urdu, Marathi, Gujarati, Farsi, Pashto, Arabic, German, French and Russian.

Such impressive language skills and wide experience of travelling to many countries enabled him to make sophisticated multilingual and multi-cultural references in his accounts. While this crossover at times makes his prose and content hard to penetrate, it enriches the text and makes it unique for the literature of that period.

While living in Kabul, Mujtaba Ali was at the epicentre of one of reformist King Amanullah's pet projects, which aimed to provide 'modern' education to his subjects through new schools, colleges and training centres for boys and girls. Drawing on the examples of Kemal Ataturk's modernisation drive in Turkey, Amanullah also pursued other reforms, discouraging the use of the veil by women and banning traditional dress for men in public, while strengthening the army and air force, with support from the newly formed USSR.

These reforms prompted resistance from religious leaders, who orchestrated a series of tribal rebellions against the 'kafir' king from the autumn of 1928. Unable to rely on the army to halt the spread of the rebellion, and with few political allies, Amanullah was forced to abdicate, and left Kabul for Kandahar in the hope of rallying support from his own clan, the Durranis. When this failed, Amanullah left Afghanistan for Italy, where he died. A brigand, Bacha-e-Saqao, who led one of the rebellions, took the throne in his place.

Mujtaba Ali was well placed to observe the tumultuous events that engulfed Afghanistan during his stay in Kabul. His young mind was curious to explore Afghan society and, with his impressive language skills, he had access to a cross-section of the Kabul population, whose ideas and experiences he chronicles with an acute eye and a wicked sense of humour.

Mujtaba Ali was inherently a freethinker and it was no wonder that he would oppose the British rule in India from an early age. The high-handedness of the British District Magistrate of Sylhet led to a student strike when he was in high school. In spite of being the son of a civil servant, Mujtaba Ali joined the strike and finally decided not to go through the British education system. This took him to a new school of learning – Shantiniketan. His views about the British empire's colonisation of India never changed throughout his life. So *Deshe Bideshe* is peppered with very strong anti-British sentiments and there are countless caustic remarks about British duplicity, cunning and tyranny. The colonial censor office would certainly not have passed the book in its current form. This could possibly have been a reason he never tried to get it published before India won independence from British rule. Mujtaba Ali's freethinking was augmented by his years of study in Shantiniketan under Tagore. Tagore's deep faith in international and universal humanism had slipped so deep under the skin of Mujtaba Ali that in all his writings he spoke out against the subjugation of humanity, like his Guru, in any form – religious, nationalistic, ethnic or political. He opposed the imposition of Urdu as the national language on the Bengali population of East Pakistan and expressed his views in a very powerful article. It was unsurprising that a man of such a freethinking bent of mind would refuse to live in a country that was built on the basis of religion. He chose to leave Pakistan for India.

Mujtaba Ali also had an acute sense of history. So he not only chronicled his times but also put them in historical perspective. This makes discerning readers think too and ask for answers to questions he had raised in his chronicles. This style of writing started to emerge in *Deshe Bideshe* and continued in his later works. *Deshe Bideshe* kindled my curiosity about Afghanistan and its history in the twentieth century, particularly the times of King Amanullah and the events that led to his departure. Mujtaba Ali had raised some suspicions about the possible British role behind the tribal insurrection against the king who had defeated them in 1918 and made Afghanistan independent. During my stay in London when I took up the translation, I decided to go through the telegrams sent by the British minister of the legation in Kabul to Whitehall to find out what was going on behind the scenes. The telegrams I accessed in the India Office of the British Library were revealing. It was clear that the British were unhappy with King Amanullah getting close to the newly formed USSR and accepting military assistance from them. So could they have had a role in the tribal insurrection against Amanullah in the autumn of 1928? Mujtaba Ali had no way of knowing during his stay or later when he was writing his account, what role the British had played during the tumultuous four months between September 1928 and January 1929 when the bandit leader Bacha-e-Saqao took over the reign of the country. But he had his suspicions and he had put his doubts in the form of questions in the final few chapters.

In Chapter 37, Mujtaba Ali makes the observation that the British Legation was at the mercy of the bandits of Bacha-e-Saqao for four days when they attacked Kabul for the first time but no harm came to the legation. Mujtaba Ali thought that was the generosity of Bacha-e-Saqao. The telegrams sent to London by the minister of the legation, Sir Francis Humphrys, make it clear how the legation was saved from looting. The telegram sent by Sir Francis on 14 January 1929 says, 'I am taking special precaution tonight. The Hazrat Sahib of Shor Bazaar and Muhammad Usman Khan, ex-Governor of Kandahar, have stationed themselves in a small house just outside the legation gates, and have sent me a message that they will remain to protect us against chance thieves on a night when excesses may be expected.'

The said Hazrat of Shor Bazaar, the most important religious leader of Afghanistan, was a kingpin in the rebellion against the king. Why did the brain behind the rebellion take personal charge to save the British Legation, who were the sworn enemies of the Afghans just a decade before that? Was there a secret arrangement between the Hazrat of Shor Bazaar and the British?

In another earlier telegram on 29 December 1928, Sir Francis lists eleven terms that the tribes gave to King Amanullah for him to continue in his position. Among the terms, there were demands that he divorce Queen Soraya, close down girls' schools, and reinstate purdah and Islamic laws as before. But the fifth condition in the list is a curious one – 'Abolition of all foreign legations except British'.

The same tribes rallied behind Amanullah when he waged the war of independence against the British just a decade earlier. Besides, the Afghans always detested the presence of the British on their soil following the first two Anglo-Afghan wars in 1839–42 and 1878–80. So why would they demand closing of all foreign legations except the British? Was that demand 'bought' by the British?

The telegrams I have accessed do not answer these questions but it only deepens the doubt of a possible British role in the rebellion through some of the important religious leaders who were instrumental in inciting the tribes against King Amanullah.

My tryst with Afghanistan that started with Mujtaba Ali completed a circle in 2012 when I was working on this translation. In the summer of that year I had the opportunity to meet the daughter of King Amanullah and Queen Soraya, Princess Hindia, who was born in Mumbai a few months after Amanullah was overthrown in January 1929. During our meeting in Kabul, I told this most beautiful and elegant grand old lady how her family's story had featured in a book in the Bengali language. She was keen to know more about the stories from the book. Sitting in her hotel suite that overlooked the Turkish and the Iranian embassies, she told me how her father gave those properties to these two friendly nations to build their missions. I had heard from an Afghan friend that Indian Congress leaders came to meet the king in Mumbai before he went into exile in Rome. My friend told me that apparently Mahatma Gandhi had suggested the name Hindia for the newborn baby. I asked her if that story was true. And the story took an altogether different dimension when she said, 'Yes, it was true that the Indian leaders came to see my father but it was not Gandhi but Muhammad Ali Jinnah who told my father, "You should name her Hindia and that way both Hind and India will remain with you always." To that my father responded, "Hind and India will forever remain in my heart but I'll name her Hindia as you've suggested."'

Mujtaba Ali lamented a number of times in his book at the fading connections between India and Afghanistan. I hope he found out in his lifetime that the king, for whom he had worked, tried to highlight that link, even as a token gesture, before leaving his country for good.

Nazes Afroz, 2015

In a Land Far from Home

ONE

I bought a pair of shorts from Chandni market for nine sikka before I boarded the train. In those days smart Bengalis travelling by train often made full use of a facility called the 'European Third'.

I was boarding that 'Third' when an Anglo-Indian shouted, 'This is only for Europeans.'

I barked back, 'Can't see any European here. So let's relax and spread our legs in this empty carriage.'

Comparative linguists say that if you add 'ng' at the end of a Bengali word, it would sound like Sanskrit; similarly, if you put emphasis on the first syllable of a word, that will make it sound like the Queen's English. Meaning, accentuating on the first syllable is like putting too much chilli powder in Indian food to hide all evidence of bad cooking. Simply put, this was barking English. The Anglo-Indian was a native of Taltola, a cosmopolitan neighbourhood in central Calcutta. He was so impressed by my English that he instantly started helping me with my luggage. I left the job of bargaining with the porter to him. His entire family had worked for the Indian railways for generations, they knew how to deal with station porters.

Meanwhile, my enthusiasm for the journey was fast fading. I had been so busy arranging my passport, buying clothes and packing that I did not have the time to think about anything else. A most cowardly thought crept into my mind soon after the train left – I was alone.

The Anglo-Indian was a good man. Guessing that I was feeling low he asked, 'Why do you look so depressed? Going far?'

I realised that he knew the rules of etiquette. He did not ask, 'Where are you going?' I had learned most of my lessons in etiquette from a padre. He had taught me that it was proper to ask, 'Going far?', as you could say yes or no – or anything you liked, if you wanted to respond. 'Where are you going' was like facing interrogation by Elysium Rowe[*] – you had to give an answer; there was no escape, and that would be rude.

I started chatting to him, which proved to be quite fruitful. Soon after it was dark, he opened a huge basket and joked that his fianceé had cooked enough food to feed a whole army. I said hesitantly that I too had some food but it was native fare and may be too hot for him. After some debate, it was decided that there would be brotherly division and we would eat à la carte.

My eyeballs froze in their sockets as he started to lay out his food. The same seekh kebab, the same Dhaka paratha, murgh musallam, meat-with-potato. I had brought the same from Zakaria Street. My menu matched his exactly – no shami kebab instead of seekh, no meat-with-cabbage in place of meat-with-potato. I said, 'Brother, I have no fianceé and I bought all of it from a hotel in Zakaria Street.'

It tasted the same too. The Anglo-Indian kept looking out of the window pensively while eating. I vaguely remembered a chubby Anglo-Indian woman coming into the hotel when I was buying my food and ordering everything that was available. I

* English jurist and judge of the nineteenth century who had served in the Calcutta High Court.

thought of asking him to give a description of his fianceé, but chose not to. It would do no good; besides he was drinking some smelly coloured liquid from a bottle. He was Anglo-Indian after all; who could guarantee that his mood would not change.

It got darker. I did not eat much as I was not hungry. I was not sleepy either. It was a moonlit night. Through the window I could clearly see that the land we were passing through was not Bengal, there were no betel-nut trees or villages lush with mango and jack-fruit orchards, only a few houses scattered here and there. There was no pond. People were lifting water from high-walled wells. The wet-smell from the earth of Bengal had evaporated and sand and dust from the scorched earth was whirling around carried by a sudden gust of wind slapping you on the face. What would this land look like in daylight if this were its face in this semi-darkness? Was this western India? The fertile-green-India? No it was not. When Bankim[*] mentioned the voices of thirty koti[†] people in fertile-green-India,[‡] he meant Bengal. It would be a joke to say that the west was fertile and green. Suddenly I saw Haren Ghosh from our neighbourhood standing by me. What? Yes! It was our Haren all right! How come? And he was singing, 'Thirty koti, thirty koti, koti koti—'

No, it was the ticket checker – come to check tickets. He was not singing 'Koti, koti'; he was shouting 'ticket, ticket'.

Anandamath
It might have been a carriage for Europeans but it was third class after all. How could he show his authority if he did not wake us

* Nineteenth century Bengali writer Bankim Chandra Chattopadhyay.
† Bengali numerical unit – equal to ten million.
‡ A reference to Bankim Chandra Chattopadhyay's nationalist novel.

up in the middle of the night to check tickets? I promptly woke up. The composition of the carriage had changed. The 'European compartment' was looking quite desi – suitcases, trunks and beddings were scattered around. I did not know when the Anglo-Indian had got off the train. He had left behind the basket of food for me with a note on top, 'Good luck for the long journey.'

He might have been an Anglo-Indian, but he was after all from Calcutta – a native of Taltola. I was a regular visitor to the Iranian restaurants there; I had introduced my Hindu friends to Muslim cuisine in that neighbourhood; watched swimming at the lake in the square; clapped and cheered when a fight broke out between a white soldier and an Anglo-Indian over a dame.

A philosopher friend from Taltola had once said that man became excessively sentimental – maudlin – if he was injected with emetine. In that state he would sob, covering his face with the pillow, if even the cat next door died. Being injected with emetine and going abroad were the same. But we should not go further. There will be ample opportunities to touch on this subject later.

I could not remember when dawn broke. The summer month of June in western India did not make any overtures. By seven the sun had entered the cars and indicated what the day would be like. I had heard that the maestros in the western region did not like to sing in slow tempo, they liked to reach the climax quickly. That evening I realised that only the early morning sun in the region was andante and the rest of the day was allegro.

The train was like the maestro. Running fast in an attempt to beat the drummer so that he could rest. The sun was running equally fast. We poor passengers were caught in the middle of this race, with brief pauses at stations. But I could clearly see that the sun was looking at the train from the corner of his eyes, standing outside the shade of the platform, like the drummer who rolled his sticks and got ready in between two songs.

When I ate, when I slept, which stations passed, who got off, who did not – I could not keep track of anything. The heat was so intoxicating; otherwise why would I write a poem?

A burnt field lay before me. As far as the eyes go to rest
On the horizon – burnt, angry yearnings. Heart at unrest
Everywhere on the earth. Only her angry, her fiery eyes
Raining at cruel speed. All of creation groaning in a rise
In forests, mountains and roads. Yamuna's dry chest
From one bank to the other – like some mother's breast
Sucked dry by some ogre. A dirge rises in all-consuming grief
The world over. I surmise: there is no hope, none to relieve
This desert with life, give it the sweet sap of a green shroud.
A demon's wrath has sapped the strength of the water-cloud,
Drained the King of Gods of his wine. Earth's breast ploughed
Dry of all green by a weary, disconsolate spectre-wombed cow.

What a poem! Drier than the dry lands of the west. The poem was not published before Gurudev[*] passed away. Guru's curse is the ultimate curse!

[*] Nobel Laureate Bengali poet, novelist, philosopher and educationist Rabindranath Tagore.

TWO

The Hindu pundit of my village primary school used to snap his fingers whenever he yawned and say, 'O Radhe,* the beauty of Braja,† take me to the other side.' I read enough Hindi and Urdu literature later in my life, I had detailed discussions with many people from various cultures of the world, but I never found anyone using the metaphor 'Take me to the other side' in conjunction with names of gods and goddesses.

I understood the meaning of this phrase only while crossing the Beas, Sutlej, Ravi, Jhelum and Chenab, the five rivers of the Punjab, whose names I had had to memorise in my childhood. I knew exactly where to find them on the map. I always imagined that our Ganga, Padma, Meghna, Buriganga‡ could not match up to them but when I looked down from the train, I had difficulty in believing that these were those mighty rivers from my history and geography lessons. Where were the fast-flowing waters and waves? There were only sand dunes bound by the two banks. You needed both telescopes and microscopes to look for

* Radhe or Radha, the lover of Lord Krishna, reincarnation of the Hindu god Vishnu.
† The town where Krishna grew up.
‡ Rivers in erstwhile East Bengal, now in Bangladesh.

8

water anywhere. At that point, I realised why the metaphor of crossing the river at the end of one's time in this world never appeared in the imagination of the people in the west. They did not need any help from a boatman let alone gods and goddesses to cross these rivers. I did not know what it was like in the monsoon, but you could not pray to the gods for only one season. The monsoon lasted for barely three days here; so it would be a total waste to pray to the gods all the time to help you cross over.

The look of the carriage had changed meanwhile. You could see that the beards had become longer and the tiki* shorter. The rugged and rustic sounds of six-foot Pathans and Punjabis had replaced the sweet voices of chubby lalas. Besides, there was an amazing display of Sikh beards bound in nets. I thought, the way men wrote poetry in praise of the long hair of women, the women in this land surely sang ghazals of enchantment for these beards. I had read in a novel by Theophile Gautier that when Frenchmen took up shaving, an enlightened woman had written, with great sadness, 'The joy of kissing is disappearing from France. The French woman, while kissing, will forever lose the touch of masculinity that comes from rubbing her face against the facial hair of her lover. It is the time of neuters from now on. It makes me shudder even to think about it.'

I thought of asking a Sardarji to give his opinion about this. The French beard, at the peak of its glory, could not come close to a Sikh one. So the women of this land most certainly had ample appreciation for these beards. But, looking at their size and rugged manner of talking, I did not dare ask the question. I still had not

---

* Tuft of hair at the back of a man's head – a custom prevalent among Hindu society in many parts of India, especially among the upper castes.

figured out what people took offence to in this country, and how they took revenge with blood. I thought it would be unwise to give my life for comparative 'beardology'. These people gave their lives easily to save the honour of their hair; no doubt they could surely decapitate a beardless head.

The old Sardarji sitting opposite me started the conversation. No more 'Going far', but a straightforward, 'Where are you going?' I replied, showing due respect for his age. The gentleman was as old as my grandfather and a beautiful soft smile was visible through the forest of his beard. Wise too. He quickly understood that the Bengali weakling was unnerved in the midst of all the guns and swords. He asked if I knew someone in Peshawar or would I go to a hotel. I replied, 'A friend's friend is supposed to come to pick me up at the station. I'm slightly worried because I don't know how he'll recognise me.'

Sardarji said, with a smile, 'Nothing to worry about. Trainloads of Bengalis don't get off at Peshawar station. You should just wait and he'll find you.'

I said, 'That's right, the problem is I'm wearing shorts—'

Sardarji broke into loud laughter, 'Do you think a man can recognise another by looking at the one-foot area that is covered by the shorts?'

I replied in embarrassment, 'It's not like that, it would have been good if I had worn a dhoti and punjabi.'

There was no way to beat Sardarji. 'It's very strange, how could a Bengali wear a punjabi?'

I decided to retreat. I did not know how he would outwit me again if I tried to explain that the loose shirt in Punjab and the Bengali punjabi were one and the same thing. It was better he talked and I listened. I asked, 'Sardarji, how many yards of cloth do you need to make a shalwar?'

'Three and a half in Delhi; four and a half in Jalandhar; five and a half in Lahore; six and a half in Lalamusa; seven and a half in Rawalpindi; then it jumps to ten and a half in Peshawar and in the heart of the Pathan-land – in Khyber and Kohat, it's the whole reel.'

'Full twenty yards!'

'Yes, that too, made with khaki shorting.'

I said, 'Let's not talk about fighting or mugging or robbery; how can they even move about with a whole reel of khaki on them?'

Sardarji said, 'Have you never been to a cinema? Even at this age, I sometimes go. How would I understand what the young people are up to if I don't? I have an army of grandchildren at home. The other day, I went to see a film based on a 200-year-old story. In that film, a woman was putting on layers of frocks – ten or twelve – I can't remember how many. She was carrying at least forty yards of cloth on her. If she could dance seamlessly wearing that, then why can't a Pathan fight with a shalwar of twenty yards?'

I gave it some thought and said, 'That's right, but it's a waste.'

Sardarji was not to be defeated. He said, 'That's a matter of opinion. A dhoti in Madras is seven to eight yards long, but you Bengalis wear a ten-yard dhoti.'

'Ten-yard dhotis last longer, you can wear them from both ends.'

Sardarji said, 'The same rule applies to shalwars. Do you think a Pathan gets a shalwar made at every Eid? Never. A young Pathan gets a shalwar from his father-in-law on the night of his wedding. As it has a lot of cloth, it doesn't stretch much – hence he doesn't need to repair it for many years. A Pathan doesn't throw away his shalwar when it starts to wear out. At first he puts stitches, then he puts patches – any colour will do. On his death-bed he gifts his shalwar to his son and his son wears that until his wedding night when he gets his own shalwar from his father-in-law.'

I could not figure out if Sardarji was trying to make a mockery of me. I asked, 'Is this true, or did someone make it up?'

Sardarji said, 'The prince meets a tiger in the deep forest. The tiger says, "I will eat you." This is a story. But isn't it true that tiger eats man?'

Irrefutable logic. Also he was backed by seventy years of experience. So I surrendered. I said, 'How could we, Bengalis, understand the intrigues of the shalwar? We live in a wet, watery land; we often have to cross rivers, canals and ponds. The way we can pull up our dhotis and lungis, you can't do that with shalwars.'

Finally, it felt I had impressed Sardarji. He said, 'Yes, it's the same in Burma and Malay. I spent thirty years there.'

Then he opened his treasure trove of tales. I did not have any litmus to check if his stories were true or works of fiction, but it seemed they were like the tiger analogy. A few Pathans had flocked around us by then. Later I found out they all had spent a few years in Burma-Malay. The way Sardarji kept on unwinding his yarn of stories in front them – I figured out that the stories were unadulterated.

The huddle became dense and the chinwag most interesting. I realised that the Pathans might look dry from the outside, but they did not lack passion in telling and listening to stories. They wouldn't get into debates, they wouldn't use intricate flowery language to make the stories more interesting – they had a simple approach, like a woodcut. There was some secret attraction in that dryness that would leave a deep impression in your mind. Most of them were military stories. Sometimes they were of clan-clashes or fighting between tribes. I learnt a lot about various tribes – Afridi, Shinwari, Khugiani and so on. I realised that Sardarji knew everything about them. At times, he would add footnotes and explanations for my sake, as if he was preparing me for an examination. In a pause between stories, he said, 'You have passed many exams by reading scandals of the English and the French. It will be of no use to you in this land. You'd better get acquainted with the names and behaviours of the Pathan clans. It will come in handy in Peshawar and the Khyber Pass.'

Sardarji was so right.

Pathans always ended their stories with evidence. One completed his story in broken Urdu-Punjabi-Pashto and said, 'After that I couldn't remember anything as if I was drunk. When it became quiet, I saw that I had lost two fingers of my left hand. See.' Then he dug out his left hand from the depth of his twenty-yard shalwar to display it.

I said, to show my sympathy, 'How many days did you spend in the hospital?'

The whole Pathan gang roared in laughter at the ignorance of the city-bred gentleman.

The Pathan said, 'Where can we find a hospital or any English doctor, sir? My wife put on a bandage, my granny applied some of her all-cure lotion and the village mullah blessed me. Now see, it as if I was born with three fingers.'

The brother-in-law of the Pathan was also there in the gang. He said, 'You had nothing to fear. Everyone knows that even the messenger of death doesn't dare come close to your village, fearing the trio you just named.' Everyone laughed. He then said to me, 'Ask him to tell his granny's stories. She once held up a full company of the British army for three hours by rolling down boulders from the hilltop.'

The sun and the heat were awash in the torrents of stories. And what a feast. Everyone was buying something or other at every station. Tea, sorbet, ice-water, kebab, bread – we did not miss anything. It was impossible to figure out who was paying. I gave up after trying to give my fair share a few times. By the time I reached the door after dodging a dozen big-bodied Pathans, somebody had already paid for it. When I tried to protest, they said, 'You are going to Pathan-land for the first time; do let us treat you, sir. You can play the host after you reach Peshawar and settle down. We'll come together one day.' I said that I was not going to stay in Peshawar for long. But no one paid any heed. Sardarji said, 'I'm the oldest here. They didn't even let me pay once. The only way to avoid the hospitality of the Pathans in this land is to not talk to them. But even that doesn't work most of the time.'

The Pathan gang chorused, 'We are poor people, we roam the world to earn bread. How can we really show hospitality?'

Sardarji whispered to me, 'What intelligence! As if hospitality depends on your wealth.'

THREE

When Sardarji began combing his hair, arranging his beard and tightening his turban, I realised that we would be in Peshawar in an hour or so. The heat, sand, coal dust, meals of only kebab-bread and lack of a bath had sucked out all my strength. I did not have an iota of energy to fold my bedding into the holdall. But the advantage of travelling with Pathans was that they very happily helped you with any task that was beyond you, doing it with the greatest of ease. The way they folded my bedding, keeping their balance on the running train, it felt like they were playing with matchboxes. It seemed as if they were moving small attaché cases and not trunks.

Meanwhile, from the stories in the train I had picked up an important tip about Pathan-land, that Peshawar belonged to the British in the daytime while at night the Pathans ruled the roost. I felt proud that the gun-toting Pathans could take on the cannon-owning British but I was not comfortable at all. We were supposed to reach Peshawar at nine at night. I was wondering in whose reign I was going to set foot when the train chugged into the station.

How could it be nine at night? There was ample daylight outside. I was so numbed by the long journey that I had forgotten to look at my watch. I looked at it now; it was nine all right. It was no time to think about such trivia, but later I learned that our clocks ran according to Allahabad-time,* so it was only natural and scientific to have daylight that late so far in the west – and it was the peak of summer too.

There was not much of a crowd on the platform. I noticed, in the midst of taking down my luggage, that someone noticeably taller than the six-footer Pathans was walking towards me. As I was trying to establish my Bengali-ness by assuming the looks of a little lamb, he approached and said, in chaste Urdu, that his name was Sheikh Ahmad Ali. Extending my hand, I mentioned my name. He caught my hand with both of his and pressed it, with a great deal of warmth. My five fingers were playing hide-and-seek in his palms. The only reason I did not shout was that subconsciously I remembered the story of the Pathan losing his two fingers and it inspired me to forget my pain. Thus the honour of the Bengalis was saved on the very first day on the platform at Peshawar. I was wondering how to retrieve my hand when he gave me a bear hug in true Pathan style. I did not know what he would have done if I had been his equal. Luckily my head only reached his chest, so he could not hug me tighter. At the same time, the translation of what he was saying in Urdu and Pashto would have sounded something like this – 'Hope you are fine; all well I hope; everything fine I suppose; not too tired?' I kept saying, 'Yes sir', 'No sir,' thinking I should have learned some Pathan etiquette from my fellow passengers. Later, when I got accustomed to their ways, I found out that you were not supposed to say anything when your friend greeted you in that manner. Both sides would ask the same series of questions for two full minutes. Finally, after plenty of shaking hands and hugging, one would ask the other,

* The mean Indian timeline that ran through the northern city of Allahabad.

'How are you?' Then you would say, '*Shukur Al-hamdulillah* – praise be to God. How are you?' Now it would be his turn to say, '*Shukur Alhamdulillah*'. At that point, you could talk about your cough and cold, but during the first barrage of questions, it would be extreme bad manners if you tried to answer.

He partly carried and partly dragged me out of the station to a tonga. By then my chain of thoughts was like this – he did not know me; I was a Bengali; he was a Pathan; so what was the meaning of this elaborate reception? How much of this was genuine and how much was perfunctory?

I would say now that a Pathan's reception was always truly genuine and heartfelt. He derived much pleasure in inviting guests to his home – more so, if that guest happened to be a foreigner and that too a five-foot-six delicate Bengali. It was not proper for a gentleman Pathan to fight. So he did not know what to do with his stored energy. He got immense satisfaction if he could take care of a weakling.

The tonga was moving in Pathan style. In our country, cars moved in a straight line and people made way for the cars. But in Pathan-land, people walked as they liked and cars had to find their own way through the crowd. No point honking or shouting. A Pathan never made way for anybody. He was 'independent'; what was the value of 'independence' if he had to make way for cars? And he was ready to pay for his 'independence' too. If a horse trampled on his foot, bloodying his toenails, he would not abuse the driver or shout or call the police. He would look at the driver with an annoyed expression and say, 'Can't you see?' The driver was also an 'independent' Pathan. He too would stare with total disdain and say 'Don't you have eyes?' End of the story, each would move on.

I saw that three-fourths of the population in Peshawar knew Ahmad Ali and he knew two-thirds. Every two minutes he would stop the tonga to say something in Pashto to someone. Then he would turn to me and say smilingly, 'Invited him to dinner with you. Hope you don't mind.'

Ahmad Ali's wife was lucky that their house was close to the station. Or else there would have been a big Pathan jirga* at his house that night.

Simple Pathans and cunning British agreed on one point. Every Pathan thought that the Bengalis bombed the British rulers; the British also had the same opinion. Ahmad Ali worked for the police – CID. A policeman brought a letter to him soon after we reached his house. He started laughing after reading the letter before passing it to me. It contained a vivid description of me, asking him to make a full and thorough enquiry and submit a report to the government.

Ahmad Ali wrote at the bottom of the letter, 'The man is my guest.'

I urged him, 'Write my name, address, reason for coming here, etc.'

Ahmad Ali said scoffingly, 'Am I going to spy on my guest?'

I could not resist showing off some knowledge. 'You ought to work dispassionately without thinking about your guest. This is the edict of the Gita.'

Ahmad Ali said, 'There are so many books in Hinduism. Why did you pick up a quote from the Gita? Whatever . . . I don't believe in work – neither passionate nor dispassionate. My religion is lying in prone position.'

I was slightly confused with the concept – lying in prone position? We liked to lie on our backs, which the British masters did not appreciate. Our masters considered 'lying supine' an

---

* Traditional Pathan gathering to settle disputes.

18

expression of laziness. I said earlier that the Pathan and the British agreed on at least one point. So I thought that the Pathan wanted to absolve himself of the sin of agreeing with the British; hence he chose the 'prone' and not the supine position. I did not know if Ahmad Ali could guess my confusion but he said on his own, 'Otherwise how will you save your soul in this land? Only a few days ago, I had gone out for a round at night. The famous exotic dancer Janki Bai had gone missing. So I was snooping around for some clues. I was walking on my own when I saw eight white soldiers marching in single file, about fifty yards ahead of me. Suddenly there were several loud bang bangs, one after the other. I went for the ground and rolled into the ditch next to the road. Lying in prone position, I lifted my head to see that the white soldiers were all scattered on the road while a dozen men of the Afridi tribe were picking up their rifles before vanishing in a flash. The Afridi's target is like the summons of death – no respite, no mercy. Thus I say, unless you lie in prone position, how will you know that you're not going to be the sitting target of an Afridi? This is the first lesson to save your life in this country.'

I asked, 'Why not lie supine?'

Ahmad Ali said, 'Never. You will only see God's sky if you lie supine. That is certainly extremely beautiful, but how would you keep an eye on bad people and their intentions from that position? How would you know that the show was over and you'd be in trouble if you stayed a minute longer? The military would come, investigate and would round up all the eyewitnesses. You should rather face an Afridi's bullet.'

I said, 'But that applies to me. You are with the CID, you would have had to submit a report about me.'

Ahmad Ali said, 'Tauba, tauba (shame, shame). Why should I report? What's my responsibility? The rifles belonged to the white soldiers and the Afridis wanted them. Man's life is hinged on one thing; he can take away or give life for that. Why do I need to poke my nose in the middle? Bengalis love to bomb the British – God knows why? Somehow they don't like rifles. The British don't like to be bombed but the Bengali is adamant that he'll do it at any cost. He is ready to give his life for that and take a few too. The third party should stay away from matters of life and death. Why should I send any report on you to the government?'

I said, 'Spot on. Bertrand Russell also said the same – no one can debate about values. I can see there are a lot of similarities between Pathans and the British. But do you want to know why the Bengalis want to bomb the British? Very simple – for independence. But you need rifles to save it once you have gained it. I suppose, that's why the rifle is so precious to the Afridis.'

Ahmad Ali thought for a while. He then said, 'I don't know what's important to save independence. Rifle or courage? Possibly you are aware that there are a couple of gangs in every neighbourhood in Peshawar. The other day there was a gang fight – no guns though, only fists and knives. One gang could not fight for more than ten minutes; they retreated. But the leader didn't quit; he stood his ground. The other gang had a free hand and made mincemeat of him before leaving him, thinking he was dead. Yesterday I was in the hospital to see him. It will take him six months to recover – if he makes it at all. Doctors are yet to figure out how many bones have broken or how many stab wounds he has.

'But I was surprised to see that he was barely five-foot-six and thin as a twig. He apparently doesn't know how to use the knife. He hardly ever uses the gun. But he possesses just one thing – courage. He has been beaten up many times. He has killed a few but has had more people killed. He has appeared in the court of law as an accused but never as a plaintiff. He says, "I adjudicate disputes; I can't go to the court seeking justice."

'It seemed the city fruit market had moved to the hospital. Grapes from Kabul, cherries from Kandahar, walnuts and dry-fruit from Mazar-e-Sharif – everything was available there, in case His Highness asked for any of it. Meanwhile His Highness was negotiating the Khyber Pass between life and death.

'The main point is he's still the leader. His stature has increased. His fame tops the list of gangsters of Peshawar.'

I saw Ahmad Ali was smiling while I was digesting his story. He continued, 'Apart from his courage he has something else – ready wit. He can quip at the drop of a hat. Apparently Judge Ijaz Hussain was really cross with him when he appeared in his court for the fifth time after being acquitted four times for lack of evidence. He said very angrily, "Aren't you ashamed of yourself? This is the fifth time you're appearing in my court."

'The leader said with a naughty smile, "Is it my fault if Your Honour doesn't get any promotion?"'

That night I wrote to my friend Motru, 'Brother, no supine position, lie in prone. This is the rule of the Pathanland. Spread the word in our beloved land too.'

FOUR

I would plead with my host every day, 'Ahmad Ali, my brother, Lord will have mercy on you, you'll go to heaven, please make some arrangement so that I can leave Peshawar and continue with my journey.'

Ahmad Ali would respond, '*Baradarey azeez-e-man* (oh my dear brother), there is a saying in Farsi, "*Der aayad dooroost aayad*" – all good things happen slowly; in Arabic they say, "*Al ajlu meena shaitan*" meaning you will follow Satan if you make haste; there is something in English too—'

I said, 'Fully understood! But I beg of you, this Pathan way will not work for me. I have heard you take fifteen days to go to Landikotal from here and it's only twenty-two miles.'

Ahmad Ali asked gravely, 'Says who?'

'That Ramzan Ali – well-coiffeured, handsome – from last night's dinner.'

Ahmad Ali scoffed, 'What does Ramzan Ali know about the ways of the Pathans. His grandmother was from Punjab; he himself spent three months in Lahore. A true Pathan never ever crosses the Indus at Aatak. A Pathan should take at least two months to reach Peshawar from Landikotal. Otherwise it will mean he has avoided all his friends and relatives on the way. The custom of the land is he has to spend at least three nights with his relatives; and each Pathan is related to every other Pathan. Now you do the maths.'

There was no paper and pencil in my hand. I said, 'Please help me. I have signed the contract to teach in the college in Kabul, I have to go.' Ahmad Ali shrugged, 'What can I do if there's no bus?'

'Have you tried?'

Ahmad Ali warned me – he faced daily grilling by lawyers and judges. So I would not have any joy if I followed this line of questioning.

Finally he said, 'Why not see Peshawar properly? So much to see; so much to learn. Traders have brought pustin* from Bukhara and Samarkand; samovars from Tashkent—'

I asked, 'What is a samovar?'

'Haven't you read in Russian stories? A metal pot – you boil water for tea keeping it on the table. The way some people try to get hold of a vase from the Ming period, likewise Peshawar, Kandahar, Tashkent fight over Tula samovars – they are ready to pay large sums to lay their hands on it. But we will talk about it some other day. Then there are carpets from Mazar-e-Sharif, red ruby from Badakshan, rosary from Meshed, from Azerbaijan—'

I said, 'That's enough.'

'So many other attractions. The traders are staying at the caravan inns. They do their business in the evening and have grand feasts and fun at night. So much fun, many murders and various degrees of sins. Haven't you heard that Peshawar is a sin-city? You will learn a dozen languages easily if you spend a month in an inn. You will start with Pashto, then move to Farsi, after that Jagtai Turk, Mongol, Usmanli, Russian, Kurdish – the rest you'll pick up

---

* Long fur coat commonly used in Central Asia.

automatically. Do you like music? No? What a surprise! You are a Bengali; I have read *Gitanjali* by your great poet Rabindranath Tagore, in Farsi translation. High quality verses. I'm sure you have interest in music. Even if you don't, how can you leave Peshawar without listening to Iddan Jaan? She is the fairy of Peshawar, can sing in twelve languages. Her fan following is spread from Delhi to Baghdad. She will be over the moon if you visit her – her reign will then extend from Baghdad to Bengal.'

I had no hope. I said resignedly, 'Yes, yes, I will experience all of that. But first tell me which poem of Tagore you like most.'

Ahmad Ali thought for a while, then said, '*Aye Madar, Shahzada Imroz*—'

I understood, it was – 'Oh mother, my prince will go today—'

I said, 'What is this, Khan? You are not supposed to like this poem. You are a Pathan. Once rejected in love, you will ride on your stallion like lightning, gather her in your arms and disappear in a flash into the distant land. After that you will sit at her feet in the caves of the mountains trying to win her over. You will caress her feet—'

I had to stop because Ahmad Ali was a gentleman; he did not interrupt. He said, 'Why did you stop? Carry on.'

I said, 'Why would you bleat like a lamb with a sad face and teary eyes?'

Ahmad Ali replied, 'Hmm, a German philosopher apparently has said, don't forget to take your whip while going to a woman.'

I said, 'Tauba, tauba, not that extreme.'

Ahmad Ali responded, 'No brother, you have to have the final say in love. Love is like a big city street, full of people. There's no "golden mean" there. Either "keep to the right", meaning bleat like a lamb, or "keep to the left", meaning carry the whip as Nietzsche has suggested. But let's not discuss any further.' I

24

understood that Pathans are silent lovers. We Bengalis could not help but wake up the whole neighbourhood in the middle of the night while expressing our love to our wives. As if Ahmad Ali could understand my dilemma, he said in an attempt to make me happy, 'No dancer manages to stay more than six months in the bazaar of Peshawar. Some young Pathan will fall in love with her. He will then marry her and take her to his village.'

'Society doesn't object? The girl doesn't cry to come back to the city?'

'Why should society object? Such marriage isn't forbidden in Islam. But who knows if she cries after two days. And even if she does, do you think the sound of her wailing will reach the city? Even Iddan Jaan's voice is not that strong. Can't say it for sure, but I think the girls prefer the peace of the village rather than the noise of the city. And there's nothing like it if she gets love.'

I said, 'One of our novelists has the same opinion; he has done enough research on these women in the bazaars.'

At that point Ahmad Ali's friend Muhammad Jaan arrived dragging his bicycle. Ahmad Ali asked, 'Why is your bicycle limping?'

Muhammad Jaan was Punjabi. He said, looking at me, 'Why have you come to this land? You would have understood what a public nuisance these Pathans are if you rode a bicycle in this city for half an hour. Three punctures in one hour – all from small nails.'

I asked sympathetically, 'Where do these nails come from?'

Muhammad Jaan said angrily, 'Why are you asking me? Ask your dearest Pathan friend Sheikh Ahmad Ali Khan.'

Ahmad Ali said, 'You know that every Pathan is a chatterbox. He can't walk a mile without chatting to somebody. He will sit down with a cobbler if he has no companion. He will tell the cobbler, "Okay brother, why don't you put some nails on the sole." The cobbler will hammer the old nails and put a few new ones – possibly another dozen. After a hundred such nails, the shoe walks on a mosaic of nails rather than the sole. Pathans don't like to spend money in replacing soles anyway. There are different sizes of nails. But the truth is, repairing the sole is an excuse; he sits down with the cobbler just to chat.'

Muhammad Jaan finished the story, 'And those nails come off and spread all over the city.'

I said, 'I thought chattering distracted people from wrong-doing. Now I see that it is not entirely true.'

Ahmad Ali pleaded, 'Please don't blame chitchatting. Blame the cyclists instead. I was telling you earlier, "*Al ajlu meena shaitan*" – you will follow Satan if you make haste; hence another synonym of bicycles is Satan's vehicle.'

The cool evening breeze in Peshawar erased all the discomforts of the hundred and fourteen degrees of the day. The roads came alive with the clip-clopping of horse carriages. Well-dressed Pathan men came out to take the air in brocade shoes and flowing poplin shalwars with razor-sharp creases. They wore long coloured shirts; and what a display of turbans – nothing in the world could compete with them. Bengalis are not accustomed to headgear. Any hat, cap or turban appears superfluous to us. But seeing the turbans of the rich and middle-class Pathans, it felt as though God had given us the upper part only to wear them. After they had finished grooming themselves, when these Pathan men were out on the streets of Peshawar, with a hint of perfume and the spectacular turbans, who would say they were brothers of the Pathans we knew in Zakaria Street in Calcutta? The evening dress-clad he-men of Hollywood would not be able to come anywhere close to them either. At the end of the scorching summer day, the cool breeze caressed my cheeks after playing hide-and-seek with the leaves on the trees, the tops of the Pathan turbans, the garlands in the flower shops and finally Ahmad Ali's massive moustache. It was like the first rain after the summer months in Bengal. It seemed as though the men and the animals had taken refuge in some underground cave to flee the tortures of some cruel pharaoh. After the sun set behind the western pyramid, the northern wind brought the message of Moses – and life sprouted from everywhere, they were free from their prisons.

And what did they need after waking up? Food. There were long queues in front of the kebab and bread shop. Burqa-clad women, toddlers, old men on their deathbeds – everyone swarmed around the shop. The bread-maker tried to keep everyone happy – calling someone 'brother', someone else 'my love', 'my master', 'my friend'. He could speak fluently in four languages – Pashto, Urdu, Punjabi and Farsi. His workers kept busy taking out baked breads from the wood-fired oven with a long spike. The glow of the hot oven turned their foreheads and cheeks reddish. Their long hair fell across their faces but their hands were so busy plucking breads from inside the oven that they did not have the time to brush it aside. The flowing beard of the shop owner swayed in the breeze. His loose turban came down to his eyes – one minute he was scolding his bread-makers, *'Zud kun, zud kun'* – faster, faster – the next minute he was pleading with his customers, 'Oh my dear brother, oh my friend, oh my love, oh my darling, I always sell oven-fresh bread; hence this delay. Would you have to wait for long if I sold stale stuff?'

One burqa-clad woman – I couldn't figure out her age – said, 'Three generations of this neighbourhood have died eating your so-called "oven-fresh" bread. What do you eat on the sly? Stale loaves? Why don't you give us some of that?'

She was merely wearing a burqa – otherwise Pathan women were independent too.

After buying bread, they would visit the flower or the perfume shop. I remembered a verse by Prophet Muhammad – If you have a penny

> Buy some food
> If you get another
> Buy some flowers, oh believer.

FIVE

The Pathan is very lazy and likes to chat a lot. But he is neither weak nor fanciful. Nor does it take a lot of money to fulfil his fancy. The doyens of travellers have opined that strong and brave people are generally very peaceful. I realised that this theory applied to the Pathans too. We often read about banditry and lawlessness in that land but there were reasons for that. It was a dry arid place; they could not grow crops. Every Pathan male could not join the army; so he had no option but to engage in banditry. He did it not to show his muscle or strength but just to fill his stomach. A Pathan does not get angry very easily – Punjabis are different in that respect. And even if he does, he does not look for his gun. But there are always a few exceptions in life and Pathans are no angels of God. If you call a Pathan a 'traitor', his blood will boil instantly to the temperature of the Khyber Pass. He will also sit down calmly to count how many bullets he would need to save his brother from his enemy. As he is no Einstein, he often makes mistakes and a couple more people than anticipated will die from his bullets. And when he faces angry questions about it, he will lament, 'But I wasted four bullets! As if that doesn't count. I understand that their families are crying but nobody is even considering my misfortune. Men are so selfish; there's no justice in this world.'

I heard such stories over dinner the other night. Guests and gatecrashers had equal rights to tell stories. But one thing proved that they were all Pathans.

That was their way of feasting. They would spread a cloth on the carpet —one yard wide and twenty yards long, depending on how many had been invited. Two rows of people would sit facing each other. After that the food would be served on the dastarkhan – the serving cloth – three plates of meat-with-potato, three plates of seekh kebab, three plates of fowl-roast, three plates of ribs and liver, three plates of pulao. Everything would be served at the same time. We Bengalis sat with our own plates and got a portion of everything that was served. The same didn't apply to the Pathans. They would be satisfied with whatever there was in front of them. Even if his life depended on it, a Pathan would never say, 'Can you pass me the fowl-roast' or 'I would like to taste the seekh kebab.' Once in a while someone would suddenly notice and say loudly, 'Can't you see, Gulam Muhammad is only chewing okra. Why don't you pass him the pulao?' Then everyone would pass all the plates of pulao to him very apologetically and start chatting again. Nobody would look at Gulam Muhammad for another hour to check if he was lost in the desert of the dry pulao or was drowned in the thick gravy of the meat-with-potato. And if you were observant you would see that the Pathan was ready to sacrifice a lot in order to take part in the chat sessions. He achieved such a state of bliss from chatting, that he would carry on eating only dry bread. The underlying reason was that it took a lot of time to look at the food and eat it. If he did that then when would he chat with his friends?

They were all gentlemen and fairly wealthy too. They got good food at home every night. But the motto of the Pathan was that it was better to eat dry bread in the company of friends than have a five-course dinner alone. Omar Khayyam too said—

I would rather die in your company
Losing my way in the scorching desert
Without you what's the point
Praying in the mosque.

Khayyam used the language of a bourgeois poet. But the proletarian Pathan expressed the same sentiment in broken Urdu –

Dost!
Tumhari roti, humara gosht!

Meaning, 'You have invited me, that's my fortune. You only have dry bread? No problem. I will give you my own flesh.'

The quality of that poetry was more like the hooch consumed by daily-wage labourers rather than the best Shiraz that Khayyam drank.

I must explain something here. The difference between a bourgeois and a proletarian Pathan was purely economical. In the realm of sensitivity, they shared the same space. The difference in ideas came from the extent of their knowledge – some had more, some less. Some had read Shakespeare and some had not. But on the question of right or wrong, they did not differ much. In those matters they all blindly followed the traditional codes of revenge, taking and giving life and the justice systems of their respective clans and tribes.

A professor of Islamia College explained these theories to me. After setting up the sociological context with a lengthy, colourful preamble, he said – 'Take for example my colleague, Professor Khudabux – an ocean of knowledge about history. He can come up with the most fascinating economic explanation to everything under the sun and pass it on to his students. Even religion. Jesus Christ founded his religion through distribution of wealth between the rich and the poor. The poor benefited most from that and hence the poor fishermen flocked around him. Muhammad too introduced equality by wealth distribution by banning the system of interest and money-lending in Arabia. Not just about worldly matters, Khudabux can give theories about the afterlife too! But I digress. The main point is that the telescope of economic history was so tightly strapped on his eyes, we often wondered if Khudabux could ever see anything else.

'About a month ago his eldest son died. He was in the final year in school, extremely intelligent and bright like his father. After the death of his son, he should have been shocked and shaken; yet there was no reaction from Khudabux. He came to college routinely. During the tea break we went to express our condolences and he gave us a lecture on how Zoroaster or Zarathustra had converted King Gustasp on the basis of some economic conditions. After three days his second son died of typhoid – but Khudabux was delving into some pitak* of Buddhism. His wife died a month later, at her parents' house. It seemed Khudabux, like a man intoxicated, was trying to solve the mystery of the economic reasons of Alexander's victory in the Indus valley region.

'We had, by then, written him off. We were convinced that by reading history all the time, he had lost his humanity. As the Pathans are the best people on earth, we had no doubt that his Pathan-ness had evaporated so long ago that even his telescope of economic history would not be able to find the tiniest trace of it.

'At that point his brother passed away. He worked in the army. And Khudabux stopped coming to college. We all went to his house to enquire about him. We saw he was rolling on an antique carpet. Books, maps, compasses were all scattered around. His

---

* Buddhist religious text.

glasses were broken too. His old uncle said he did not touch a thing, even water, for two days.

'He kept howling, "My brother is no more." We had never seen anyone breaking down like that. We tried to console him in many ways but he had just one sentence, "My brother is no more."

'Finally I said to him, "You are a learned man. And you are breaking down like this? We know your capacity to absorb pain and loss. We didn't see you breaking down like this when your wife and two sons died recently."

'Khudabux stared at me as if I was a lunatic. But at least he said something. "Even you are saying this? My son died – so what? I can have another son. Wife passed away – so what? I can marry again. But where will I get another brother?" Then he started to roll again saying, "My brother is no more."'

After the professor stopped speaking, I said, 'Ramachandra also had broken down like that when he lost Lakshman.'*

Ahmad Ali said, 'Lakshman? Ramachandraji? I know this is a very good story from Hindu mythology. Please tell us. You only listen to us but never say anything.'

Oh God! They wanted me to narrate the story by the first poet, Valmiki, in my broken Urdu? I said, 'Ask Khudabux. There are some economic explanations of the *Ramayana*, I have heard.'

The professor asked, 'Ramachandra was a great fighter. Right?'

I said, 'He most certainly was.'

The professor said, 'That is the crux of the theory. Every great fighter and brave man loves his brother. And you can't find any people braver than the Pathans.'

I said, 'But Khudabux wasn't a fighter.'

---

* Lord Ram and his brother Lakshman whose fourteen-year exile in the forest is the basis of the *Ramayana*.

'That is a matter of perception,' the professor responded. 'He may teach in college and be able to explain the theories of economic history very well. But that is only a thin veil. Just rub him a little and you will see his true colour will come out in no time.'

Another guest, Major Muhammad Khan, said, 'You don't have to be a Pathan to love your brother. Yusuf (Joseph) also loved his bother Benyamin (Benjamin) greatly. Isn't it so?'

The professor said, 'Let's not discuss the Jews. Didn't one son of Adam kill the other?'

I said, 'But aren't the Pathans one of the twelve lost tribes of Israel? I read somewhere that when that tribe realised that this arid dry land had been allocated to them, they created such a hue and cry – which is called Fagan in Farsi. Hence they are called Afghan. And aren't you really Afghans? You are Indians now just because you live in this country.' The professor gave the smile of a learned man, 'We would have appreciated this theory had you said it thirty years ago. But now things have changed. We didn't know then that all major races in the world were claiming to be Aryans. Until then the theory was that you had to be some animal in the zoo of the Bible from the time of Judaism to be considered as people with history. Now things have changed. We are all Aryans. You have something called Veda in Hinduism. We read that too. We defeated Sikander Shah – Alexander the Great. The Gandhara art is our handiwork. Gandhar and Kandahar are the same. In Arabic there is no letter for "G" hence Arab geographers used the letter K.'

I was about to drown in this sea of knowledge. But the police normally help you when you are in trouble. My policeman, Ahmad Ali, said, looking at me, 'Don't take notice of the professor. He picks up such theories in the teachers' room of the college and now he's serving them to you, after distillation, in a nicely coloured glass. The crux is, the Pathan never bothers or loses his sleep over such trivial theories. The Afridi thinks that he's the best. The Momand says that is all nonsense. If there is one tribe that God loves most, it is the Momand. They don't even consider themselves as Afghans.'

I asked, 'Is that the reason you don't want to be a part of independent Afghanistan? You will live as independent Pathans in an independent India?'

All the Pathans present said in unison, 'Never. We will live as the independent frontier – and that land will be known as independent Pathan-land.'

The professor said, 'Haven't you heard the Pathans' soapbox lecture? One says, "Okay my brother Pathans, let's blast everything – democracy, autocracy, bureaucracy, communism, dictatorship – everything." So another Pathan shouts, "Are you an anarchist?" The first Pathan replies, "No, we will blast anarchism too."'

The professor asked, 'Do you understand now?'

I said, 'Certainly. Tagore also said, "First get drowned, then get drowsy, then high and finally become nothing." Like that?'

The professor said, 'Exactly.'

I said, 'You don't have to be a part of independent India, but please stop the Russians at our borders.'

All chorused, 'Certainly, certainly.'

SIX

If you want to go to any country, all you have to do is to get hold of a passport and reach an entry point. But that was not how it worked if you wanted to go to Afghanistan. You had to obtain a new permission after reaching Peshawar. That permission remained valid only for three days as there was no certainty whether or not there would be any trouble around the Khyber Pass. Hence this arrangement. Even if you had the stamp, in the event of trouble, the bus might turn back after reaching the Khyber.

I was returning home after getting the permit when I saw a few colourful buses, loaded with passengers, going west. I asked Ahmad Ali, 'Where are those buses going?'

He scolded me, 'They are not going to Kabul.' Then he asked, as if to create a diversion, 'Tell me a story from Bengal.'

I said to myself, 'All right my friend I have a story for you', but told him, 'I can't tell stories but I can see that there is at least one similarity between the Pathans and the Bengalis. Let me narrate that to you. Listen –

'The way most of the businesses here are run by the Punjabis or Sikhs, similarly in Calcutta most businesses are run by non-Bengalis. Even when a Bengali decides to go into business, he conducts it in a very odd way.

'I lived on Elliot Road where most shops were owned by Anglo-Indians. There were a few non-Bengali Muslim tailors and laundries. That's all. In the middle of all that a young Bengali Muslim man opened a shop – quite a fancy one. It seemed from his appearance that he was from an urban educated family. So I decided to patronise him because he showed the guts to come into business.

'It was a very hot day – that too, it was two in the afternoon. I was roaming the city for work, but I didn't buy a bar of soap I needed – because I had decided to patronise this educated young man.

'When I got off the tram at Elliot Road, I saw that he was happily taking a snooze, snoring loudly. His pet bird was sleeping in its cage; and even the hands of his clock were asleep exactly at twelve.

'I called softly, "Hello." Getting no response, I called again, "Excuse me."

'Still there was no response. My temper was rising in tandem with the temperature outside. Now I shouted, "Excuse me, sir!"

'The man half-opened his bloodshot eyes, "Yes." Then he went back to his siesta.

'I asked, "Do you have soap, Palmolive soap?"

'He said with his eyes closed, "No."

'I said, "What nonsense! I can see them, there, on the shelf."

"Those are not for sale," he responded.'

When I finished my narration, I asked Ahmad Ali, 'Isn't the Pathan way of doing business similar?' He laughed for a while then said, 'Why do you ask?'

I quipped, 'You just said, those buses don't go to Kabul!'

Ahmad Ali stopped on the road, turned towards the wall and went into peals of laughter. It was no ordinary laugh, but waves of it. I stood there wondering when it would stop. At last he replied. He said, 'These buses go up to the Khyber Pass.'

I asked, 'How could you laugh so much with this puny little joke?'

'Why can't I? Do you think laughter is embedded in stories? No, sir. Laughter comes from the heart. I told you that independence does not come with rifles; it comes from courage, with blood. Want to hear a story? Let's go and sit at the tea stall.'

A Pathan is a true democrat. It was a tea stall for tongawallahs and tobacco-sellers.

Ahmad Ali was well aware of his body-mass, so he sat very carefully – on the corner of the bench. And I parked my slender body in the middle. He said – 'One night Omar Khayyam, even though very thirsty for his wine, decided that he was not going out to drink before finishing five Rubaiyats.* You know how complicated his poetry is. It was early morning when he finished. He rushed to the bar almost at dawn and shouted, "Get me the best bottle of Shiraz." The bar owner said very apologetically, "Sir, you are too late. I've run out of wines." Omar told him to give him whatever was available. The owner said, "I'm so sorry sir, not a drop left." To which Omar replied, "No problem. Collect the few drops left in those glasses on the tables and give it to me. Getting drunk is my business."'

Before we got into any complicated and lengthy theories on courage, laughter and the ability to get drunk, I saw the half-Pathan – Ramzan Ali – going by. I brought that to Ahmad Ali's notice. And the inevitable happened. 'Oh Ramzan Khan, jaane man, baradarey man, please come here.' Then he turned towards me and started scolding, 'Aren't you a strange man? If I didn't call, would you have let him go away? In this heat? What would have happened if he had a heatstroke? Are you not afraid of God?'

Ramzan Khan came to where we sat and said, 'My brother-in-law is not well. I'm going to send a telegram.' Then he readily

* Farsi poems.

parked himself on the bench next to us. Ahmad Ali consoled him, 'It's okay, it's okay. All will be done. The telegraph wires are made of very strong material. They will not wear out in a few hours but there is some good news. Syed Sahib has just now told me a very funny story.' He then narrated my half-baked story adding lots of sauce – tomato and Worcester both. Finally he kept repeating the punch line, 'This soap is not for sale; this bus is not for Kabul. The orange hue of the sunrise from Bengal and the crimson red of the sunset in Peshawar – identical, same colours.'

Ramzan Ali said, 'Understood. But on one count, Pathans and Bengalis are very different.'

'How?' I asked.

Ramzan Ali said, 'You are aware that I have fallen foul of Ahmad Ali by crossing the Indus river. This story is from the same river valley – but much further south where the river is really wide. On one hot summer's day eight Pathans were sweating, sitting on the sand dunes in the riverbed. They ran a business of camel trains and had earned ninety-six rupees that day. But they couldn't manage to divide the money equally. Sometimes someone was getting less, sometimes they were left with some extra. They kept doing the calculation from scratch again and again, but without any success. With the heat making them sweat, they were getting more and more impatient and their voices were rising. At that point they saw a trader passing by on the other side of the river. The Pathans asked him to cross over to their side and help them to divide the money. The trader told them with a lot of gesticulation that it would take too much time and he really was not in the mood to cross the river. Then he asked how many of them there were and how much money was to be divided. They said there was four scores and on top another ten and another six and that was to be divided between eight of them. The trader said in a flash, "Take twelve each." The Pathans said, "Wait please, let's see if it works." And surprise – it indeed worked out. Then their leader thundered, "How come it worked out? We have been trying for hours and we couldn't figure it out. That trader's son must have palmed off some money; hence it worked out this time. Let's catch that bastard."'

Finishing his story, Ramzan Khan said, 'You can understand, the trader was in deep waters while trying to be helpful. But luckily the Indus was quite wide there and traders can do one thing very well. They can run as fast as an Arab stallion. So he saved his neck that time.'

I said, 'Very good story. But what about the main point – the difference between the Pathans and the Bengalis?'

Ramzan Khan said, 'Didn't the Bengalis tell the British the height of the world's highest mountain, sitting at home, without climbing or measuring it with a tape?'*

I said, 'But the British took all the credit.'

Ahmad Ali interjected, 'Is that why angry Bengalis want to bomb the British?'

I scratched my head and said, 'That may be a very minor reason, but Sikdar didn't bomb Everest.'

Ramzan Khan said angrily, 'Well, he should have.'

I said, 'But there was a technical problem. When the mountain was being measured and named, Sikdar was in Calcutta and honourable Sir George was drawing his pension sitting in his London home. So you see—'

---

* Bengali mathematician and cartographer Radhanath Sikdar first measured the height of the tallest mountain of the world in the 1850s. He worked for the Survey of India all his life. Peak XV, measured by Sikdar was later named after the retired Surveyor General of India, Sir George Everest.

The Pathan and the half-Pathan exclaimed with dropped jaws, 'What? What does that mean? The measurement didn't even happen under the supervision of Everest?'

I said, 'No. But why are you so surprised? I can't even count how many times your people conquered Kabul, but I know that every time the British took the credit. Whenever you chose not to fight, they were butchered. And what did they do? They blamed the defeats on you while they wore lots of medals to hide the humiliation. Even this time when Amanullah, armed with only a few Mughal era guns and cannons, gave them a solid beating,* didn't they tell the whole world that they were defeated because of the treachery of the Pathans?'

Ramzan Khan asked, 'Why do Bengalis know so much?'

I said, 'Please don't take any offence and forgive me for saying this; we will be better off if you people care to know a little more.'

They both listened to me silently. Then Ahmad Ali said, 'Syed, please don't mind. You people bomb the British; you organise political agitations; the British do fear you. These are recent stories. But tell me something. The world didn't know the name of an arid, rocky land called the Frontier where a group of mountain tribes lived. What could they have done? The British would have liked to wipe them from the face of the earth. No crop grows on this land. You can't find gold, silver or oil under the rocks here. The women walk for three hours in early morning for just a drop of water. Only the stupid Pathans have grown roots here. Who knows for how many centuries? When the green pastures across the Indus and the wet monsoon air of the east tried to mesmerise us, so many tribes left the place – except the Afridi and the Momand.

* King Amanullah defeated the British in a short campaign in 1919 and gained independence for Afghanistan.

'When the British couldn't kill us by fighting, didn't they try to lure us by recruiting us in the army? Tens of thousands of men joined the military. What could they have done? In the Mughal period they had nothing to worry about. The doors to the army were open, but that army didn't enter our villages to take away food from our plates, they didn't force our women to wear clothes produced in mills in England. The Emperor of the world, the owner of the throne of Delhi, couldn't stand the heat of India and returned to Kabul every summer. The Pathan came to pay his respects to the Emperor when he passed through this land. It made the Emperor happy and the Pathan got his due. The Emperor's ministers threw gold coins on the road. The Pathan shouted, "Long live the Emperor." That cry of a thousand voices used to resonate in the rocks of the Khyber and come back at the feet of the Emperor as the voices of millions to pay more respects. Now there is no gold coin, the cries of the Pathans don't echo in the rocks any more. But the Pathans have fought for their independence with their blood. That's why it's still called "no-man's land". Now tell me what else could the Pathan do?'

I said apologetically, 'I didn't mean that. I was talking more about the gentry and the middle-class. But even the middle-class has played its role. If they didn't agitate, the soldiers possibly would have fought against Amanullah.'

Ahmad Ali said, 'Let's not talk about the educated gentry. The sooner they die and go to hell to meet Satan, the better it is.'

Ramzan Khan said disapprovingly, 'The fighting styles of the educated gentry and the Pathan soldiers are bound to be different. When the time comes, you'll see which side this useless Ahmad Ali takes.'

I looked at Ahmad Ali questioningly. He had his answer ready: 'I can't hear everything clearly; by God's grace I'm a little deaf.'

SEVEN

There is a saying in Arabic, '*Yom oos safr, nisf oos safr*' – meaning 'Half the travel is done on the first day.' Even in our East Bengal people say, 'Half the journey is completed if you can cross the courtyard.' It took me a full seven days to cross Ahmad Ali's front yard. On the eighth morning Ahmad Ali took me to the bus station, found me a seat next to the driver and left me at his disposal – my life and my luggage. At Howrah station, I had thought, 'I'm alone', but now it seemed like 'I'm frightfully alone.' Be it the Khyber or the no-man's-land or Afghanistan, the crux of the matter was that you were responsible for your own life. I heard that there were police outside Kabul, but murder had not been recognised as a cognisable offence in this land yet. You would pay for your stupidity if you did not hit the ground in prone position, Pathan style, at the time of a robbery. It was not the job of the Afghan government to teach you how to travel on those roads, any more than the government in England took you to school to teach 'keep to the left'. And in case you died, your relatives could very easily take revenge – one did not have to mortgage one's property or get a permit, to buy a bullet.

This was what ordinary people on the streets did. But Afghanistan was a civilised and independent country. Its government, like other civilised countries, could not afford to be oblivious to murders and crimes. So to prove its concern, the government sent a few policemen to the crime spot for a couple of days. But why should they get involved if they heard that the smart relatives of the murderer had shut the eyes, ears and mouths of the relatives of the victim with a big bundle of the rare shiny metal? Or they found out that that your relatives were taking your death very philosophically – in this journey of three days in this world, how did it matter if someone left two hours early or late? How did it matter if someone died in a roadside ditch or on his bed taking the name of Allah? So my dear sir, why should the police create more trouble for everybody by dragging the murderer and his relatives to court; what was the benefit? The philosophy of detachment was not exclusive to you. The police could also lay claim to this universal philosophy. But yes, there was one consideration. In this world they needed to buy bread and kebab; the salary that the government gave was often not sufficient and when the Lord had given enough wealth to the murderer's family, then – ? Why should we blame the Afghan police?

The Afghan government was careful that the situation did not spiral out of control. If the word got around to Bukhara, Samarkand, Shiraz, or Tehran that the highways of Afghanistan were not safe, then trading would stop; thus the government would lose its goose that laid the golden eggs – by which I meant the customs tax.

Sardarji – the Sikh driver – was sitting on my right. He was almost sixty, had a long flowing beard and I later found out that he was night-blind. An officer of the Kabul government sat to my left. He had gone to Peshawar to get equipment for the radio station released from the customs house there. Apparently he knew many languages but with me he conversed only in Farsi. He pretended that it was your fault if you did not understand his English. He then used the six words of French he knew. After that he blabbered a bit in Urdu because you still did not understand what he was saying. Finally he gave a haughty look – as if it was such trouble to talk to a bunch of philistines. Later I realised that he was quite friendly and was always ready to help others. Even later I found that he had to show off his knowledge of languages to me because he had got his job at the Kabul radio station by claiming to be a polyglot. He would be travelling with me for two days. He was afraid that he might be in danger of losing his job if I told everyone after reaching Kabul that he was really a small fish in the smallest of ponds. But actually he had nothing to fear; he did not know that all his bosses were aware of his ability or the lack of it. The only reason he still had the job, was that others were even worse. He was a simple man. He was always so busy trying to hide his own lacunae that he never realised how ignorant others were. Learned people said, 'A closed fist very close to our eyes obstructs the views of even the mighty Himalayas.'

There was a bunch of Kabuli traders in the belly of the bus. They were carrying cigarettes, gramophone records, pots and plates, chandeliers, equipment for electricity supply, books – essentially, 'everything under the sun'. Afghanistan had only three industries – guns, bullets and winter clothes. They had to import everything else, mostly from India and a little from Russia. You did not have to read the reports of the Afghan Ministry of Industries to know this. One round in the bazaars of Kabul would be enough.

But more on this later.

It was a hundred and fourteen degrees the previous day – that too in the shade. You would not be able to spot, even with the most powerful binoculars, a single green leaf in this land through which we were travelling. All you could see was thick tufts of burnt yellow dry grass on the rock faces, here and there.

A boy, in my college hostel, had burnt his face while trying to put more spirit in a burning stove. The whole stove and the bottle caught fire and burned his eyebrows, eyelashes and newly grown soft moustache, which created the most shocking and horrible crinkles on his face. It was like that here too. It seemed that Mother Earth had taken her face too close to the sun god who had slapped her with scorching heat – her eyebrows, lashes, hair – everything was burned beyond recognition.

I had never seen such a scorched land in my life. Deserts were different. There, everything had been burned back to the elements long before we were born and the rest had left the country – nature never tried to grow grass and plants in a row there. But here there was a horrible naked contradiction. It would be wrong to say it was a contradiction – it was actually cruel, heartless torture. Mother Earth could not leave this land altogether – she had been trying her best, however feeble that might be, but she got beaten down mercilessly. It reminded me of the landless and poor peasant rebels in East Bengal. They would try to build homes on the river islands and the landlord's goons would burn them to ashes, again and again.

It was a ten-mile drive on the plains from Peshawar to Jamrud fort, where our passports were checked. Then we entered the Khyber Pass.

I admit with folded hands that I cannot describe that experience. I do not know what Pierre Loti would have written on the conditions through which I crossed the Khyber. I mention Loti here because he had the amazing ability to paint, with words, the true picture of an unknown land. I am yet to come across such skill in any other writer. Even the 'King of Poets', Tagore, did not like to describe something unknown to him. There are no mountains in the plains of Bengal. I did not find a single description of high mountains in his two and a half thousand poems. The most beautiful sight of a cold country is the snowfall – Tagore had seen that at least fifty times but never described it.

It would have been easier to describe the journey if one had passed through the Khyber Pass in this heat at least a dozen times. Sri Ramakrishna[*] had said, living through the pleasures and pains of life was like the camel trying to eat thorny bushes. It filled his stomach but his mouth got bloodied. So I imagined that once you had absorbed the heat of the Khyber, you may be able to extract some moisture of literature.

The bus in which I was travelling did not have any moisture. It seemed like it was prepared for a military campaign, in the way that it negotiated the roads built in Mughal times. It was covered on all sides by thick corrugated tin. They had removed the windscreen as if to prove that glass was breakable. One headlight was broken, no glass cover on the other. There is a line in praise of the one-eyed in the Book of the Song in the Bible – 'Thou hast ravished my heart, my spouse thou hast ravished my heart with one of thine eyes.'

I had read many books of Concord, the Christian doctrinal teachings from the fourth to the sixteenth centuries, based on the Holy Scripture, searched many footnotes for years but never managed to understand the meaning of that line. By the grace of my Guru and the Khyber bus, I deciphered it now in a flash.

There were thousand-foot high naked rocky mountains on both sides of the road. Two winding roads stretched side by side towards Kabul. One road was for motor cars, the other for horse,

---

[*] Bengali Hindu reformer and philosopher of the nineteenth century.

mule, camel, and donkey caravans. The narrowest point of the pass would not be more than thirty yards wide. Like a drunken man, the roads ran so unsteadily that at some points you would see mountains on all four sides.

The midday sun had descended straight down that hellhole – and the rocky mountain faces were throwing it around as if it were a session of catching practice. In this pass, where once a thousand Afghan voices had echoed, amplifying them into a million – one sun turned into a thousand suns. Millions of tongues of flame were not only satisfied with licking our bodies, but they were penetrating our eyes right through our closed lids. I saw that even without his evening dose of rum, Sardarji's eyes were bloodshot like the evening sky. The Kabuli had made an eye-pad with his handkerchief. Who could face a firing squad with eyes opened?

Did Gandhari,* the daughter of Kandahar, become blind in this heat? There was no other way to Delhi but through the Khyber Pass. Who knows why the creator of the *Mahabharata* did not write about the reason for her blindness? Possibly out of pity for Dhritarashtra and to console the blind queen.

I saw that the pustin traders of Bukhara were going towards India with their mule trains wearing two-inch-thick fur overcoats. I asked Sardarji to solve the mystery. He said, 'It's very comfortable, for people who are used to it, to wear such thick dress. The outside heat can't get in; the body stays cool. And people don't sweat in this land. Even if they did, it wouldn't matter much. They don't care.' I saw that the intense heat made his tongue dry in no time. I decided not to chat any more.

---

* Gandhari was the wife of the blind Kaurava prince Dhritarashtra. To empathise with her husband Gandhari decided to blindfold her eyes forever.

A mosaic of culture and a medley of people from so many countries was travelling in those caravans. So many different kinds of hats, so many coloured turbans, so many varieties of weapons – from various ages – from the age-old musket to the modern Mauser. The famous handsome sword from Damascus, Jamdhar – like the ones I had seen in Mughal paintings – stuck in silk belts. Some were carrying stout sticks with metal tips, some had a lance. The camels were loaded with colourful woollen carpets, samovars of different shapes. Sacks of pistachios, almonds, walnuts, raisins and prunes were heading over to garnish and flavour the Indian biryani. I heard some whispers that they also carried dope – opium, hashish, cocaine and other substances – hidden under their belts, in the linings of those overcoats or in the folds of their trousers.

Everyone was moving very slowly. A friend who once visited Mansarovar lake in Tibet, had told me that one should walk very slowly when one got tired at high altitudes. You would offer your life to the angel of death for sure if you wanted to hurry in those conditions of extreme cold. I realised that the same rule applied in extreme hot weather too. My Pathan friend had said it twice, I now accepted his wisdom wholeheartedly. '*Al ajlu meena shaitan*' – you will follow Satan if you make haste.

Tagore also said something similar; how would you cope with pain if you did not experience it? He actually meant that there was no point trying to avoid pain in haste, it would run its course anyway.

Christ too said, 'Verily I say unto thee, thou shalt by no means come out thence [prison] till thou hast paid the utmost farthing.'

Who said there were no miracles in the twentieth century? All my problems were solved with a loud bang. The Kabuli quickly opened his eye pad and looked at me with a pale face and I looked at Sardarji. He parked the bus on the side of the road very calmly and said, 'Puncture. It happens in this heat. Happens every time. It'll be an exception if it doesn't.'

When the Creator assumes such devastating looks, one should never hurry. But, I thought, in this summer heat, He would be able to attract more followers if He had chosen to show His cool kind face.

There was no need, yet Sardarji reminded everyone that the two roads in the Khyber might be government property but the land on both sides belonged to the Pathan. He was hiding somewhere behind the rocks. There would be a bang if you stepped out there. After that they would rob you of everything. How? No need to elaborate. What does a hunter do to the deer? He does not even spare its skin. I heard that the broad grin that you had on your face before getting shot floated in the air and the rest vanished in no time.

The British gave a tax of two rupees to the Pathans who lived on both sides so that they did not commit robbery on the roads. They also extracted another condition with a lot of difficulty, that two Afridi clans would not fire at each other across the roads.

I did not remember how long it took to change the tyre. Apparently in a state of delirium, people lose track of time. Next day when I asked Sardarji why it took him two hours, he replied that it had taken only half an hour.

The bus moved again. The Kabuli had lost his voice. Yet the essence of what he was muttering was this—

'No worries, monsieur – we will reach Kabul tomorrow. Then we will jump straight into the Kabul river. You will cool down in the ice-cold water that has come from the mountains. After that we shall have grapes frozen on ice for the next two months. The water in the ditches will start to freeze from September. In

October, the early winter wind will cover the whole city with a thick carpet of dry fallen leaves. We will bring out our pustin overcoats in November. It will start to snow in December. We will then take a walk on that snow. Oh, what cold, what comfort.'

I told him, 'May God bless you.'

What was that ahead of us? Was it a mirage? Why was the road closed with a gate? The bus stopped. We had to show our passports. We had entered Afghanistan. There was a signboard with bold lettering:

> It is absolutely forbidden
> to cross this border into
> Afghan territory.

The Kabuli said, 'The biggest test in this world is to pass the Khyber Pass. Al-hamdulliah – thanks be to God.'

I said, 'Amen.'

EIGHT

Finally we made it through the Khyber Pass. I thought that the killer heat would now ease off a bit. It certainly did, but at least there was a tarmac road in the Pass. Here there was a semblance of a road, rather, some thousand-year-old track created by the caravans. The caravans could easily negotiate it but for a bus passenger the experience was a nightmare. It was similar to travelling in a bullock-cart at night in the eroded open lands of Birbhum in Bengal. The only difference was that the cart did not travel at twenty miles an hour and had a thick padding of straw. The surface of the road consisted simply of rocks and pebbles.

Ahmad Ali had put a huge turban on my head before I left Peshawar. It saved me from sunstroke in the Khyber Pass. Now the turban, acting like a buffer state, saved my head from serious injuries as it bumped against the ceiling of the bus.

I asked Sardarji if turbans had any other use. He said, 'There are many; but right now I can think of only one. In some situations, when you want to hang yourself and can't find a piece of rope, then turbans come in very handy.'

I thought the heat and the trouble of driving on this excuse for a road had finally got to him. Otherwise why would he think of this perverse example?

I felt sorry for him. He was at least sixty. He should be sitting under the shadows of the tamarind tree in his backyard and recounting stories from his military days to his grandchildren. Instead, here he was, regularly commuting between Kabul and Peshawar in this blazing heat. Considering the climate, the condition of the road and his mood, I gave up on my intention of having a chat with him.

What a country! There were fields of rock and pebbles – on either side – for miles on end. On the horizon there were faint outlines of mountains. It was difficult to say for sure from a distance, but I guessed that there was no life in those fields, cruelly battered by the sun for millions of years. The bus stopped once to refill the radiator and I saw that there was not a single blade of grass between the rocks. Nor any insects. No wonder. How could they survive? What would they eat? There was no sign of a trickle of water anywhere. In this massive purgatory that extended up to the horizon, the Ford bus was like a mother-ghost travelling with her children under her wing. It felt as if some invisible keepers of this vast expanse of desolate land would appear out of nowhere and make this smoke-belching car vanish, restoring silence to the land.

Then we came across death. Nature refused to create life in this land, but she was certainly not averse to taking it. The huge carcass of a camel lay by the road. Even the scavenger birds or animals avoided this land for the fear of death. Hence the bones were not scattered. The flesh had turned into dust in the dry heat. A complete clean white skeleton was lying there as if waiting to be a museum piece.

Dakka fort was only ten miles from Landikotal.* In this desert, the fort looked imposing. The high walls had been built by mixing

---

* Landikotal is the entry point into the Khyber Pass on the one side, then in India, now Pakistan, and Dakka fort is on the other side, in Afghanistan.

straw with mud – matching the colour of the land – dull yellow. There was a row of small holes towards the top of the walls; the sentries could easily shoot the enemy from those holes. From a distance, the holes looked like gouged eyes.

But my eyes were soothed as we approached the fort. The Kabul river was flowing to the left – creating a strip of green on its bank. This dry land had produced corn on that patch of moisture brought about by a little silt.

I stared in surprise. The sight of the river, like a piece of green wet cloth, wiped all tiredness and pain from my eyes.

The Kabuli said, 'Let's go inside the fort. We need to show our passports here. We are government employees, so they will process us quickly. In that case we'll reach Jalalabad before evening.'

The officer of the fort showered me, the foreigner, with courtesy. It was unlikely for a place like Dakka to have an icebox. As I drank the glass of water he offered me, I wondered how it was possible to get such cold drinking water from earthen pitchers.

The officer was an educated man. He was very lonely; he had no companion to talk to. He was so delighted to have me in his office that his lonesome thoughts started to spill out in no time. He recited a few verses from Hafiz and Sadi. He spent his time in this exile in the desert to find the inner meanings of these poems and he shared some of it with me. I asked him, in my broken Farsi, if this lonely life was difficult or not. He said, 'I work for the military. Can't resign. So I keep myself busy with the Kabul river. Every evening I sit out there and feel as if she were flowing only for me. A few other people also go there but they want to cool themselves on her banks. I do too, but I don't spare the winter either. I was selfish in the beginning. I only used to admire her beauty. I used to see her dancing, I used to hear her music, and I used to sit on her green lap. But now we have a special relationship. Tell me, have you ever heard the river flowing on a pitch black night?'

I said, 'Many times – lying in a boat.'

He said approvingly, 'Then you will appreciate what I am saying. I feel that it's not only the sound of the flowing river, if I try for a few more days, I'll be able to understand her mysterious language. You think I am trying to write poetry? Never. The thunder in the clouds scares us but I feel the river brings some message of hope. I don't know if that message has come from the faraway sea or she is singing here after waking up from the bounds of the snow peaks of the Kabul mountains.

'It's very hot now. Please come back here during your winter vacation. I will tell you many mysteries of the river. Food? No problem. Plenty of chicken and lamb. But no vegetables.'

I began to seriously worry about the mental health of the officer as I listened to him talking. But I buried all my doubts instantly when he drifted from his allegory of the lap of the Kabul river to chicken and lamb. He said, 'My job is to stamp passports and keep a log of all goods being imported and exported. Not a very difficult job. There, in Kabul, the king is trying his best to turn Afghanistan into a strong and energetic country. Many people have flocked around him. I hear that Kabul is full of new green grass. But there is the British ram on this side and the Russian goat on the other. Both will overgraze the hills of Kabul if they get an opportunity. By God's grace we have the barriers of the mountains on all sides. The other advantage is if the ram eyes the grass, the goat tries to jump over the Amu Darya* and chases him intimidatingly with his horns. If the goat acts funny, the ram bleats to alert the whole world that the goat not only wants to

* River Amu in Central Asia.

overrun Afghanistan but the rice fields of India, China and Iran too.'

I said, 'Why should the ram only bleat? He also has a pair of strong horns.'

'He had once. India still thinks he does. But he has lost his sharpness by trying to lock horns with the rocky mountains of this land. So he now has gilded them – I mean, you have seen the pomp and shine of the British army. Indians are still scared and awestruck because of that shine. Meanwhile Saad Zaghlul Pasha[*] in Egypt, Kemal Pasha[†] in Turkey and Ibn Saud in Hijaz[‡] have showed the ram the door after properly whipping it. But it's an animal after all, not easily defeated.' I almost jumped. Total sedition! No, not here. I had forgotten that I was sitting in independent Afghanistan.

The officer went on, 'I'm very glad to hear that Afghanistan and India are going to work together. But you will have a hard time there. Kabul is a very tough place. It's covered with rocky hills and the people there are even harder than those rocks. The king is trying to grow fresh grass in the cracks on those rocks and you are going to help by watering it.'

I interrupted, 'It's nothing. I have a very small job there.'

The officer said, 'We will take stock of that some other time. Until now only people from Peshawar or Punjab came to Afghanistan. I'm really glad to see that the invitation of Afghanistan has reached the faraway land of Bengal.'

I saw that Sardarji was calling; everyone was ready; he would

---

[*] A revolutionary and a nationalist leader of Egypt, who led the anti-British movement in the 1920s and became the prime minister in 1924 when Egypt attained independence from the British in 1922.
[†] Ruler and founder of modern Turkey.
[‡] Saudi Arabia.

leave as soon as I boarded the bus.

The officer said, 'You are going in Amar Singh Bulani's bus? The best driver and mechanic on this route. There is no bus here that hasn't got a few slaps or been caressed by him. If some car behaves badly, all you have to do is to open the bonnet and whisper, 'Witch-doctor Amar Singh is coming.' The car will start instantly, unaided, without the self-starter and run for its life. The driver will barely get a chance to get in.

'But you'll often see that Amar Singh is driving the most broken down bus. Let's have some fun.' He called out to Amar Singh and said, 'Sardarji, I'm buying a new bus, coming soon from America. Would you like to drive it? You will get the same salary that you're getting now.'

Sardarji looked happy when the officer called him. But his smile vanished after hearing his proposal. He fiddled with one end of his turban and kept his eyes focused there too. Finally he said, 'Sir, it would be an honour to drive your bus, but I'm still contract-bound.'

The officer said, 'Is that so? What a shame. Let me know when your contract ends. Okay, you go now, I'll send your young Agha[*] soon.'

Then he said, turning towards me, 'Did you see? He doesn't like to drive new cars. The contract isn't an issue at all. It's all rubbish. On this route no owner would dare to throw the contract at his driver if I decide to hire him. It's nothing like that. Amar Singh doesn't have any fun driving new buses. How could he show his skills if there was no puncture on every road, if the engine didn't stop or if the roof didn't blow away? Even a burqa-clad woman can easily drive a new bus.

'You know what I think? His wife is dead. He gets the same

[*] Gentlemen are referred to as Agha in Farsi.

57

thrill in finding an excuse to open the bonnet of the bus as one does when one unveils one's newly-wed wife. You don't get that chance in a new car.'

I asked, 'Why do you need an excuse to unveil your wife?'

He said, 'Oh yes. Certainly. Even kings need one. Listen to what the King of Kabul, Badakshan and half of India, Humayun, said to Zubeidi—

> Still, if I pleaded with you like a beggar,
> to appear before me in mercy;
> you tell me, "Veiled shall I remain,
> this visage you shall not see".
> Distanced shall be thirst and quenching
> in the form of this pointless veil?
> Keeping your beauty from my pleasure,
> never shall a veil prevail!
> What game of war is this twixt you and I?
> Pray forgive, I seek relief;
> The inner meaning of me thou art
> the life of this life I live.'

NINE

The Afghan officer was not only a poet but a prophet as well. Just as he had predicted, we had three punctures and the engine ceased twice. The handyman changed the tyres – under the supervision of Sardarji. With the application of a lot of oil and solution the bus-beauty was taken care of, but Sardarji had to intervene himself in order to make her talk. He had to peep into her veil, pleading and cajoling all the while, even threatening to use the starter handle. We did not know what the final agreement was, but at last she moved unwillingly to go to her in-laws house, making all sorts of strange noises on the way.

But a few miles before Jalalabad, her belt or bra – whatever you chose to call it – broke into two pieces. That was also when I learned that Sardarji was night-blind. The radio employee announced into my ear, mistaking it for a microphone, 'That's the end of tonight's act. We will gather again at seven tomorrow morning.'

There was an Afghan inn about half a mile away. The broadcaster and I started walking towards it while the rest of the passengers followed behind pushing the bus. I was told that in this country, before boarding a bus, one needed to sign a contract to 'carry the beauty on his shoulder' if needed.

Sardarji hurried everyone, 'Walk quickly. They will close the door of the inn after it is dark.'

It looked like a fearsome fort rather than an inn. The mention of an inn usually conjures up an image of a nice quiet little resting place, but this one had an unimpressive yellow wall thirty feet high on all four sides, one of which had a high door in it. It was so big that camels, elephants, double-decker buses – all could easily pass through it. It felt like we were walking into the belly of a beast and would never come out.

I stopped the moment I stepped in. I did not know how many years of collective odour jumped on me but I could say that I was pushed back three yards. It did not take me long to figure out what it was. This region was outside the range of monsoon clouds; so it hardly ever rained here. It was not high up enough for it to snow here either. As there was no river close by, there was no concept of washing or cleaning the place with water. So from the time of Alexander the Great till today, the faecal matter of horses and sheep was only superficially cleaned with brooms but it left layers of stink over thousands of years. You had to cut your way through that solid odour to go inside. You could even scoop some of it with a spoon. There were high walls all around; so the fresh air from outside probably refrained from entering, sensing that there was no way out of this maze. I knew about pitch black, but here I experienced 'pitch odour' for the first time.

There were some open coupés – not rooms – along the walls. The broadcaster rented one such coupé for us after bargaining a little with the innkeeper. They also arranged a cot for me, which was placed outside in the veranda. I went inside the coupé once – man sometimes makes such grave mistakes. By Jove – if an unconscious man did not wake up with smelling salts, he should be sent in there for only half a minute.

The traders were taking care of their animals in the dim light of kerosene lamps. If the camels started to back off, then the mules would try to get towards the baker's corner, braying cacophon-ously. If the bus switched on its headlights to look for parking space, all the animals would scatter around the courtyard, and their owners would scramble around in search of them. Animals were fighting over the hay; people were bargaining at the baker's shop; there were sounds of the bus being repaired; a Pathan was snoring in the next coupé. His nose was hardly six inches from my face. There was no way I could change position; in that case my feet would face west[*] and my face would touch the tails of the camels. I did not want to imagine what it would be like if the camels decided to back up a little.

But it was true that one would not be disappointed if one could penetrate the stench and filth of the inn in search of knowledge or a most interesting session of repartee. There were speakers of as many languages as described by Ahmad Ali, besides a few wise pilgrims who were going on Hajj on foot from India. There was no sign of weariness on their faces because they walked very slowly and they learned the trick of living with filth at the Frontier. They did not have any possessions – they only depended on God and the alms of the people on the way.

There were tell-tale signs of various sins. But I will leave them to Hirschfeld[†] to describe.

I had left Peshawar after a modest breakfast of bread and eggs and had not eaten the whole day. The sorbet in Dakka could not even reach my stomach; my parched tongue and throat had sucked that in. There was so much filth around that I did not

* Muslims in the Orient are not supposed to sleep with their feet facing west where the holy city of Mecca is located.
† German physician and sexologist Magnus Hirschfeld – an outspoken supporter of the rights of homosexuals. It is believed that homosexuality is rife among the Pathans.

feel like eating anything. I was getting annoyed with myself. What kind of royalty was I that I could not eat anything without taking a bath and was about to pass out in this two-thousand-year-old odour when hundreds of people were sleeping peacefully after a happy meal? At least the animals were in the courtyard and I was on the veranda. The Virgin Mary did not even get some space in the inn and finally gave birth to Jesus in the stable among donkeys and mules. Western painters tried their best to paint the place hiding all the dirt and filth, without much success.

'What is the difference between a stable in Bethlehem and one in Afghanistan? It rains three drops and snows two and a half ounces in Bethlehem too. Who told you that the Jews then were cleaner than the Afghans now? Here your body is revolting in this Afghan stench, but the Jewish stink was so strong that a stinking goat would run for its life by bolting the stable door.'

But these were theoretical debates. One could read the holy books to a man, but the sinner also lived inside him. He had only one answer, 'Why are you reading the good words of the holy books, I have no appetite for it.' Besides my mind was ready with another argument: 'If the lovers' spat between Sardarji and his bus hadn't taken place just before the evening, we would by now be at the government guest house in Jalalabad, sleeping happily under the chinar tree after a bath and a hearty meal.'

The rebel inside me knew a few theories too – otherwise how could it live in the same room with my conscious-self? It started to debate in a whisper, 'The story of Virgin Mary giving birth to Jesus in the stable is a scandal from the Bible. According to Islamic writings, she gave birth to Isah[*] under a date-palm tree.'

* Jesus Christ according to the Islamic faith.

Conscious-self – 'What nonsense. Mother Mary gave birth to Jesus in winter in December under a tree?'

Rebel-self – 'Why not? The Bible says that after the Lord was born, the Magi went to the shepherds to give the news. If they could spend the night in the open fields, then why couldn't the wife of a carpenter? Besides, she was in labour – she must surely have been sweating a lot.'

But I never cared much for religious debates, so I banished both of them from my mind and closed my eyes.

A loud announcement atop the forty- or fifty-foot high watch-tower in the courtyard woke me up in the middle of the night. It was the innkeeper saying, 'If the inn is attacked by bandits at night, then my good travellers, it is your responsibility to save your property and lives.'

That was the last straw. I had, so far, taken everything in my stride by entrusting my safety in the hands of the innkeeper. I reached the state of absolute bliss when the innkeeper passed that responsibility back into our hands. There is a saying in Urdu, '*Nange sey Khuda bhi darte hain*' meaning 'Even God is scared of the naked man'. With a slight variation, the saying sounds poetic in Bengali, 'One who is lying in the sea doesn't bother about the night dew.'

Meanwhile some doubts, mostly linguistic, clouded my thoughts. The broadcaster was fluent in Farsi. So I asked him, 'Isn't it odd the way the man said just now "maal-jaan" – property and life. Shouldn't that be constructed as jaan-maal – life and property?'

In the dark I could not see his face, so his voice reached me as a radio broadcast, 'In Iran they say jaan-maal but in Afghanistan, jaan, I mean, life, is cheaper; hence here we say maal-jaan.'

I said, 'Possibly true. We also say the same in India.'

By then I had opened up a 'brain-trust' with the broadcaster. He asked, 'There is no fear of dying from bullets after you cross the Frontier. So why do you say so?'

I replied, 'There are so many ways a man can die. Malaria, cholera, tuberculosis. Above all that, there is the universal royal way of dying of hunger. You don't need an inn or hospital for that.'

The broadcaster said, 'Dying of hunger is the sole property of the Orient. To live forever is "the white man's burden". But we Afghans are poor people; we carry our own burden. The missionaries tried to give us a shoulder by offering to share some of it. Hence they are forbidden in Afghanistan. Under no circumstance is a missionary given a visa. We treat the British like the missionaries. We try not to let them in. We tolerate the presence of a few of them in the British Legation in Kabul – and that too with a lot of reluctance.'

These two bits of information soothed my mind as though someone was reading me the gospels of Mark and Matthew. They killed every bit of stench by blowing in the fragrance of the rose gardens, bringing sweet sleep to my eyes. 'Long live Afghanistan!' – Let there be millions of bedbugs in the cot, I did not mind them.

TEN

I woke up with the early morning azaan. A pustin trader from Bukhara led the prayer. I wondered how such a good Arabic accent could survive in Turkistan. I queried the broadcaster. He said, 'Why don't you ask him?'

I asked, 'Wouldn't he mind?' The broadcaster was surprised by my reticence; I understood that in this part of the world it was quite normal to face queries from a complete stranger. Later I found out that they felt happy if you asked a question.

I picked up the thread and delved into a conversation to take stock of the previous night.

The Great Eastern in Calcutta was a hotel, so was this inn. I had some knowledge of the comforts of the plush Grand and the Great Eastern hotels at home. Here, I had experienced the very basic facilities of the inn. You could say, even without reading Marx that an inn was a poor man's place and the hotels were for rich people. But could you explain all the differences by that? In that inn there were at least eight traders who could easily have stayed in the best suites in the Great Eastern. I talked to them as I had done in the past with guests in the Grand or the Great Eastern hotels.

The difference was in their attitude. The eight rich traders could have flocked together and spent a few thousand rupees on food and drink as well as gambling. Their servants would be there at their beck and call and would have kept others away from their masters.

Instead, they did not sit in a silo, creating their own coterie. The rich and the poor from the same caravan already knew each other. After getting some rest, they sat down to enquire about one another. In no time at all, they were engaged in easy banter. The difference between rich and poor was visible only in their clothing, but not in the way they were conversing with each other. There were some yes-men among the rich who were sucking up to their masters but the leader of the gang of the poor also had such people around him. They discussed everything – trade, religion, the condition of the roads and the Khyber Pass, tension between Britain and Russia, treatments for a rabid camel bite, the eccentricity of our Sardarji – everything. People were diving in and out of the pool of such chitchat but the poorer lot never tried to partake of even a little share of the food served for the rich traders.

Some fights broke out in the courtyard. The chattering lot did not cast an eye on that as long as it remained verbal. But someone or other from the group would intervene and mediate if they saw any indication of it becoming physical. It reminded me of English films; the onlookers would make an excited circle when two white men got into a fight. The two men would take off their jackets and throw them down. The 'concerned' onlookers would catch them so that they did not get dirty. Then they would start to fight, boxing and punching – bloodying each other. Others would enjoy the fun for free and leave the act when it ended after applying the lotion of 'their-own-private-matter' on their conscience.

There was no concept of personal space in the inn. Everyone would carry on with their own business as they liked and you could not object. You could do yours too, no one would stop you either. Everything was permissible as long as there were no fisticuffs.

There was both good and bad in this attitude. People learned how to tolerate each other in spite of the thirst and hunger and the scorching heat. At the same time they would dirty the place beyond imagination.

On the one hand, there was this concept of a tightly knit communal living, on the other there was individual freedom. There was a sense of community but no civic responsibility.

I realised that I had started to form lots of theories regarding the Afghans and the Turkmen. Immediately I shut the windows to my inner self. But what was there to see outside?

The same land or, to be precise, the same lifeless rocky mountains.

I said to Sardarji, 'It would have been good to have some betel nut when I was feeling a bit queasy at night. But I didn't see any shop for paan.'

Sardarji said, 'Where will you get paan? The last paan shop is in Peshawar. I haven't seen any paan shop west of Peshawar – in Afghanistan, Iran or Iraq. I have travelled to all these countries working for the army. Pathans don't chew paan. Punjabis are the only customers of the paan shops in Peshawar.'

When debating democracy, one wise holy man from southern India had said, 'Then everyone should go to bed. There is no difference between people when they sleep, they are all equal.' I understood the meaning of the theory sitting in that heat. In spite of the rattling of the bus, dust, hard seats, hunger and thirst, both the broadcaster and I were dozing off. Sometimes his head was resting on my shoulder and I was trying my best not to disturb him by staying stiff. But he would wake up with a sudden jerk and apologise to me. With all my good intentions, I could not help but doze off on his shoulder at times.

With my eyes still closed, I felt the touch of a cold breeze; I woke up to the sight of a lush green valley – with fields of crops on both sides of the road. Sardarji introduced me: 'Jalalabad.'

With help from the same Kabul river that we had seen in Dakka, Jalalabad looked green – with trees, plants and crops. As it was not too rocky as Dakka had been, the valley looked wide – once you entered, it was difficult to gauge its expanse. Both sides were green, lined with houses. It was hard to imagine how a small river could perform such magic with the smallest of opportunities. Jalalabad was an example of that. The Pathans on the streets looked much gentler than the Pathans of the Frontier. I noticed that Pathan women were working in the fields. Pathan men would vehemently criticise the disregard for the purdah by city women. The same Pathan would not object if his mother or sister worked in the fields and even looked at the bus. I raised the issue with the broadcaster and he said, 'As far as I know, poor women in any country do not observe the purdah, at least in their own village. They will sometimes wear the veil in town to imitate the middle class women but it is inconvenient when they work; so they stay unveiled in their village.'

I asked, 'But what about the Arab Bedouin women?'

He replied, 'I have seen them shepherding in Iraq – without the veil.'

Let us put these discussions aside, I thought. Let me see the country first, we can talk about the customs and rituals of the land later.

The bus entered the city. The Kabulis came out from the belly of the bus and disappeared in no time. No one even asked when the bus would leave. This was my first journey, so I asked Sardarji, 'When will the bus leave?'

He replied, 'When everybody is back.'

I persisted, 'But when is that?' Sardarji replied, rather irritated, 'How do I know? Everybody will now have a proper meal. Only after that.'

The broadcaster said, 'What are you doing standing there? Come with me.'

I directed my question to him, 'Where did they go? And when will they be back?'

The broadcaster replied, 'Why are you so worried about them? You are not responsible for their jaan-maal.'

I said, 'It's not like that. The way all of them disappeared, it seemed like they would not come back any time soon. Then how can we reach Kabul this evening?'

He answered, 'You have high hopes. They are not in a hurry. When there was no bus service, it took them fifteen days to reach Kabul. They are happy to be there in four days now. At least they don't have to look after their camels, mules and horses. They don't have to load and unload their goods at every stop. They have reached Jalalabad. All of them have a few relatives here, uncles, aunts, in-laws – someone is surely here. They will go to meet them, eat a proper meal and only then will they come back.'

I went silent. I had told the officer in Dakka that I wanted to have the same experience as the rest of the passengers. Now I understood that every man had the ability to be prophetic – but some did it with proper knowledge and some did it unknowingly.

There were five main cities in Afghanistan: Kabul, Herat, Gazni, Jalalabad and Kandahar. Jalalabad was the winter capital.

So there was a royal palace and some fine quarters for the civil servants, the broadcaster informed me.

I believed the broadcaster; surely there were such places when he said so. But I saw nothing impressive in the city and its bazaars; the same dirty dull-yellow-walled houses and rickety shops. The bazaar was full of cheap Japanese goods, plenty of tea stalls and millions of flies. People were not at all bothered by the flies – just as in the inns in the Himalayas.

Suddenly my eyes were attracted to sugarcane, on display outside the shops, cut into small cubes. Flies squatted on the cubes, creating a thin greyish film. I set aside all my revulsion and bought some. It tasted sweeter than the sugarcane from our land. No wonder Emperor Babur was impressed by the sugarcane from Jalalabad and sent samples to Badakshan and Bukhara. Then I came across a medley of melons and cucumbers. That corner of the bazaar looked bright with stalls full of dark green and golden yellow fruits. There was a sweet intoxicating smell in the air too. No need to bargain. As they did not have the opportunity to export, everything was already very cheap. The broadcaster wanted to show off his knowledge, 'People who love fruit spend the whole summer eating it. During winter they have dry fruit and nuts – pistachio, walnut, raisins and almond. Sometimes they eat some bread and cheese. Only occasionally a slice of meat. Those people live longest.'

I said, 'Don't they face bullets? Or is the water of Jalalabad so magical that bullets don't harm them?'

'Why should the people of Jalalabad face bullets? They live in the city; they don't know a thing about fighting; they are law-abiding citizens.'

The main attractions of Jalalabad were outside the city limits. If you were interested in geology, you could establish your knowledge by digging around the city. If you were an anthropologist, a plethora of tribes and sub-tribes would provide you with volumes of research material. If you wanted to write on the Oriental context of Marxism, all you had to do was to bring Engel's *Origin of the Family* along with you. The rest was here – the villages around Jalalabad exemplified the family structures while Kabul, just a hundred miles away, would explain the pinnacle and the power of the state. If you were a historian, you could check, first-hand, narratives of the campaigns of Alexander, Babur and Nadir or the story of Gandhari. If you were interested in economic geography, you could study how a small river could fight famine downstream of the Kabul river from Jalalabad. And if you were searching for the confluence of Indo-Greek art, then you could go to Hadda village – only a few miles from here. You would find everything you wanted to look at – the meditating Buddha, the skeletal or Amitav Buddha – every style of Gandhara art. Only a few were visible in the open, but there were many more underground. Even the most untrained eye could find them under the surrounding hills.

If you wanted to scoop a big share in the market of knowledge, you would agree that the recent discoveries of Mohenjo Daro in the Indus valley, the Babylonian-Assyrian civilisation by the Euphrates and Tigris or the Egyptian civilisation on the Nile were all pre-Aryan ancient civilisations. I heard that some pundits had been excavating, with a lot of zeal, around the Narmada river in Central India in an attempt to post some profit in the same market. You would be totally cornered in that crowd and be bankrupt in no time. Luckily if you found something original, you could become one Rakhal Banerji.* But the fact was, that a flock

* Bengali archaeologist and historian Rakhal Das Banerji who discovered and led the excavation of Mohenjo Daro in the nineteenth century.

of birds of prey were flying overhead and in no time, they would swoop onto your raw material. Then, using your own original material, they would throw three fat volumes at you. Didn't you hear the saying, 'The conman is to be blamed if you are conned for the first time. But you will be blamed if it happens again.' Hence I say, 'Go to Jalalabad and find the younger version of Mohenjo Daro. You will make India proud. The Afghans will benefit from it too. There are no vultures in Afghanistan to gobble up your work.'

But a wise man has to be cynical. You may say, 'Okay, agreed that there's not only gold dust on the ground, there are gold mines too. Then why haven't the magpies already gathered around in cacophony so that they can steal it?'

The broadcaster had explained it the previous day. Afghans do not like white magpies. In the realm of knowledge, all the birds are white and they are forbidden to enter the skies of Afghanistan. But you are brown, a neighbour too. The Afghans have known you for centuries – you may have forgotten him, but your brethren are still doing business in many corners of Afghanistan. The Afghans will not look for a club to beat you if they see that you are trying to dig here and there.

You will still not pay heed to what I am saying? That is why I always say that you have to be a scholar to spoil good ideas.

ELEVEN

The bus left late in the day. So there was no possibility of reaching Kabul that evening.

Peshawar to Jalalabad was one hundred miles and Jalalabad to Kabul another hundred. The timetable said that the bus would leave Peshawar in the morning and reach Jalalabad in the evening, and the same the following day – it would reach Kabul in the evening after leaving Jalalabad in the morning. I should have understood that very few buses actually travelled according to that timetable. Only the mail buses did.

Children in the villages around Jalalabad were playing on the streets. One of the games was to create a zigzag path for the buses and cars, right in the middle of the street. They arranged the hard skullcaps that the Pathans wore under their turbans, in such a way that you would most certainly crush a few if you were not careful. Whenever Sardarji saw those caps, he slowed down and wound his way around them, swearing under his breath. After he had negotiated a few such hurdles, I told him, 'Why don't you crush a few. That will teach them a lesson.'

Sardarji said, 'By God's name, never do that. I don't want any more punctured tyres.'

I said, without understanding the riddle, 'How can these caps puncture your tyres?'

Sardarji replied, 'You haven't understood the cunning game. They have put long nails under the caps; so my tyres will be intact only as long as I can manage to save them. I'll be shooting myself in the foot if I drive over them.'

I said, 'So the kids want to teach you that you will suffer if you want to harm others?'

Sardarji said, 'You have such a clear brain.'

The broadcaster joined the conversation, 'But the question is, where did this teaching come from?'

I asked him to explain.

He said, 'There are Buddhist teachings in this kids' game. You know, once upon a time, this was the heartland of Buddhism.'

'So I have heard.'

He said, 'What do you mean, you have heard? You will reach Hadda if you walk a little to our right. You should go there just to see how many statues of Buddha have been dug out. Do you think those are the relics from some museums of ancient times?'

It was like a question in your university exam, 'Were there any museums in the Gandhara period?'

I failed. The Bengalis, however, may not be able to do many things, but they can argue. It is in their blood and they can argue non-stop. So I said, 'But when I heard the chilling warning about saving your jaan-maal, sorry, maal-jaan – at the inn last night, it didn't sound like Buddha's teaching.'

The broadcaster said, 'Right. Buddhism is the religion of innocent children and women. The religion of the strong, fighting, adult men is Islam.'

'Oh certainly,' I responded sceptically.

Sardarji said grimly, 'I'm a follower of the Guru Granth Sahib, but I will say it a thousand times that if any religion can tame these half-human Pathans, it is Islam.'

For a moment I was scared that this comment might start a fight. But the broadcaster answered him calmly, 'You are a foreigner. The eldest here and most experienced too. You have seen enough in life. I'm very glad to hear your opinion.'

I was very surprised. I whispered to Sardarji, in Urdu, 'What was that? You abused his people by calling them half-human, but he didn't take offence; rather, he seemed very pleased.'

Sardarji was even more surprised, 'Why should he take offence? He's a Kabuli.'

I was now in deep waters. I asked again, 'Kabulis are not Pathans?'

By then Sardarji had figured out my ignorance. He explained, 'Pathans are inhabitants of Afghanistan. But pure Kabulis came from Iran and they control the city. Their language is Farsi. The Pathan's mother tongue is Pashto. Your broadcaster friend doesn't know a word of it.'

I said, 'But the Kabuliwalas of Calcutta don't understand any Farsi.'

'That is because they are not from Kabul. They are from the Frontier, Khyber, at most Chaman or Kandahar. A true Kabuli never leaves Kabul. The few who do make such journeys are all traders, and their limit is Peshawar.'

But Sardarji was not satisfied after doling out so much knowledge to me. He asked, 'Why did you say Kabuliwala? The inhabitants of the city should be called either Kabuli or Kabulwala. So why this business of Kabuliwala?'

I was caught off-guard. Even Tagore had written it as 'Kabuliwala'!* How could I save his honour? But I had to, because my motto was – 'My guru may be drunk, but he's my guru after all.'

* A famous short story by Tagore where the central character is an Afghan.

I went on a counter-offensive. I said, 'It is like the way you say Jawahirat! Jawahar* is singular; Jawahir is plural; yet you add a double plural and say Jawahirat. How come?'

You can cover an odour with perfume. But can you cover an odour with another? That can be debated in any other country but here in Pathan-land, the rule was 'an eye for an eye'. I had somehow saved my honour.

Yet it was not necessary. Sardarji was busy taking a turn. I remembered the road to Kabul went straight. Then why was he taking a turn?

The broadcaster said, 'Good. Since we can't reach Kabul tonight, let's spend it in the Nimla Garden.'

I could see, from a distance, the rows of chinar trees. The chinar is taller than a betel nut tree – almost touching the sky. Half of its trunk has no branches, the rest sways in the breeze with its soft, smooth, thick leaves. The only comparison one could come up with would be that of a long plait of bamboo leaves intertwined with the newly grown soft leaves of Ashoka trees. But the chinar's trunk was unrivalled – unique – nothing like any other tree. For centuries, Iranian poets had untiringly compared the shapely bodies of attractive women with the chinar tree. When the chinar swayed from head to toe, even the dry Pathan looked at it with admiration. The swaying resembled the betel nut trees in my land but betel nut trees were rough – devoid of any green.

The broadcaster knew nothing about Indian history. I did not expect any better from Sardarji. Yet he informed us that the Nimla Garden and the Taj Mahal were built around the same time. The palace in the Nimla Garden could not withstand the attacks and invasions over the ages. Thus there was not a single ruin left to see,

---

* Meaning jewel.

but according to Sardarji, Emperor Shah Jahan had planted the trees in the garden. A study of botany could prove the historical veracity of what Sardarji said. But why bother? I felt so thrilled imagining that I was in a place founded by Shah Jahan. What was the point of spoiling that illusion? There was nothing special in the garden that someone would object if I gave the credit to Shah Jahan. Besides, Shah Jahan had the Taj to his credit; he did not need the Nimla Garden to augment it.

But one had to admit that it had been turned into a magnificent garden with very little effort. Rows of chinar, a canal in the middle to water the garden and a profusion of nargis flowers. The Greek king Narcissus used to sit by the river all the time admiring his own reflection. The gods eventually turned him into the flower. Even now the narcissus – nargis in Farsi – looks at itself in the water.

I spent the evening sitting by the canal, next to the forest of nargis, listening to the sound of the swaying chinars. The cook in the guesthouse served us food soon after sunset. After dinner, I slept by the canal on a cot.

I awoke early in the morning with an ethereal feeling. Suddenly I heard the sweet sounds of flowing water next to me and felt as though I were being touched all over by the fragrance of a beautiful woman.

In the early morning when the boat leaves the lake to join the river, the sound of the flowing river wakes you up. The scent of the jasmine tree next to your bedroom window will arouse you in the autumn dawn. There in Nimla Garden, I experienced both sensations simultaneously – the sound of the water and the scent of the flower. I had heard the music of flowing waters many times but had never been caressed by such a sweet fragrance.

In the dim light of the dawn I saw that the dry canal was overflowing, touching the feet of the nargis plants. During daytime the water was stopped by some gate upstream. Now with the call to morning prayer, it was the turn of Nimla Garden to receive water; the gate had been opened and water was flowing into the canal. The music of the water blended with the fragrance of the flower.

The chinar trees, at whose feet the music and the fragrance were creating an orchestra, were waiting with their heads held high for the first sun. In no time, the chinars wore a crown of gold and the morning crier called out from the scented forest of the flowers.

> The day today threw
> A door in some house ajar;
> The sunrise this morn
> For whom did it come so far?[*]

[*] Poem in Bengali by Tagore.

TWELVE

Sardarji started honking soon after the early morning prayer. It seemed he was determined to reach Kabul that evening by any means.

The broadcaster too was full of energy. He started chatting to Sardarji and filling me in with necessary information about Afghanistan as well as regaling us with various colourful stories. I was not equipped to estimate just how much of it was real, how much his imagination and how much was blatantly untrue. But I was thoroughly enjoying the one-sided conversation. In reference to one such story he said, 'Listen to this; see how some small things change the entire course of one's life.

'Some thirty years ago, about forty prisoners and their guards spent the night at Nimla Garden on their way to Jalalabad. In the morning the guards realised that one of the prisoners had escaped. They were in dire straits. They could not imagine what would happen to them if they failed to produce the same number of prisoners as they had left with from Kabul. They had neither any prior experience nor any legal knowledge. Some said they would be hanged; others indicated a firing squad; and some even talked about live skinning. But all of them were sure that they would face prison terms. As they were prison guards, they knew only too well the conditions of Afghan prisons. Once one went in, he never came out unless to face the firing squad or to be brought out horizontally in a coffin. So all the prison stories that you might hear are all lies as no one ever left alive.

'The guards were out of their minds with fear. Finally one of them came up with the idea of catching someone from the streets to fill up the place of the missing convict.

'So they went out on the streets at dawn before anybody found out about the escaped convict. They were looking for someone alone who they could catch. It was still dark and one man was out on the street to respond to the call of nature. They immediately put him in chains and left for Jalalabad along with the others.

'On the road, the guards had scared him to death. They had warned him not to say anything, "When the jailor asks your name, you will only say, '*Ma khu chihel O panjom hastam*', meaning, 'I'm number forty-five'. Nothing else."

'Either the man was utterly stupid or was so scared that he thought that as a matter of principle they caught the first person they saw on the street when they lost a prisoner.'

The broadcaster continued, 'I heard the story from at least five people. There were some variations in the narrative but why he didn't try to tell the jailor what had actually happened remained the real mystery. '

Sardarji asked, 'Why didn't the other prisoners say anything?'

The broadcaster said, 'They must have had many reasons to keep quiet. All of them were from the same gang of bandits, so they thought that their runaway mate would be able to get some help for them. They also might have played a role in his escape. So it would have amounted to grassing on their own mate if they said anything.

'Anyway, that ill-fated man entered the hellhole of the Jalalabad prison. Within a few days, he understood, after talking with other prisoners, that he had made a terrible blunder. He then tried to send a petition to the king through various people. But it was almost impossible for any petition to reach the king from inside the belly of the Jalalabad prison. Meanwhile the jailor was possibly scared too. He might have thought that he would be equally blamed for incarcerating the man without checking properly. He might also have thought that the man was either telling a fib or had gone mad.

'It was not as if there was an abundance of ink and paper in the prison. The poor man would get a petition written by someone once in a while but he could never find out what happened to it.

'Believe it or not, not a few months or years, but sixteen years went by like this. It was difficult to say what was happening in his mind, but eventually he gave up the idea of sending any more petitions to the king.

'At that time, the whole of Afghanistan was celebrating either the wedding of the Crown Prince or the birth of his eldest son. The happy King Habibullah doled out a lot of money to the poor and his mercy also reached the prisons. An order was given to parade all the prisoners of Jalalabad in front of him. He was in seventh heaven; so he decided to reduce their prison terms after talking to them.

'Many prisoners were released, and many had their sentences reduced. Finally the poor man of Nimla stood in front of him.

'His Highness asked, "Tu keestee?" (Who are you?)

'The man said, "*Ma khu chihel O panjom hastam.*" (I'm number forty-five.)

'The king kept on asking his name, address, the crime for which he was jailed, but he had only one answer, "*Ma khu chihel O panjom hastam.*" At first the king thought that he was mad. He asked him, to determine his mental state, other questions, like on which side the sun rose and where it set, if the mother fed the baby or the baby fed the mother – questions like that. He gave all the right answers but whenever he was asked any question about himself, he said, "*Ma khu chihel O panjom hastam.*"

'After saying it for sixteen years he was fully convinced that he had neither a name, nor a home; neither sin nor good deeds; there was no incarceration in the prison and no freedom outside – his whole existence was hinging on the hymn of one line, "*Ma khu chihel O panjom hastam.*"

'Habibullah had many defects but he had at least one virtue. He could really untangle any knot if he got hold of one end of the thread. Finally, with the help of some members of the old bandit-gang he solved the mystery.

'I heard that even after his release, that poor man from Nimla could never recover from the spell of "*Ma khu chihel O panjom hastam.*"'

I had goosebumps by the time the broadcaster came to the end of his story. The old Sardarji with the white beard said, 'Allah Malik, God is the master.'

Meanwhile, the uphill journey to Kabul had begun. The seven or eight thousand feet of climbing started soon after the Nimla Garden.

Winding roads and hairpin bends would not be anything new for people who had travelled from Sylhet to Shillong or driven from Dehradun to Mussoorie or crossed the Western Ghats close to Mahabaleshwar. The only new element here was that no one repaired these roads or put up railings at the bends. Neither did anybody control traffic at landslide points. You would be stuck for hours if there were a landslip, until the drivers themselves cleaned it up with shovels. I heard from regular travellers that in the winter they often cleared snow and ice. History said even Emperor

Humayun had given a hand to clear snow on this road when he was fleeing India after being chased by Sher Shah.[*]

The drivers on the routes near Shillong or Nainital would try to cheer you up by saying accidents generally did not happen on those roads. If anyone said the same here, you needed only to look down the thousand-foot gorge to spot the skeletons of vehicles. I heard that the authorities in some hill town had thought of a unique way of warning drivers. They displayed a smashed car by the side of the road with a signboard in bold lettering, 'The same will happen to you if you do not drive carefully.' On this road you did not need any such signboard – there were plenty of examples strewn all around in the gorges.

Sometimes after taking a sharp turn you might face a caravan of camels. There was the steep mountain to one side and a sheer drop of a thousand feet to the other. There would be a gap of hardly a yard in between the bus and the mountain. Let alone lanky camels, a nice tame donkey would not be able to pass through that gap. As a half-a-mile-long camel caravan could not simply back off, the bus needed to reverse for several hundred yards to a clearing. Not a single passenger had the nerve to look over his shoulder at that time. They either closed their eyes or recited verses from the Koran. And there was an even greater surprise after you opened your eyes. The camels were passing through one by one but suddenly one of them decided to block the clearing by half-turning and standing firm. Experiencing a blockage, the other camels then scattered along the road with a huge cacophony – like the way water spilled when the flow was

[*] Pathan fighter who had defeated the second Mughal Emperor Humayun and ruled north India for a couple of decades before Humayun regained the empire after his death.

blocked. At that point at least five people would pull the stubborn camel from the front and another twenty shouted from behind. It was almost like a novice driver blocking a narrow road while trying to take a three-point turn. But in that case there would be no sheer drop on one side of the road and you might be enjoying the fun, smoking a cigarette with your mates, sitting on the front porch.

In this situation all hell would break loose if another caravan came from behind. The area would then look and sound like a big animal market.

Bukhara-Samarkand, Shiraz-Badakshan would get mixed into that whirlpool; everyone would shout abuse at each other; everyone would try to untangle the knot; the knot would open and get tangled once more. They would rest for a bit and then start all over again.

If you could establish truth with the help of your memory, then all I remembered was that I was holding my head with both hands. I clearly remembered the jumble but I had no recollection of how it was undone and when the bus moved.

THIRTEEN

Radio France started its broadcast with '*Ici Paris*', meaning 'Paris here'. Kabul followed Paris if they had to mimic anything European, so they too said, '*In ja Kabul*' meaning 'Kabul here.'

Our broadcaster made the announcement, '*In ja Kabul*.' It was evening by then and hence my chance of seeing the city was as slight as seeing Paris or Kabul through a radio broadcast.

There was no possibility of seeing anything in the headlights of the bus. One of the lamps was already broken. Sardarji discovered that the other one had gone blind too, like the way Gandhari had in the heat of the Khyber Pass, when he tried to switch it on. But, of course, Sardarji did not need any light for himself – he was night-blind. A lantern was borrowed from one of the passengers and the bus' helper sat on the bonnet holding it for the benefit of pedestrians who were in the same mental state as 'I'm number forty-five'.

I asked Sardarji, fearfully, 'Aren't you finding it difficult to drive in such dim light?'

He said, 'Certainly. The light is dazzling my eyes. I could have driven faster without it.' I remembered that the boatmen in our country did not like to have lamps in front of their boats either.

Even though the Kabul valley was flat, there were some cross-roads. I would close my eyes at each turn. I conveyed this to

Sardarji. All my fears were gone with his answer, 'I close them too.' After hearing that piece of information I closed my eyes forever, like Gandhari.

The only reason I reached Kabul in one piece was that the detective would never die in a pulp novel; possibly the same rule applied to travel writers.

The gumruk* had closed by then. They did not release anything, not even my bedding. I hired a tonga to go to the French Legation – my only acquaintance lived there. He had been my Farsi teacher in Shantiniketan and was now working at the legation.

Three minutes after we set off, I figured out why Moscow Radio asked the proletarians of the world to unite. I realised that there was no difference between the proletarian tonga drivers of Kabul and the taxi drivers of Calcutta. Just like the cabbies of Sealdah station, he worked out his strategy after taking me for a half-wit.

The broadcaster had given him detailed directions to the French Legation. He swore on his life and his mother's grave to take me straight there. But within two minutes, he stopped the carriage to ask someone the way to the legation. He kept repeating this act and I felt that he was seeking directions from the most ignorant group of people in the city.

We had many pieces of advice; one even said the French Legation was in Paris, so if we wanted to go there—

I completed his sentence, '– we have to take the ship from Bombay. Right? Okay, driver, take me to Peshawar or Kandahar whichever is closer. Then to Bombay.'

The tonga driver was clever. He understood that I was not a half-wit after all. Finally he reached the legation via Lab-e-Dariya,

* Customs house.

86

Deh-Afghanan and Shahr-Ara. Surrounded by the hills, Kabul was a small city. He had already circled it at least three times through the same roads.

He had pretended throughout the journey that he could not understand a single word of my broken Farsi. Now it was my turn. At the time of settling the fare, I gave a catatonic look when he tried to convince me with a lot of gesticulation that I was under-paying him. In a bid to bring some novelty and a bit more life into the conversation, I kept taking away some money from his hand saying in my most broken Farsi, 'Oh I understand – you are an honourable man. As a foreigner, I'm ignorant of the fare and I'm paying you a lot more than you deserve. Right? You don't want so much? *Masha Allah, Subhan Allah* – by the grace of God, good things will happen to you, you will live long, your children . . .'

The more money I took away, the more animated he became. He kept taking the name of God and all the prophets and reciting verses on honour and honesty from Rumi and Sadi. At that point Professor Bogdanov, my host, came down and arbitrated. The driver measured me from head to toe with keen eyes and asked under his breath before leaving, 'Which country are you from?'

It was surely for his future protection.

Who said that Bengalis were inferior? Did we not occupy Sri Lanka* at one point?

Night was the right time to talk to Igor Bogdanov. He used to read all night and sleep all day long. That was probably the reason why, of all the birds in India, he liked owls the most. Nandalal

---

* An ousted Bengali prince, Bijaya Singha, went to Sri Lanka to seek his fortune and became the first king after occupying it. The name Sinhala came from his surname.

Bose had painted an owl on the wall of his classroom in Shantiniketan. He admired him greatly for that.

Bogdanov was Russian, a resident of Moscow and a staunch Tsarist. He fled Moscow at the time of the Bolshevik revolution in 1917 and reached Tehran through Azerbaijan. From there he came to Bombay via Basra. As he knew Pehlavi* rather well, the Zoroastrian organisation in Bombay, the Cama Institute had commissioned him to translate a large volume of old scriptures. At that time Tagore had responded to an international campaign to assist the Russian scholars in exile. Having met Bogdanov in Bombay, he brought him to Shantiniketan even before he founded Visva-Bharati University.

Bogdanov was posted to Tehran for eight years while working for the foreign ministry, before 1917, and had learned Farsi well during his stay there. Later, when Tagore went to Tehran and searched for a good Farsi teacher, he was told that nobody could match Bogdanov. I gathered from the leading critics in Kabul that his writing style in modern Farsi had attracted a lot of admiration.

He knew many European languages and had mastered various Turkic languages and sub-languages like Jagtai and Usmanli. In a multi-lingual city such as Kabul, he could easily converse with people of many nationalities in their own mother tongue.

On the one hand he was a vast ocean of knowledge, on the other he was full of superstition. All hell would break loose if he ever saw the moon over his left shoulder. He would blame the 'accident' of sighting the moon thus if his pet cat vomited three months later. You were doomed if you walked under a ladder, broke a mirror, or put a bunch of keys on the floor. He would try

* The pre-Islamic language of Persia.

to ward off your bad luck by praying in front of the Icon for an hour, wish you well before all the saints of the Orthodox faith for the whole night, and sprinkle your face with holy water in the morning. After that he would keep an eye on you for three years so that there was no bad news. Three years was a long time. Something or the other was bound to happen. He would then walk to your house, sit in front of you with his head down and say, 'Didn't I tell you?'

You would become an expert on superstitions if you spent three days with Bogdanov and would start to believe in them in a month.

He was an extremely generous and friendly man, and always happy. The French professor Benoit used to describe his generosity by saying, 'He bought the machine to make a hole in the macaroni.' In simple Bengali, he would even buy a crow's chick if his friends needed one.

Bogdanov was the centre of attraction for all foreigners living in Kabul – an institution by all accounts. For that reason, I had to talk at length about him.

FOURTEEN

An old woman once said, 'Mothers with grown-up, unmarried daughters get a headache when they are invited to attend any social gathering. It will feel like a bone stuck in her throat if she leaves her daughter at home; on the other hand she will get snide comments if her daughter accompanies her.' Meaning she would worry if the daughter stayed at home alone, and friends and family would criticise her for not having her married off, if she accompanied her to the gathering.

Travel writers too have the same dilemma. After reaching one's destination, should one give the historical backdrop of the place? You will constantly worry if you do not – would it have been good to have done so? You will face a barrage of critical comments if you do. It was particularly true for Afghanistan. Like a grown-up unmarried daughter for whom no match was found, nobody had ever written a proper history of the country. The real history of the country was buried beneath the soil, much like the way that Indian history was hidden in its Puranas, *Mahabharata-Ramayana*. Afghanistan is a poor country; Afghans do not have the time or the resources for archaeological excavations to write their own history. Even if they had the resources, they would be digging to look for coal and oil. There is not enough erudition in Afghanistan to delve into the Puranas. I often doubted the scholastic skills of our own people. One could spend one's entire life in figuring out how much of the stories in the Puranas was history and how much was made up. The writers of the Puranas possibly wanted to have some fun at the expense of history-mad people.

The recent history of Afghanistan is strewn across at least four countries, in Farsi manuscripts. Some scholars in India had been sifting through the material from this country – through the lives of Mahmud[*] or Babur[†] – to write the history of the Pathan-Turk-Mughal era.[‡] But not a single Indian historian had yet travelled to Kabul, Hindukush, Badakshan, Balkh, Maimana or Herat to trace Babur's life, carrying with them his autobiography – the *Babur-nama*. They were not interested in writing the history of Afghanistan. Yet there was hardly any doubt that you could not complete India's history without linking it with the history of Afghanistan. In the same way that it was not possible to keep India's Frontier Province under control without understanding the politics of Afghanistan.

It would get complicated if you looked at the north of the country. The history of Afghanistan's north, meaning Balkh and Badakshan, was linked with Turkistan beyond the Amu Darya river in Central Asia (Bakshu in Sanskrit); the western region of Herat had connections with Iran; and the east, meaning Kabul and Jalalabad, was intrinsically linked with India and Kashmir's history. It was easier to write the history of Switzerland with its four languages and three races.

---

[*] Sultan Mahmud – the ruler of Ghazni in central Afghanistan between 997 and 1030 AD. His empire extended from Iran to north-west India.

[†] A descendant of Timurlane from his father's side and Zhenghis Khan from his mother's side, Babur founded the Mughal dynasty in India by conquering Delhi in 1526. He came from Andijan in the Farghana province in present-day Uzbekistan as a military adventurer and set up his kingdom in Kabul in 1504.

[‡] The first Muslim rulers of north India between 1206 and 1526 AD.

Meanwhile the scholars were waiting with the swords of their own interpretations in the few books that had been written so far. You would face their wrath if you wanted to poke your nose in there. They would charge at you, asking 'Where is it?' if you wanted to write 'Gandhar'. They would draw their swords if you said 'Kamboja'[*] and demand an explanation, 'What do you understand by Kamboja?' 'Kombugreeb' or 'Kombukonthi' means someone who has three stripe marks on his throat, like the ones seen on conch shells. Buddha had those marks on him. So did Kamboja indicate a country like Afghanistan marked with stripes of mountain ranges and valleys or the place where one found Kombu or conch shells like Baluchistan – the region by the sea? There was no consensus even on the spelling of some of the names. Take for example Balkh – sometimes its original name was spelt as Balhika; sometimes Baalhika and somewhere it had been spelt as Balheeka. Was that the same Balkh, mentioned by Firdausi,[†] where Zoroaster converted King Gushtasp in the Avesta?[‡] Do the Kabulis get saffron and heeng from there nowadays? Was that why these two were known as Balhikam in Sanskrit?

Bertrand Russell had said, 'The fool should not try to say something about which there is a difference of opinion among scholars.'

But my position was just the opposite – I thought it was the right moment to give your opinion – as the pundits were divided, you would be spared their combined attacks.

The gist of what the pundits and fools had agreed on Afghanistan was like this—

---

[*] A region in the north-west in ancient India.
[†] Highly revered Iranian poet, 940–1020 AD.
[‡] Primary collection of sacred texts of Zoroastrianism.

The Aryans reached India through Afghanistan and Khyber and not via the Pamir, Dardistan[*] and Kashmir. If they came after the destruction of the Mitanni kingdom of Bogazkoy,[†] then the myth of the Afghans being one of the lost Israeli tribes would not be entirely wrong. They would be right about the mythical country but not the people.

Gandhari came from Kandahar. The writer of the *Mahabharata* had described her as the mother of a hundred children, possibly after taking into consideration the size and strength of Pathan women.

The history of northern India and Afghanistan took a clearer shape with the advent of Buddhism. We could find mention of Gandhar and Kamboja in the history of sixteen kingdoms in northern India. But the pundits would show you their swords if you wanted to find out more about their expanse and influence.

In antiquity, there had not been any defining borders between Afghanistan and the Indo-European plains of Persia, just as there were none between India and Afghanistan in present times. In ancient Indian literature, the land on both sides of the Bakshu, or Amu river, had been shown as part of India. Similarly the old Persian literature claimed the same land as Persia's own.

After that, the Persian king Cyrus[‡] (Kurush) occupied the whole of Afghanistan and proceeded to the Indus valley in India.

---

[*] Ancient region in north-eastern Afghanistan, northern Pakistan and Kashmir. The region was inhabited by Dard tribes speaking Dardic language.

[†] A kingdom in northern Syria and Anatolia in Turkey between 1500 and 1300 BC. Bogazkoy (modern name Bogazkale) village of north-central Turkey has ruins from that period.

[‡] Cyrus the Great was the ruler of one of the biggest empires in ancient Persia between 600 and 530 BC.

It remained thus until Alexander the Great conquered Afghanistan and reached the Indus valley.*

Alexander entered India from northern Afghanistan but his main army made its way to Peshawar through the Khyber Pass. The mountain tribes from either side of the pass had put up so much resistance that the Greek general took revenge by burning down and razing all the villages and towns along the way. Alexander's conquest of the Indus valley was a milestone in Indian history. Similarly, during the Greek occupation of Afghanistan, various geographical regions, Arakhosia (Herat), Gedrosia (Balkh), Paropanisodai (Ghazni) and Drangiana (Kandahar) began to emerge.

Within a few years after the death of Alexander, Chandragupta Maurya† conquered northern India and faced the Greeks in the Indus valley. Finally he took control over the whole of Afghanistan except for the Balkh area, north of the Hindukush. Afghanistan remained part of India until the decline of the Maurya dynasty and the emergence of the Sunga‡ era.

The four Vedas of ancient India and the Avesta of the Iranian Aryans originated from the same civilisation. But the Maurya period saw the rapid spread of anti-Vedic Buddhism in the region. Persian and Greek architectural art also flourished at that time. The polish of Emperor Ashoka's iron pillars was Persian but the inspiration was Greek. The truly indigenous Indian art from that period was still rough and ready, while at the same time pregnant with future potential.

---

* Macedonian king Alexander the Great reached the Indus valley in 327 BC.
† Chandragupta Maurya from Magadh in Bihar founded the Mauryan empire in 321 BC.
‡ Northern Indian empire from Magadh between 185 and 73 BC.

Ashoka had sent a monk named Madhyantik to Afghanistan to preach Buddhism. There was no way of proving if the whole of Afghanistan adopted the religion, but certainly the rugged arid land was detrimental to the four-caste system of Hinduism. It was easy for the people to convert to Buddhism, which had a much simpler structure. In the span of two hundred years, many Greeks, Scythians and Turks in Afghanistan embraced the teachings of Buddha. At this confluence of history the heritage of the Vedas from Indian civilisation and the Avesta from Persia maintained its influence through Buddhism for a period of time.

The Balkh province was part of the Greek empire at the time of the Maurya dynasty. After the decline of the Mauryas, there were conflicts between the Greek rulers of Balkh. These rulers crossed the Hindukush to conquer Kabul and then proceeded further east after entering Punjab. One of those kings, Menand (King Milind of the Pali[*] holy book *Milindponghor*), apparently carried out his campaign up to Pataliputra[†] in the east and Karachi in the south.

There was no historical source for learning more about the Greek kings of central and southern Afghanistan and western India. Except for one. Thousands of gold coins made in that period had been retrieved during excavations in the Bagram[‡] valley, thirty kilometres north of Kabul. Those coins carried the names of twenty-nine kings and three queens between 260 BC and 120 BC. There were Greek and Kharosthi[§] inscriptions

---

[*] Middle Indo-Aryan language. Most Buddhist religious scriptures were written in Pali.
[†] Modern day Patna, the capital of the eastern Indian state of Bihar.
[‡] Valley now an American military base after the anti-Taliban war in 2001.
[§] Ancient script used by the Gandhara civilisation.

in the earlier specimens and Greek and Brahmi* in the later ones.

Many battles were fought between the kings of Afghanistan and western India but the connection between the two countries remained intact.

Then came yet more trouble. The Saka† people, after being defeated by the Yuezhi‡ tribe, entered Afghanistan in large numbers and spread all over the country. They took over Kabul and moved towards both the east and the west. The region was named Sakadwip in Sanskrit and Sakistan in Persian following their permanent settlement in southern Afghanistan, Balochistan and in the Indus valley. The barbarian Sakas became somewhat civilised after coming into contact with the Persians, Greeks and the Indians but they could not contribute much to Afghan history.

The Indo-Parthians§ defeated the Sakas. Their last king Gondopharnes was apparently baptised by Jesus' apostle St Thomas. St Thomas brought Christianity to the Africans of Abyssinia and the Hindus on the Malabar coast and Tamil Nadu in India. His tomb was traced to a hill close to Madras. Therefore, it was possibly a myth that he preached Christianity in Afghanistan.

The history of the Kushan¶ dynasty is well known to Indians. The second Kushan king Bim defeated the Sakas and the Iranian-Parthians to conquer Afghanistan. The great Kushan king

---

* Ancient Indian script – origin of most modern South-Asian scripts.
† Scythian tribes from ancient Persia or Iran.
‡ Ancient Chinese tribe.
§ Parthian tribes contemporary to Scythians in ancient Persia came to north-eastern India to establish the Indo-Parthian kingdom a little before the first century AD.
¶ The Kushan empire expanded from Central Asia to the whole of north and central India in the first and second century AD.

Kanishka expanded his empire from the borders of Iran in the west and to Kashgar,[*] Khotan[†] and Yarkand.[‡] Just outside Peshawar he built a stupa, in which the relics of Buddha were kept. Kanishka employed a Greek architect to build the stupa. There was no point debating whether he was an Indian-Greek or an Afghan-Greek as there were no cultural differences between the two.

Kanishka had stored the proceedings of the last Buddhist conclave engraved on a bronze plaque in a stupa. This stupa has not yet been found. Afghan historians should not be surprised if it is eventually discovered among the many unopened stupas close to Jalalabad. If Kanishka was considered an Indian king, then there should be no objection to calling him an Afghan king as well. Religion was irrelevant, as the Afghans had taken the blessings of Lord Tathagata[§] long before Kanishka.

The Kidara Kushans[¶] ruled Afghanistan for two hundred years after the decline of the Kushan empire in India.

The pinnacle of that era could be found in the Gandhara school of art.[**] Indian and Greek artists jointly contributed to this art form that was shaped by Buddhism. Its evidence could be found in India until the twelfth century. But its peak was in the sixth century in Afghanistan and eastern Turkistan. The history of the influence of Gandhara art on the culture of the Gupta empire[††] has not yet been written. Narrow-minded nationalist Indians

---

[*] Oasis city in the Taklamakan desert in the Uyghur region in China, an important centre on the ancient silk route.

[†] Ancient kingdom on the edges of the Taklamakan desert.

[‡] City in the Uyghur region in the Gobi desert in China.

[§] Another name of Buddha.

[¶] Kidara or little Kushans.

[**] Gandhara art flourished in the Kushan period between the first and fifth century AD.

[††] The Gupta kings ruled most of north India between 320 and 550 AD.

often looked down upon the art from Gandhara. If we approached it with an open mind, we would acknowledge that the attempt to separate the history of India and Afghanistan is a recent one. In the realm of sensitivity, India shaped some universal ideas and concepts that were heavily influenced by Buddhism. Nothing like that has happened since that period. More discoveries of Gandhara art and a greater volume of its history written, would one day force India to accept its debts to Afghanistan.

During the Gupta dynasty, traditional Vaishnavism[*] emerged as the main religion in India; however, Afghanistan had not yet deserted Buddhism. The Gupta emperors did not try to invade Afghanistan like the Mauryas, but the Saka rulers of the country had been weakened by then. The Chinese pilgrim and traveller Fa-hien[†] did not enter India through Kabul and the Khyber. Quite possibly, he chose the far more difficult route through the Pamir and Kashmir in order to avoid the anarchy in the border region.

After that, the Persian king Firoz died in an attempt to stop the invasion of the barbarian Huns. The Hun campaign reached India after destroying many Buddhist monasteries. The stories of the battles between the Guptas and the Huns can be found in Indian history. The present-day Rajput race came about as a result of the mixing of the Huns and the Afghans.

Hiuen Tsang[‡] reached Kabul in the seventh century through Tashkent, Samarkand and by crossing the Amu Darya. By then

---

[*] A sect of Hinduism – followers of Vishnu, the protector of the universe according to Hindu mythology.

[†] Travelled to India, Nepal and Sri Lanka between 399 and 412 AD and wrote one of the most important travelogues of that time.

[‡] Famous Chinese Buddhist monk, traveller and scholar, renowned for his seventeen-year-long overland travel to India starting in 629 AD.

the ripples of the resurgence of Hinduism* had reached Kabul. When the timid Indians could not hold on to Buddhism for long, it was no surprise that the fearsome fighters of Afghanistan found it difficult to practise the message of love and kindness to all living beings. Hiuen Tsang had shown Kandahar, Ghazni and Kabul as part of India in his writings.

Then it was the turn of the Arab historians. They said that Kanishka's descendant, King Turki, was ruling over Afghanistan when the Arab invaders reached Afghanistan. But his Brahmin prime minister later overthrew him and established a Brahminical kingdom. In 871 AD, Yakub ibn Lays conquered Kabul. The Hindu Shahi rulers, as a result, moved to Punjab, and their last king Trilochon Pal was defeated by Ghazni's Sultan Mahmud in 1021. The remaining history of the last Hindu rulers of Afghanistan could be traced to Kashmir.

Following this, the Indian scholars put a big full stop. I was no scholar but I felt that there was no need of a pause. From the first advent of the Aryans, or possibly even before that, Afghanistan and India had been trying to keep the continuum of the same tradition through friendship and conflict until the nineteenth century. If someone said that they had a different history after they became Muslims, then I would say there was no problem when they worshipped fire, or the Greek idols, or chanted the anti-Vedic Buddhist hymns. So how could it be a blasphemy when they embraced Islam? By accepting Buddhism as their religion they never become Magadhi;† similarly by adopting Islam

---

* Following the decline of Buddhism, the resurgence of Hinduism took place in north India and Hinduism again established itself as the main religion of the land.

† Magadh in Bihar in eastern India was the capital of the Maurya empire.

they did not become Arabs. If you tried to exclude the history of Muslim Afghanistan – especially Kandahar, Ghazni, Kabul and Jalalabad – from the history of India, then you would have to exclude the Frontier, Khyber, Bannu, Kohat[*] and even Punjab.

So where was the difference? The difference was that there was no written history of India before Mahmud of Ghazni. After Mahmud a great deal of history and geography had been written in every period.

There is no need to restate Mahmud's history. But one needs to mention Al-Biruni, a doyen of his court. If one prepared a list of six greatest scholars in the history of the world, then Biruni would most definitely be one of them. There was no Sanskrit-Arabic dictionary then, none even now. There was no intermediary language between Al-Biruni and the Hindu Brahmin scholars. It is a mystery that in spite of that difficulty this great man learned Sanskrit and wrote the massive encyclopaedia on India called *Tahqeeq-e-Hind* after mastering Hindu knowledge, science, philosophy, astronomy, literature, grammar, physics and chemistry.

Al-Biruni wrote the encyclopaedia on India in the eleventh century, but in return no Indian scholar ever wrote any history of Afghanistan. Apart from Dara-Shikoh,[†] no one had shown that level of mastery of Farsi and Sanskrit. Even in the twentieth century only a handful of people would be equally fluent in both languages.

[*] Both Bannu and Kohat are towns in the North-West Frontier Province or NWFP.
[†] Eldest son of the fifth Mughal emperor Shah Jahan, a Sufi and an erudite scholar. He was the crown prince but was imprisoned and blinded by his youngest brother Aurangzeb who took over the throne after the death of Shah Jahan.

The Pathan and Turk-Afghan rulers of India never cast their eyes on Afghanistan, yet the cultural connection between the two lands was never severed. Only one example was enough. The poet laureate of Alauddin Khilji,* Amir Khusrau, wrote poetry in Farsi. He was not known in Iran but his fame had spread to Kabul and Kandahar. Appreciation of his work equalled that of Hafiz and Sadi. There was no maulvi in Afghanistan who had not read his 'Ishqia' – the love story of Debala Devi and Khijir Khan.

With continuous inputs from Afghanistan, especially Ghazni, Farsi literature, Byzantine-Sarrasin-Iranian architecture, history writing, Unani† medicine and philosophy flourished in north India. It was Afghanistan that helped create Gandhara art acting as the conduit between the Greeks and the Indians. Afghanistan married India and Iran together during the Pathan and Turk-Afghan period.

Then came the campaign of Taimur.‡

After Taimur died, his descendants engaged in establishing new forms of art in Samarkand and Herat. The Afghan city Herat very quickly overtook Samarkand in Turkistan. Taimur's son Shah-Rukh introduced a new style by inviting Chinese artists and getting them to work with the Iranian form. Taimur's daughter-in-law Gohar Shaad was no less erudite than Queen Elizabeth or Catherine the Great. After he saw the mosques and madrassas built with the direct patronage of Gohar Shaad, Taimur's great-great-grandson Babur was filled with admiration. Herat was the only place worth seeing in Afghanistan. The few minarets still left

---

* One of the early Muslim rulers of Delhi in the thirteenth century.
† Ancient Muslim medical practice.
‡ The formidable Timurlane (1336–1405 AD) who conquered west, central and south Asia to establish the Timurid dynasty in Central Asia.

intact, in spite of the barbaric acts of the British, were all in Herat. They remained as evidence of how various Central Asian architectural and art forms combined to create an oasis in this arid land.

Al-Biruni to Gohar Shaad, and then to Emperor Babur.

The racism of the white scholars was exposed when they tried to establish that Julius Caesar's autobiography was superior to that of Babur. But let us set that discussion aside for the time being.

It was enough to carry only the *Babur-nama* with you while travelling through Afghanistan. Babur's descriptions of Kandahar, Kabul and Ghazni were not very different from what one would see even now.

The writer Babur was not the king of Farghana,[*] nor the emperor of Afghanistan and India; he was but an ordinary man. He was excited by the onset of the monsoon in India; he profusely praised the sweet taste of the sugarcane of Jalalabad, taking it back to his own land, Farghana, through the Hindukush in a pot. Similarly he transplanted the art created with the patronage of Gohar Shaad from Herat to Delhi, thinking that it would grow into a great tree in future.

It did. The Taj Mahal.

Babur did not love India. But he had the deep insight to understand that it would be foolish for a conqueror to leave the throne of Delhi for Farghana or Kabul. He founded a new empire in Delhi, risking his own life, but gave instructions that his dead body was to be sent to Kabul for burial.

Babur's mausoleum was the only monument worth seeing in the whole of Kabul.

The Mughal dynasty that followed with Humayun, Akbar, Jahangir, Shah Jahan and Aurangzeb, matched the Maurya empire.

---

[*] Southern valley in Uzbekistan.

Nadir Shah[*] ransacked northern India and was killed in Afghanistan on his way back. Ahmad Shah Abdali[†] captured his loot and wealth. He founded the first ever dynasty encompassing the whole of Afghanistan. 1761 was the battle of Panipat.[‡] Sikhism received a new spurt of life and inspiration in 1791.[§]

Meanwhile, history was playing a cruel game with India in the form of white invaders. For the first time some people came to this land, who did not accept India-Afghanistan as their own country. They remained invaders forever like Taimur and Nadir.

In the nineteenth and twentieth century, the British either tried to conquer Afghanistan on their own or to prop up a puppet regime to counter the influence of Russia. It was not so hard to conquer Afghanistan but it was mighty difficult to occupy it. Especially for the 'kafir' British. The ignorance of the Afghan mullahs equalled the heights of the country's mountains, yet they understood the British well.

The British were lucky that Amir Dost Muhammad[¶] had

---

[*] The king of Iran who invaded India in 1739 and defeated the Mughal army in the battle of Karnal. Under his order his army plundered Delhi and ransacked the city to avenge the killing of some of his soldiers.

[†] King of Afghanistan in the eighteenth century.

[‡] The battle between the Afghan king Ahmad Shah Abdali or Durrani and the Maratha army from western India. After the decline of the Mughal empire, the Maratha confederacy from Maharashtra gained power and proceeded to the north and northwest, where their paths crossed Ahmad Shah Abdali's.

[§] Ranjit Singh became the ruler of a small Sikh state at the age of thirteen. He created a large and powerful Sikh state, which included all of the Punjab, through clever diplomacy and waging numerous wars against rival Sikh princes, Muslim rulers, and Afghan invaders. Throughout his long and successful rule, he avoided conflict with the expanding British empire.

[¶] Ruler of Afghanistan between 1826 and 1863.

shown them friendship. They were luckier that Raja Mahendra[*] could not inspire Habibullah[†] to invade India in 1915.

But the penny finally dropped. Amanullah[‡] won independence easily by bashing the British a little. Possibly that was why Kabulis said '*Khuda-dad*' Afghanistan – 'God's gift' Afghanistan.

Zindabad Khuda-dad Afghanistan – long live God's gift Afghanistan.

---

[*] Raja Mahendra Pratap Singh (1886–1979) was a revolutionary social reformer and nationalist fighter against the British rule in India. In order to garner support for independence, Raja Mahendra travelled to Europe in 1914. His anti-British stand led him to make an alliance with Germany during the First World War and he came to Kabul in 1915 to form a government in exile. He encouraged the Afghan king Habibullah to invade India but Habibullah never took on the British.

[†] Son of Amir Dost Muhammad, his successor.

[‡] Youngest son of Habibullah and his successor.

FIFTEEN

I rented a house in the village of Khwajamollah, about two and a half miles away from Kabul. I acquired a servant too, along with the house.

I shared the house with Principal Girard, head of the college where I was going to teach, and his wife. Professor Girard was French. He introduced us formally, 'His name is Abdur Rahman. He will do all your bidding – from polishing your shoes to killing your enemies.' It meant he was my '*Harfan-Moula*', my 'Jack of all trades.'

Girard was a busy man. He spent his whole day fighting in the offices of various ministers. That was called work in Kabul. 'Au revoir, see you in the evening,' he would say every morning, and with that he was gone.

I had seen two giants in Kabul. One was this Abdur Rahman – I will talk about the other one later.

I once measured him from head to toe with a tape – he was six feet four inches. His width was proportionate to his height. His arms came down to his knees and his fingers hung from there like a bunch of plantains. His feet were the size of a small boat. His shoulders were so broad that if he had been Amir Abdur Rahman instead of my chef, he could easily have carried the entire weight of Afghanistan on them. His mouth stretched from one ear to the other – he could have swallowed a whole banana sideways. His nose sat atop his face like a rugged mountain, and he had no forehead. His head was covered with a big turban but I had no doubt that it was so small that a baby hat would have come down to his sideburns.

His skin was fair, but so cracked and creased by the harsh winters and summers that it had formed contours that resembled the relief map of Afghanistan. His cheeks were red, as though someone had slapped him. But who would have that courage? He was not likely to put on any make-up either.

He was wearing a shalwar, kurta and a waistcoat.

I could not see his eyes. He stood there, his head hanging down, looking at the carpet. He hardly ever raised his eyes from the patterns of the carpet during his stay with me. One was not supposed to look at one's master or elders in my country – possibly such a custom existed in Afghanistan as well.

But I did see his eyes at times. They looked like two round black balls floating in giant china bowls.

I felt reassured by his size and strength. But I was slightly apprehensive too. He would cook for me like Bheem[*] and like him he would be my bodyguard too. But what if he ever grew angry with me? Then? I was searching for an example, when suddenly it came to me. A philosopher had once asked Dwijendranath[†] to have quinine when he had fever. Dwijendranath said, 'Quinine will get rid of my fever but who will rid me of the quinine? Who?'

[*] A character from the *Mahabharata* – the second of the five Pandava brothers. He was renowned for his strength and power. He was a very good cook too.
[†] Dwijendranath Tagore was Rabindranath Tagore's eldest brother – a poet, composer, philosopher and mathmatician.

Dwijendranath did not have the quinine. But I am a Muslim. I had to do the opposite of what the Hindus did. So Abdur Rahman instantly got the job of being my majordomo, chef-de-cuisine and handyman – three in one. When I informed him of this, he muttered, 'I will try to make Sahib happy with my chashm, sar and jaan' – meaning, with my eyes, head and life.

I asked, 'Where did you work before?'

He answered, 'In the army, in charge of the mess. I finished there just a month ago.' 'Can you fire a rifle?' He laughed heartily. 'What can you cook?' 'Pulao, qorma, kebab, faluda . . .' I said, 'You need ice to make faluda. Is there an ice-factory here?'

He said, 'From the mountains of Paghman.'* He pointed at the snow peaks through the window. It was mid-summer, yet one could see the white snowy ridges on the high blue mountain peaks. I asked in surprise, 'One goes up so high to get ice?'

Abdur Rahman replied, 'No, Sahib, in the winter, people make big holes in the ground at a much lower level to store ice. In summer they dig the ice out and bring it down to the city on donkeys.'

He proved to be resourceful too. I discovered that there were no utensils or crockery in the house. I told him, 'Go and buy everything from the market. You probably won't be able to cook tonight. Make lunch tomorrow. And, by the way, I need tea in the morning.'

He left with the money.

I too left for Kabul in the early afternoon. There was a nice breeze, and I was enjoying the stroll. On the way I saw Abdur

---

* Mountain range about twenty miles west of Kabul.

Rahman returning, carrying a mountain of goods on his back. I said, 'Why did you have to carry it all by yourself? You could have hired a porter.'

The gist of what he said was this – who in Kabul could carry a load that he was unable to carry?

I told him, 'But you could have shared the load.'

I guessed he either did not figure that out or did not want to.

He was carrying the load in a big net bag. I could see firewood, oil, salt – everything in there. He said, as I resumed my stroll, 'Sahib, come back home for dinner.' The way he said it, I did not have the courage to get into an argument with him on this deserted road in a foreign land. I started walking fast towards Kabul, saying, 'Okay, okay.'

I had not gone very far when I saw Monsieur Girard returning on a clip-clopping tonga.

As my boss and the head of the college, he was within his rights to scold me, and he did so now. He said, 'You neither have the strength nor the weapons that one needs to be out at night in Kabul.'

It was always best not to disagree with your boss if you lacked enough grey matter in your head, especially when his better half was sitting next to him and supporting him, '*Oui, certainement, évidement*' (yes, certainly, evidently).

I had heard that there was only one occasion when there had been an agreement between Queen Victoria and Prince Albert. But apparently it was the opposite in France; there, one's spouse agreed with one all the time.

Abdur Rahman came to the living room once to make sure that I had paid heed to his threat and obeyed him.

It was not the month of Ramzan. Yet I thought that if I was lucky I might get my dinner by sehri time.

I dozed off while waiting for the meal and was awoken by a sound. I saw Abdur Rahman waiting with an aftaba* and a bowl for me to wash my hands. It was summer, yet as I was washing my face I sensed how cold the water of the Kabul river was. I was sure that it would create contours of relief maps on my face in no time.

Looking at the dinner table I had no doubt that my servant Abdur Rahman had indeed been in charge of the army mess.

A kilo of lamb qorma was swimming in a thick gravy of onion and ghee, not in a small bowl but in a big dish, a few nuts and raisins were playing hide-and-seek here and there, while one outcast potato was trying to kill itself by drowning in one corner. There were eight jumbo-sized shami kebabs on a plate. A big serving dish was full of pulao with a roasted chicken sitting on top.

Seeing me speechless, Abdur Rahman hurriedly said, 'I have more in the kitchen.'

You could scold someone if he served three portions of food to one person. But what could you do if he served food for six people and said that there was more?

The cooking was excellent and I was hungry too. So I ate much more than an average Bengali normally would. That was the opening night and Abdur Rahman was checking out my ability to eat like the way a student of medicine concentrates on his first cadaver dissection.

When I could eat no more, I said, 'Bas – enough. Fine cooking, Abdur Rahman.'

Abdur Rahman disappeared. He returned with a plate of faluda. I told him, taking care to show a great amount of appreciation, that I did not like desserts.

Abdur Rahman disappeared again. This time he came back with a tumbler full of crushed ice. I was at a loss, 'What is this?'

* Water jug used for washing hands.

He showed me by removing the ice. There were grapes underneath. He said, 'Barki grapes of Bagh-e-Bala – the best in Afghanistan.' He then sat down with some ice and grapes on a saucer and started rubbing each grape very gently with the ice – in the way that women in our land rub lime on a pumice stone to prepare it before making pickles. I figured out that the grapes were not cold enough; so it was a special way of making them colder. It was not necessary – my tongue and palate froze when I tried to bite the grapes. I ate about eight of them with the courage of the Khyber Pass just to prove to Abdur Rahman that his master was not an uncivilised barbarian. I could not manage any more. I told him, 'Enough, Abdur Rahman, now you go and eat properly.'

But who was going to listen? Now Abdur Rahman appeared with arrangements for tea. Kabuli green tea. It had a pale yellowish hue when you poured it. Sugar was added in the first cup and nothing in the second. Like that, the third and fourth cups followed – Kabulis drank about six cups. But the cups were small – like coffee cups.

After the tea ceremony, Abdur Rahman vanished for about ten minutes. I thought of bolting the door in case he came back with something else. Possibly he had forgotten his roasted camel.

Abdur Rahman re-emerged with a sackful of almonds and walnuts and a small hammer. He took position in the corner of the room with his legs folded and started to crack nutshells.

He came to me with a handful of nuts. He said, with his head lowered, 'Sahib did not like my cooking?'

'Says who?'

'But you didn't eat enough.'

I said, annoyed, 'What nonsense? Will you compare your size with mine and guess how much I am capable of eating?'

Abdur Rahman did not get into a debate. He went back to his corner to crack open more nuts.

He kept on saying to himself, 'The climate in Kabul is not good at all. Water here is like stone, it doesn't move in your stomach after you drink it. Kabul's air has the feel of a blaze; how can one get hungry here?'

Then he asked, without looking at me, 'Have you ever been to Panjshir, Sahib?'

'Where is that?

'In the north! My country – what a place; heaven. You drink a glass of water after eating one whole lamb and you'll feel hungry again. You inhale the air facing the sky, you will feel like running with horses. People of Panjshir don't walk on the ground, they float in the air.

'What snow in the winter! Fields, mountains, rivers, trees all will be covered; there will be no activity in the farms; roads will be invisible in the snow. There will be no work, no hurry, no way of going out of the house. Ah, what comfort. You will make a charcoal fire in an iron pot and sit next to the window covering yourself with a blanket. You will see that it is snowing outside; snowing and snowing and snowing – two days, three days, five days, seven days. You are sitting there and watching the snowfall, you are watching – *che tour barf mebarad* – how it's snowing.'

I asked, 'I will sit for seven days next to the window?'

Abdur Rahman gave me a pitying look as if he had never seen such a philistine. He said, 'Come once, sit by the window and then if you don't like it, Abdur Rahman's head is there for you to chop.'

He picked up the thread, 'So many types of snowflakes. Some are straight, like cotton wool from broken pillows, and you can see the sky and the earth through them. Sometimes it will be so dense – it will come down like a sheet, like pulling down the window shutters. Sometimes there will be a strong wind – storms. The wind will churn the piles of snow and whirl it around. The snow dust will run mad in all directions – right and left, up and down. Sometimes it will run straight, beating the wild horses. Sometimes it'll be dark all around, and you will only hear the howling – at times it'll sound like a whistle of the engine at Darul-Aman. One has no hope if one gets caught in that snowstorm. It blows a man away, he will fall unconscious on the snow and a blanket of snow will cover him – piles and piles of it. But that snow also keeps one warm. People have been rescued even after two days from those piles of snow.

'One morning, you will wake up to see that it has stopped snowing. The sun is out. You can't look out in the glare of the snow. You will go out wearing the dark glasses that you get in the markets of Kabul. The air you will inhale will not contain a speck of dust. The ice-cold air will enter your chest like a knife, cutting you inside. But it will sweep out everything impure inside your body. Your chest will swell six inches every time you inhale. Each inhalation will rid you of hundreds of illnesses. Each will add one year to your lifespan.

'After the walk, if Sahib doesn't eat a whole lamb, I will shave off my moustache. You will kill me if I don't serve double the amount of food that there was tonight.'

I said, 'That's settled, Abdur Rahman. I will spend the winter in Panjshir.'

Abdur Rahman melted with joy and said, 'It will be my pleasure, Sahib.'

I said, 'Not for your pleasure, but to save my soul.'

Abdur Rahman looked perplexed.

I explained to him, 'If you sit there by the window for seven days, who will cook for me?'

SIXTEEN

Seeing a pair of rubber gloves in a shop window, one Irishman asked another, 'What's their use?' The second one was equally bright. He replied, 'Don't you know? It's very convenient to wash your hands wearing these. You can wash your hands without getting them wet.'

If a lazy man ever wanted to make a trip but did not want to go through the troubles of sightseeing, then the best place for him to go to would be the narrow Kabul valley. Because, there was nothing worth seeing in Kabul.

When you returned home after spending three years in Kabul, if anybody asked whether you had seen the influence of the lotus flower in the motif atop the mehrab* in the old mosque that stood at the corner of the Deh-Afghanan and the education ministry, you could confidently say, 'Nope.' That is because there was no such old mosque in Kabul.

Those smart-pants might ask if you had seen the bunch of Iranian rosaries engraved with paintings of the master miniature artist Behzad, which the Amir had brought with him while fleeing Bukhara. You could say 'no' without batting your eyelids, as no such rosaries existed in Kabul.

---

* The small cubicle in the mosque from where the maulvi conducts the prayer.

We were not talking about the scholars. Someone in Kabul might be growing aubergines in the backyard of the stable where Alexander had kept his horse. The scholars would be absolutely delighted if they found that location with their compasses. They would make a great noise if they found a rock had once touched a tuft of Lord Buddha's hair. I was not talking about them. I was talking about ordinary tourists who had seen the shrines of Delhi, Agra or Secundra Bagh. There was nothing in Kabul to dazzle that lot.

So you would not have to go on sightseeing tours after reaching Kabul. You would not have to walk barefoot on a hot stony terrace at midday for six furlongs; you would not have to climb steep spiral stairs through the stench of bat droppings.

Like in the Irishman's story, you could wash your hands without getting them wet.

Hence Kabul was a beautiful city. And the best part was that you could see the city without much trouble. Some friend or other would take you to one of the gardens to spend the whole day.

Gulbagh was close to the city; one could walk there or get there by car or tonga.

It had high walls on three sides; the Kabul river was on the fourth. They had made a little bay by building a bund on the river. There were plenty of apple and pear trees in the garden, nargis plants and lawns of deep green grass. Possibly, the carpet-weavers of Kabul had drawn their inspiration from these lawns. Friends and friends of friends would spread a carpet on the soft grass and recline on cushions. Within five minutes they would all be flat on their backs.

Through the thick foliage of the tall, shapely chinar beauties you would be able to see the translucent pale blue sky and white clouds playing around on the slopes of Kabul's hills. Not only playing, you would see some making desperate attempts to climb the mighty peaks. With a definite plan, one lot was pushing another in a bid to cross over to the other side. After making some progress, they would come down again as if hit on the head with a club by the invisible guardian of the peak. They would then change their tactic; a few would mingle to form one little group and start climbing again. One or two would suddenly reach the peak and then disappear on the other side, after waiting on top for a bit to display their success.

If you looked straight beyond the chinar trees and the peaks, you would spot one cloud lying lazily on the deep blue carpet like you, looking down, nonchalantly observing the attempts at mountaineering – exactly like you. There was no way you could send him to India as the Meghdut.* His demeanour would tell you that he had been lying there possibly from the time of the Mughal emperor Babur Shah and he had no plans of going anywhere. My Abdur Rahman from Panjshir had possibly learned the trick of sitting by the window from him.

You would smell a medley of scents of so many unknown flowers. If it were the end of summer, the smell of overripe apple and apricot would be mixed in it too. As the garden was enclosed on all three sides, the sweet fermented aroma would make you intoxicated. Your eyes would become heavy and close gradually – then you would only hear the light sound of swaying branches and leaves, and the tireless tweeting and cooing of birds.

Those scents would be drowned by the aroma of the qorma and pulao being cooked in the corner of the garden. Your mouth

---

* Fifth-century story written in verse by the poet Kalidasa. One banished demi-god, or yaksha, sent his message of love to his fiancé through the monsoon clouds.

would water while you continued to doze. There would be a sudden resolution of all that reverie and contradiction by a loud boom that would resonate in the hills for a minute.

It was the sound of the cannon fired daily at twelve noon from the highest hill in Kabul. Everyone would take out their pocket-watches – very few used wristwatches – to check the time. This was a standard practice in Kabul. It would be considered snobbery if you did not open your watch – 'My, my, he's such a show-off – his watch is so good that he doesn't need to check the time . . .'

Those, whose watch hands did not show that it was twelve, would indeed be relieved. Apparently the cannon of Kabul never fired exactly at twelve. So, any watch that showed the time to be twelve was suspect. Everyone present would then stare at the watch with the saddest of faces – like the Buddha statues from the art of Gandhara.

My senior colleague Mir Aslam used to speak classical Farsi with a heavy Arabic influence – like our Brahmin pundits who spoke Bengali steeped in Sanskrit. He asked me, 'Oh my brother, did you ever try to find out the meaning of the phrase, "*chahar-magz-shikan*"?'

I said, '*Chahar* means four and *magz* is brain. Shikan means breaking into pieces. So it would mean something with which a brain can be split into four pieces. Must be some Arabic grammatical riddle.'

Mir Aslam said, 'It is right that "*chahar-magz*" means "four-brains" but when they are conjoined, it means "*akhrot*" – the walnut. So "*chahar-magz-shikan*" means iron hammer.' Then he turned to our other colleague Saiful Alam, the owner of the suspect watch, '*Aye baradare azeezey man* (Oh my dear brother), that object you call watch is nothing but "*chahar-magz-shikan*". Why are you carrying it so close to thy chest like your lover, hidden in those heathen clothes? Give it up, give it up now. Can't you see that our servants are sweating there trying to break walnuts with mere rocks in the absence of a proper instrument? Is your heart made of stone?'

Ownership of a faulty watch had such a numbing impact on Paris-returnee Saiful Alam that he could not give a ready answer. He muttered in simple prose, 'My turn will come too.'

Mir Aslam said, 'Oh brother, that ancient cannon apparently fires with a plume of smoke from that thousand-foot-high hill everyday at midday and apparently the inhabitants of Kabul can hear the sound. I heard that once, at midday, the gunner realised that he had run out of gunpowder. He asked his younger brother to go to the city armoury and fetch some explosives. His brother walked down the thousand-foot hill, entered an inn to rest for a while, drank eight cups of tea, collected the gunpowder and finally walked up the thousand feet. The gunner then fired the cannon. The Kabulis did hear the boom of the cannon before the daylight was out. But my brother Saiful Alam, did your "*chahar-magz-shikan*" watch indicate twelve on that day too?'

I said, 'In our land we too have such watches and we throw them at the mango-tree to get mangoes down.'

Everyone except Saiful Alam and Mir Aslam asked, 'What is a mango?' At least Saiful Alam had travelled to Paris from Bombay. But what about Mir Aslam?

He was ready with an answer, 'A mango is a very special sweet pulpy Indian fruit. I still haven't been able to figure out who I shall name the king of all fruits – grapes or mangoes.'

I asked him, 'When did you eat mango?'

Mir Aslam said, 'I studied theology for fourteen years in Rampur Deoband.* After that I have to face this question from

---

* Oldest Islamic seminary in the current state of Uttar Pradesh in India.

you? But no, I will not break down. I have witnessed your thirst for knowledge. In one auspicious moment I shall give you a lecture on the cultural connection between Afghanistan and India. But currently, if you turn round, you will see that your obedient servant Abdur Rahman is trying to draw your attention.'

Where did he come from? What a pain.

I saw him waiting with a towel and clothes. He said, 'Lunch will be ready soon. So, Sahib, you may want to take your bath.'

A few friends, by then, were already in the water. They were all Kabulis, therefore did not know how to swim. Only one swam across the river like a steamer, heaving, creating waves and splashing lots of water. There was plenty of applause on this bank, and some proud bows from the other. The Kabul river was not even twenty yards wide at that point.

That day the sky fell in Gulbagh. Kabulis had never seen underwater swimming.

I crossed the river twice myself, but had never experienced such cold water in my life. On a winter's night the water in even a stagnant pond in our country never turned that cold. After swimming for only a few minutes, I had to stand in the sun for one full hour with chattering teeth, shivering like a bamboo leaf.

Mir Aslam said encouragingly, 'You won't get pneumonia from bathing in the water coming straight from the icecaps of those high mountains.'

I concurred with him, 'Nothing to fear as people don't die after bathing in Mansarovar.'* I understood why my friend Vinayak Rao Masoji had to run around for two hours after taking a dip there. At least the Mansarovar was at seventeen thousand feet and Kabul was only at seven.

---

* A lake on the Tibetan plateau – a pilgrimage for Hindus.

Except for Mir Aslam and Saiful Alam, everybody was convinced that I was shivering because I had come back from the jaws of death by drowning. Finally I said, annoyed, 'Okay, I will show you again how to do it.'

Everyone stopped me by dragging me back, saying, 'What are you doing, what are you doing?' It is the noble duty of a Muslim to save another from certain death.

Bengalis and Kabulis shared the skill of making an oven with three rocks and cooking an excellent meal on the fire of but a few twigs and branches from the garden. Mir Aslam had received his education in India in the nineteenth century tradition, where the disciple had to cook for the teacher. The meal that was cooked under his supervision was comparable to a superlative ghazal by Hafiz.

When I woke up after the meal, the entire garden was snoring – all except our hookah. As long as we were up, it was snoring all the time. Now it was time for it to get some rest. But Kabuli tobacco was very strong – it could easily have killed Prahlad.* Prahlad could not be killed by the feet of an elephant or crushed under heavy rocks. But he would not have survived a puff or two of this tobacco. People coughed more than they inhaled it. Being a cold country, Afghanistan produced good quality tobacco, but the Afghans never learned the art of mellowing it with molasses. They also had not learned how to make slow-burning briquettes.

In the fading light, the line of tall trees had created lovely stripes on the grass. The garden was sleeping like a plump zebra with green and black stripes. The nargis flowers were yet to wake

---

* Hindu mythological character – an ardent follower of Vishnu, the protector of the universe. His father disapproved of his faith in Vishnu and ordered him to be killed.

up fully, but they were slowly opening their eyes. I could not say for certain if it was my imagination, but I did feel a slight scent blowing in from the flowerbeds. As if they were in a rehearsal before the full concert in the evening. The water, the shade, the breeze and the lush green garden – next to it was the thousand-foot-tall naked rocky hill. There was no sign of any pity – as if a naked yogi with his dreadlocks was engaged in the most difficult meditation.

At his feet, by the Gulbagh, the Kabul river was weeping. But the yogi was unperturbed.

I could not do any work after coming back home. After lying down in bed, I asked Abdur Rahman to open the window. Orion showed up on top of the hill. I closed my eyes saying, 'Ah'. That day I had seen so many unknown flowers, trees, made acquaintance with new people and more so the ugly, dry and hard rocky hill. Now seeing this constellation, I felt homesick – my body and mind craved for my own land, the known corners of my home.

I dreamed that night; mother was sitting on the north veranda after finishing her Esha namaaz* and looking at Orion.

* The last prayer of the day for Muslims.

SEVENTEEN

The second attraction of Kabul was its bazaars. People who had been to the old bazaars of Agra, Amritsar or Benaras, would know what they looked like. Narrow lanes with small cubicles on both sides, at chest height, double or treble the size of roadside kiosks. The front would protrude like a box eating up road space. Some shops had hinged doors so that at night they could put them up and close their upper halves.

There were small holes beneath the shops, which were either used as storage space, or by cobblers plying their trade. In fact cobblers occupied thirty per cent of them. If the Pathans of Peshawar had their shoes mended once a week, the Kabulis did it three times. A man who had no work would park himself in a shop while the cobbler would stick a few new nails in his shoe or sandal.

You thought that they had to buy something if they sat in a shop? Never. Kabuli shopkeepers were not at all worried about selling their merchandise. A 'quick turnover' was a concept alien to the Orient. Even Calcutta was laidback; the shawl-sellers of Chitpur or the attar sellers of Bara Bazaar still kept this tradition going.

They would talk about everything, except for politics. Even that would be discussed but you had to be a trusted friend in order for them to do that. The habitués of the bazaar of Kabul were very clever – in three days they would find out if you had been a frequent visitor to the British Legation or not. It was unlikely for an Indian to be a spy for the Russians or the Afghan foreign office. The bazaar would share all its 'bazaargap' with you once they had established that you stayed away from the places of high politics. And what 'bazaargap'! From women's liberation in Turkistan in Bolshevik Russia; to Janakibai, the exotic dancer of Peshawar; to how the wife of the Viceroy in Delhi managed to get diamonds and emeralds without paying a penny. Such colourful stories! After keeping your ears and eyes open for a few days, you would be in a position to figure out how much of what you heard was true and how much concocted. You would begin to understand if two-thirds or three-quarters of it was cooked up.

This 'bazaargap' was very important for the traders. I had read in Mughal history that the whole of India and even Turkistan and Iran were within the ambit of the Indian hundi.[*] I had heard from scholars that the Khan of Bukhara would give out cash with his eyes closed, upon receiving the hundis of Jagat Seth[†] of Bengal. To keep this sprawling business going, the Indian tradesmen had to keep their own postal system going. There were special needs too. Say, the emperor in Delhi had dismissed the Subedar of Ahmedabad – the order for dismissal would take seven days to reach there. Meanwhile the Subedar had just borrowed money from the local moneylender to buy two thousand horses. Once dismissed, he would leave for Delhi straight away. Then it would be impossible for the money-lender to recover his loan. Until the Subedar again got into the good

[*] Method of unofficial money transfer – a note from a money-trader to another underwriting a loan.
[†] A very influential trader and lender in Bengal in the eighteenth century; was instrumental in subverting the then Muslim ruler of Bengal Siraz-ud-daula and helped the British to win against him in 1757 at the battle of Plassey.

books of the emperor and got a new posting, he would not return the money and the lender would have to write it off.

So the trader's horse would start for Ahmedabad on the same evening as when the emperor signed the dismissal order. The clever trader in Ahmedabad would then tick the name of the Subedar in red, would try to recover as much money as he could and finally would leave for a 'pilgrimage' to avoid giving him a new overdraft. After receiving the dismissal order three days later the Subedar would understand why the moneylender had suddenly left for 'pilgrimage'.

The same system still existed in Afghanistan. It was impossible to do profitable business without knowing if the king was clipping the wings of the governors of Herat or Badakshan. So the traders had to keep their ears open to all sorts of 'bazaargap' and you would make a greater profit than others if you were gifted with business acumen and ingenuity.

The Indians still controlled banking in Afghanistan. But it would be wrong to say that they were Indian. Almost all of them were Afghan subjects. Nobody had yet researched their lives, society, festivals or lifestyle.

It was very strange. The proponents of 'Greater India' had bored us with article after article and out of focus photos of the ruins of Borobudur,[*] but they never showed any interest in this Indian footprint in a neighbouring country. Dead Borobudur came to be part of our family, but this very much alive Indian settlement had been relegated to the status of an outcast.

Kabul's bazaar was poorer than that of Peshawar, but far more colourful. People of at least twenty-five nationalities did their

---

[*] Ali describes Borobudur in a note as the ruins of a Hindu civilisation in Indonesia. However, they are more commonly recognised as Buddhist.

trading there, keeping their sartorial and linguistic distinctions. Hazara, Uzbek, Kafiristani, Qizilbash, Mongol, Kurd – the traders of Kabul could easily tell who was from where, their businesses, methods of trading, whether spendthrift or generous, from their dress, hat, pustin and riding boots.

They would walk the same streets happily, accepting this diversity. We Bengalis, while doing business with Marwaris or Punjabis, would never forget that they were non-Bengalis. After completing business, neither party invited the other to his house for a meal. But here business and social contacts were intertwined.

It was like a dream folk-theatre. The original Kabulis were trying to buy and sell loudly, taking the names of God and all the prophets. The foreigners were trying to bargain, their merchandise strapped on the backs of donkeys or mules. The elderly trader of Bukhara would enter the shop with a slow gait, as if he wanted to have all his meals and spend the night there. His servants would follow him carrying his tobacco and hookah. He too would have a mule-load of carpets. You would try to leave, but the shopkeeper would not let you go. They might be doing good business with substantial profits; and since you did not have much work, you could also share a meal with them.

Many young boys loitered on the streets. The elderly trader would tell one of them, 'Bacha – lad, ask the tea-seller to send over some more tea.'

They would then unfold the carpets. So many colours, so many intricate patterns; so soft to touch. Apparently the study of carpets was a big subject – there was no end to it. At least thirty kinds of carpets were sold in Kabul. There were various sub-groups and distinct patterns among them. They would be classified based on their place of origin, colours and patterns. Some patterns were woven with special wool. You would not find anything cheap here.

There were only three special things that one could buy in the bazaars of Kabul – carpets, pustin, and silk. Among smaller items there were metal samovars and brocade shoes. The rest were all cheap products from the mills of Britain and Japan – entering Afghanistan through India.

Kabul's bazaar was becoming poorer with the emergence of Russia and Iran. The Russians had created a barrier on the northern borders of Amu Darya, and turned the flow of trade from Central Asia towards Moscow. The Iranians had started selling their products directly to the British or the Russians. As Kabul did not have enough money, it could not buy from India. Besides, our own silk, textile and muslin industries were struggling too. The British had dug them all into their graves.

Emperor Babur was amazed to see Kabul's bazaar. In his auto-biography he had given a list of languages he had heard there – Arabic, Farsi, Turkish, Mongol, Hindi, Afghani, Pashai, Prachi, Geberi, Bereki and Lagmani.

Prachi was the language of eastern India – from the Ayodhya region. The Bengali language had its roots in it. Gone were those days – now you could hardly find three people from northern India in this bazaar.

It contained life and was full of happiness. There was a big inn at the end of the bazaar. At the end of the day's work and after the evening prayer, the traders would gather there to revitalise them-selves. The Mongols would start dancing in a circle on the terrace, with their rifles on their shoulders, wearing heavy riding boots and tossing their long hair. Mongol songs from across the Amu Darya would reverberate around the hills of Kabul in tandem with clapping and the thumping of boots. They would lower their heads with the beat of the dance, their long hair falling over their faces. Then they would jump up, drawing lines in the air with their legs, thrusting out their chests, throwing back their heads, their hair falling across their green shirts. Sometimes they would bow, clapping in a slower tempo; sometimes they would whirl with both hands high in the air. They would move in a circle and whirl – all the time.

As you took in the scene, you would notice that one Iranian, disregarding all the noise, was sitting in a corner with his sitar next to his ear, singing verses from Hafiz. A few listeners would gather around him with their eyes closed as if intoxicated with the images of roses and bulbuls and the long-separated lover.

In another corner some holy men and pilgrims were recounting stories from different countries, Meshed and Karbala, Mecca and Medina. People were listening to them intently; the older men wondering when God would be kind to them and take them to Medina—

> *Labon par hai dum aye Muhammad samhalo*
> *Mere Moula mujhe Medine bola lo.*

> My last breath is nigh, save me Oh Muhammad
> Oh Lord, take me to Medina.

A poetry session was in progress in the room of the pustin trader. A clean-shaven young poet with a hint of a moustache and kohl in his eyes, sat with his legs folded in front of a candle reading poetry from a parchment. Others were repeating each verse – and expressing their appreciation by saying *marhabba, afareen* – well done, superb.

Four Sikhs played three records repeatedly on an old gramophone—

Hardi botlon
Bhardi botlon
Punjabi Bolton
Laal botlon

Yellow bottles
Filled bottles
Punjabi bottles
Red bottles

Alas, bottles were forbidden in Kabul! And the main gathering was around the Tajiks of Kuhistan.

They were singing loudly in unison, breaking the walls and the stones, creating ripples in the air

Aye Fatu, Jane Ma—
Fatujan
Fatujan
Bar tu shoum qurb—a—a—n.

The long-drawn out *qurban* was to keep up with the beat. It was no classical music but their singing came from their hearts—

Oh my Fatujan
My love
for your sake
I shall die.

In reply, Fatujan was saying sceptically—

Chera rafti
Heech na gufti
Door Hindustan?

Meaning

Why then
Did you leave me
For far Hindustan?

When the answer to this question could not be found in the greatest of love songs and poetries of the world of all ages, then you had to be quite stupid to expect it from the young illiterate Tajik poet. Radha had the same question for Krishna when he left Braja to conquer Mathura.[*] Even Krishna, the creator of the Gita that answered all human dilemmas, had no answer.

The lover of Balkh was silent too.

---

[*] The greatest love story from Hindu mythology. Krishna, the reincarnation of Lord Vishnu, was born in Mathura but his uncle tried to kill him at birth fearing Krishna would one day kill him and conquer his kingdom. Krishna's mother left Mathura for Braja where he was brought up. Young Radha, married to Krishna's maternal uncle was madly in love with Krishna but they were never united. The love saga of Radha and Krishna forms the body of a rich literary and musical heritage in all languages of India.

EIGHTEEN

Kabul's social life was divided into three groups and no group overlapped with the other two.

The first was the original Kabulis, who were divided into two groups – zenana and mardana – women and men. The women in Kabul stayed strictly behind the veil. Except for very close relatives, no other men – Afghan or foreigner – could meet them. The menfolk were also divided into two categories; one was the traditionalist as well as the mullah community and the other was the Paris-Berlin-Moscow returnees and their Europeanised young friends' circle. Each ignored the other but at least they had to meet and talk regularly, because in the same family the father might be the Janab and the son would be the Monsieur.

The second group comprised the Indians, meaning the Punjabis, the Muslims from the Frontier province and the few thousand exiled Muslim Mujahirs who left India in 1921 at the start of the Khilafat movement.* Some of them had married Kabuli women; hence they had some contact with Afghan society through their in-laws.

---

* A movement led by Muslims around the world demanding the restoration of the post of the Khalifa, or the Islamic religious leader, of the Ottoman empire. Britain abolished the post after occupying Turkey following the First World War.

The third segment was the British, French, German, Russian and other embassies and legations. Afghanistan was a small and poor country. There was no economic reason for foreign legations to crowd the city, but there were many geo-political reasons. The French, the Turks, the Germans, the Italians – everyone firmly believed that the bullfight between Britain and Russia would take place in the Khyber or the Hindukush sometime soon. So the others needed diplomatic missions here, to keep an eye on both.

There was at least some contact between the first two groups – the second group was either engaged in business or teaching. So it was impossible for these two groups to stay aloof from one another. But there was no acquaintance between the first and the third and likewise for the second and the third.

If someone tried to achieve that impossible task, he would then be considered a spy.

Only one man moved about in these three societies seamlessly, without any fear. I met him in Professor Bogdanov's living room. Dost Muhammad – a true Pathan – a professor of Amania college. When we were introduced, he said, shaking my hand, in pukka English style, 'How do you do?'

Our second meeting was on the street. From a distance he began asking in Pathan tradition, '*Khub hasti, jor hasti*' and so on; meaning 'Are you fine? All well? Hope nothing is wrong. Hope you're not tired.'

We met for the third time in front of his house. He shouted, '*Bafarmaid, bafarmaid*' (please come in, please come in); '*Qadame taan mubarak*' (wish your feet become pure and sacred); '*Chashme taan raushan*' (your eyes become brighter); '*Shanaye taan daraz*' (hope your chest and shoulders become broader).

The local police would have locked me up if they heard what he wanted for me after the initial flurry of greetings.

I said with slight embarrassment, 'What nonsense are you talking?'

Dost Muhammad said forcefully, 'Why not? Of course I will. I'll say it a hundred times. Am I an Iranian from Kabul that I would say everything except the truth? I'm a Pathan – our horses don't have reins and neither does my tongue.'

Then he whispered, after taking me inside, 'Hope your house is in order now. Have you got servants? Kitchen is in order? Let me know if you need anything. I can arrange everything except the throne of Kabul. I can even get that for you but, you know, there'll be a lot of hullaballoo and they will look for it, as there is only one throne here. Besides, there's no point – it's too hard to sit on – I have tried.'

I said, 'Everyone knows that it's very hard to sit on the throne of Kabul.'

His face became grim. I felt uneasy. Was my joke out of place? But I was reassured by his answer. He said, 'Oh ho, ho, you have saved my life, my brother. You have a good sense of humour. I have interacted with your folks. They are too dry, too serious. As if the whole burden of gaining independence from the British is resting on their shoulders.'

A strange man! He said obscene words in public; but whispered when offering to help me set up my home; his face looked grim when he was happy with a joke. I thought he would burst with laughter if I hurled a few swearwords at him.

By then he was lying on the carpet resting his head on a cushion. With his eyes closed he said, 'What will you have? Tea and bread, pulao with meat, grapes and pears – anything you want. You will get everything in the market. There is nothing at home.'

Then he jumped to his feet before I could answer, 'No, no, I have, I have something. I have cigarettes. Wait.'

He first went to the door, craned his neck out and looked from side to side before closing the door slowly. Then he tiptoed to the back of the sofa, squatted and brought out a pack of cigarettes, lifting the corner of the carpet.

I was surprised no end. It was only cigarettes; it was not alcohol or nude photos of Parisian women that he needed to hide so carefully.

All of a sudden, Dost Muhammad started wailing loudly, 'You wretched Agha Ahmad, I will kill you today. You better bring the rifle with you. You traitor, I will go to the gallows and become a martyr by killing you. He turned to me saying, 'What a heartless act! I bring out my pack of cigarettes after closing and bolting the doors as if it's the magic lamp of Aladdin. Yet Agha Ahmad – my servant – could find the packet. And what a shameless chap! He has stolen all ten! Oh my . . .'

Meanwhile Agha Ahmad had entered the room showing no hurry. He went straight to the back of the sofa without looking at anyone and brought out a pack full of cigarettes, putting his arm deeper under the carpet. He handed the pack over to me.

He stopped on his way out. Casting a glance at Dost Muhammad, he said, 'The empty packet was mine. I put it there.'

Dost Muhammad stopped wailing. After thinking for a while, he said, 'What a naughty trick! You see how the bastard has created the ruse to fool me. Not only today, he does it every day.'

Then he said, nodding his head, 'But bacha, wait. I too know what to do. The goldsmith hammers very delicately but the black-smith bangs his hammer with force.' Then he said to me, 'His five years' salary, three hundred rupees, is with me. One day I will disappear with it in the mountains with my rifle on my shoulder; then he'll learn his lesson.'

I asked, 'Why don't you put a lock on the door before going to college?'

He said, 'I did so once. When I returned from college I saw an even bigger lock on top. I tried to break it but gave up. By that time the whole neighbourhood had gathered there – there was no sign of Agha Ahmad. What could I do? I sat on the porch in the biting cold. Agha Ahmad came an hour later. You know what the wretched man said? "That lock was not strong enough, so I put on a stronger one." When I was about to manhandle him, he said, "What injustice, you get abuse when you try to help people."'

I said, 'So no lock?'

'What's the point? Agha Ahmad is Afridi. They can open any lock in no time. You know, one Afridi laid a wager and stole the bedsheet from under Amir Habibullah.'

I said, 'If you don't put a lock on the door, one day Agha Ahmad may flee with your rifle.'

Dost Muhammad said happily, 'Oh, I can see that you are intelligent. But I'm not that much of a fool. Agha Ahmad's elder brother gave me six hundred rupees to buy a good rifle at a bargain. I bought this one with that money. Agha Ahmad doesn't know that. If he disappears with this rifle, I'll instantly write to his brother, "Sent your rifle with your brother. Let me know if you have received it." After that the two brothers—'

I said, 'Will fight like Sunda and Upasunda.'*

---

* Two demon brothers from Hindu mythology. The two brothers had conquered heaven after defeating the gods. When the gods could not defeat them, they created a mirage of a beautiful woman to distract the two brothers. Both brothers fell in love with that mirage and fought over her killing each other.

Dost Muhammad asked, 'Did they fight for a rifle?'

I said, 'No. Over a beautiful woman.'

Dost Muhammad said, '*Tauba, tauba*! How can one fight over a woman? That can only take place over a rifle. If you have the rifle, you can kill the woman's husband and get the widow. Good arrangement. The husband will get his houri – the virgin, by going to heaven and you get your beauty in this life.'

He came out on the street to see me off and said, 'I've noticed that you're talking to me too formally, addressing me as "Mister" and all that, and I'm already being informal with you. But you can't carry on like this for long. Nobody in Afghanistan addresses me formally – not even Agha Ahmad.'

As I was getting into my tonga he said, 'Wait.' He ran inside and came out with a book. Handing it over to me, he said, 'A great book. The custom of revenge in Corsica and Afghanistan is identical.' I looked at the book – *Colomba* by Prosper Mérimée.

NINETEEN

About ten days later, I saw Dost Muhammad outside my window. I scrambled to the door to welcome him, saying in true Kabuli style, 'Are you well? Everything all right? Not too tired I hope.' Dost Muhammad did not respond; he was muttering something under his breath. I gasped when I went close and heard what he was saying: '*Kamarat ba shikanad, khuda tora kor sazad, ba pundi, wa ba tarqee*' and so on.

In translation it would mean, 'May you break your hip, may God blind you, may you blow up like a balloon and then burst.'

I somehow controlled myself and said, 'Dost Muhammad, what nonsense are you speaking?'

He gave me a bear-hug and two loud kisses on both cheeks and said, 'I never talk nonsense.'

I asked, 'Then what's the meaning of all this?'

He said, 'This is to ward off evil eyes from you. Haven't you seen that in this country people put a spot of kohl on the foreheads of babies after they have been bathed and dressed? That is to stop people casting an evil eye upon them. I couldn't put such a spot on you, so I did it with words. The person who I am abusing will live longer – death will not be able to take him sooner. Understood?'

Dost Muhammad reminded me that it was the wedding of the Paris returnee Saiful Alam's younger brother. Saiful Alam had sent Dost Muhammad to pick me up. The carriage was ready.

I offered him a cigarette, 'Care to smoke?'

He said, 'No, ask Abdur Rahman to get tobacco.'

I asked, 'Do you know Abdur Rahman?'

His response to this was, 'Who knows you here? You are but a migratory bird, you will leave after three days. And who knows me? I have come down from the mountains and will disappear there at some point, taking Agha Ahmad's money. Who am I? I may be the professor of Amania College, but how many people know that fact? You go to the bazaar, and you'll hear that I'm that fool on whose shoulders Agha Ahmad puts his gun to train his eyes for hunting. Who are you? The one on whose shoulder Abdur Rahman has put his gun – we'll see if he hunts or not. So masters are recognised by their servants.'

I said, '*Beshak, beshak*' (Certainly, certainly). Then I said in Bengali, '*Gonpher ami, ghonpher tumi, ghonph diye jai chena.*'

Dost Muhammad said, 'Translate.'

I explained, 'Mine of whisker, thine of whisker, you're known by the whisker.'

Dost Muhammad was delighted by this translation. He kept saying, '*Afareen, afareen*, bravo, bravo, such nice lines, pure gold.' He instantly translated it into Farsi,

'*Maney burut, taney burut, burut sanaktdar.*'

Then he said, 'I have dabbled quite a bit in Arabic, Farsi and Turkish languages, but I have hardly ever come across good humour. Practically nothing in poetry. Is there a lot of such material in Bengali?'

I said, 'No, only two and a half books.'

Dost Muhammad said disappointedly, 'Then what's the point of learning Bengali?'

I found a common trait between Peshawar's Ahmad Ali and Kabul's Dost Muhammad – both loved humour. The only difference was that Ahmad Ali's life ran in a usual pattern – like any other person – in a straight line. But Dost Muhammad was like an unfettered mountain stream, flowing and jumping from one rock to another and creating rainbows with the slightest hint of sunlight. I tried to talk to him about worldly affairs, but it did not reach his ears. As if he was constantly looking for a fairyland where he could create his own nonsensical world.

But I felt sorry for Dost Muhammad when we took our seats among the who's who of the city at a wedding ceremony. I saw he was muttering something to himself. I leaned over to his side to hear what he was saying, 'Is the education ministry known because of Faiz Muhammad or is Faiz Muhammad known because of the education ministry? Is the post of the foreign ministry famous because of Mahmud Tarzi or is it the other way round? The Bengali poet has so rightly said, "Mine of whisker, thine of whisker, you're known by the whisker."'

I said, 'Keep quiet. The ministers are all looking at you. They will bury you alive if they hear you.'

'Yes, that is right, especially that Faiz.'

I asked, 'Faiz Muhammad Khan? The Minister of Public Instruction?'

He replied, 'No, the Minister of Public Destruction. He is already destroying the brains of so many young people. No wonder he will want to kill me too.'

I could not blame Dost Muhammad. It was hard to figure out on what basis these people had become ministers. They were all Einsteins in their qualifications! They never tried to learn about the world around them. All of them had visited Europe once or twice. When interacting with them it became quite apparent that they had not brought any wisdom or knowledge back with them, only some suspicious diseases, the result of their debaucheries while in Europe. The younger lot that joined us, at least had a few degrees in education. You could make out by conversing with the older generation that if anything, they had experience. But this gang of ministers could neither fly nor swim properly; they were like toads that hopped about awkwardly. One could feel sorry for the city of Kabul after seeing many institutions, but you would remember this line from Confucius after meeting these ministers – 'I shall quit society and take up the begging bowl in my hands.'

Saiful Alam came over and whispered, 'Come out of the door to the left in a while. I'll wait for you there.' Dost Muhammad nodded his head to indicate that he too was coming, even though he did not hear what was being said.

I could breathe properly once I had exited the room. Dost Muhammad said, '*Ta ba guluyem rasid, gharghara shudam*' (Stuffed up to my throat, I'm nearly throttled).

After that we had entry to the real wedding gathering. I saw there were about twenty young people; some sitting; some reclining; some lying down – all chitchatting. Someone had muffled the speaker of the gramophone with a towel and was listening to music. Three were playing cards, and the serious scholar Mir Aslam was reading a book in one corner. An old gentleman was sitting in the other corner, leaning against the wall with his eyes closed, possibly sleeping, with a great white turban, long flowing snow-white beard, and a jet-black long robe. He had a saintly face – there was a small sitar by him. It was a gathering of young people apart from Mir Aslam and the white-bearded gentleman. There was no furniture in the room except for the expensive carpet and colourful cushions.

Some of them greeted us, '*Bafarmaid* – please come in.'

I asked Dost Muhammad, 'Why didn't we come here in the first place?'

He said, 'No respite; no chance of promotion unless you suffered the suffocation in the main gathering. But you, sir, were sitting there with a happy face. I started having doubts and worries about your future when I failed to see you fidgeting. You know what's the qualification for becoming a minister in this country? To sit among the bores without being bored. Be careful, my brother, very careful; unless you take care, one day they will catch you and turn you into a minister.'

Saiful Alam cordially invited me to join them.

The gathering of the youths was not much more exciting than that of the older generation. But, as this place was not bound by decorum, you had the licence to do anything you liked. They were discussing politics without fear and there was no bar in talking about the subjects that occupy the mind in youth. The main difference between the Indian youth and this lot was that here there was no sign of cynicism. They did not hide behind the tales of past glories, and neither did they create a sense of an unreal fairyland about the future. They were strong too – oblivious of physical stress and pains. One of them was narrating how, in the previous autumn, he had reached Kabul from Badakshan, crossing the Hindukush, after getting a transfer order. He could advance only three miles after a day's walk as the caravan had to cross the same river six times at different points – sometimes by swimming, sometimes by scrambling over the rocks. Two mules were washed away with all their food. Two of the team of seven died of hunger.

I was not hearing such a narrative for the first time. But there was no attempt to romanticise it; it was neither laced with the usual boastfulness of travellers nor was there any criticism of the Afghan government's mad transfer policies, implemented at the wrong time. His attitude was more like, 'I got wet because I had no umbrella. I will go out tomorrow if need be – can't say for sure that I will carry the umbrella.' Meaning he would not object if he was asked to go back to Badakshan again next autumn.

But we learned that he had lived very comfortably on four hundred marks a month when he was studying in Berlin.

We were invited to the feast quite late at night. In the hot climate of Bengal late-night wedding feasts could be cold, so it was no wonder that in Afghanistan it would be even colder.

Mir Aslam served me some meat, 'Have this well-done skew-ered lamb. It will warm you up inside.'

Then he asked Dost Muhammad, 'Hope you got enough of everything, that there was no shortage.' Dost Muhammad said '*Ta ba guluyem rasid, gharghara shudam.*' This was the Farsi way of saying that you had enough of something.

You did not have to come to Kabul to discover that everyone would eat plenty of food at an Afghan wedding. But the lesson was that they did not have the barbaric habit of wasting food like the 'civilised' Bengalis.

The chitchat and the conversation became more interesting after dinner. Only Dost Muhammad went off to sleep facing the wall, resting his head on three cushions. I felt like going back home. But I guessed from the mood of the gathering that the custom here was to enjoy the conversation or go to sleep without any inhibition. Neither the noise of the wedding nor the bright electric light could disturb an Afghan's sleep.

Gradually almost everyone went off to sleep as the night progressed. Saiful Alam served us another round of tea.

Mir Aslam's language became more and more archaic but suddenly he stopped. I saw that the old gentleman had picked up the sitar on his lap.

Mir Aslam whispered in my ears, 'At last you have good luck in this third quarter of the night.'

The whole evening the old man had not said a word. When he struck the first chord, it felt like he had a lot to say.

Dost Muhammad sat up the moment the sound from the sitar spread – as if he was waiting for this instant.

Before the sound of the sitar faded away, a humming voice came out of the old man's throat; no, it was not from his throat, nor from his chest or his heart; it was as if the voice came out of his entire body; from every pore of his skin. We did not know when the sitar was tuned but it felt as if his body had been tuned by the master of all master tuners to give the perfect pitch that night.

It was not simply classical music – it seemed like sprites appeared from nowhere with his voice, dancing in tandem with the resonance of the sitar.

It was a Farsi ghazal. The old man's eyes were shut, his face calm and serene, his eyelids motionless, only a steady humming emanated from his slightly parted lips. The sound mixed with the air and filled the room like the scent of a fine perfume.

How could one listen to the lyrics? The voice and the sitar were in unison, as if the deep blue sky, spread with the crimson red of the sunset, was gradually turning orange from deep purple. I could not say for the others, but I had such an experience for the first time, like a blind man opening his eyes at sunset. I was drowned in colours – I could not make out the sea, the beach, the trees, the entire landscape was awash in a blaze of colours. Mesmerising us with his voice, the old man was now whispering his secret hymn in my ears—

Shabi agar, shabi agar, shabi agar . . .

If only for one night, only for one night, only for one . . .

I felt like asking at the top of my voice, 'What? What? What?

What if only for one night?' But there was no need – the maestro knew the answer.

Aaz labe yaar boseyee talabam.

I get a kiss from my lover's lips.

At first he said it very calmly, yet filled with hopelessness. Gradually the hopelessness started to disappear, you were filled with the paradox of hope and desperation, you became more and more desirous, and finally you were left with this firm belief, 'I will get it. I will certainly get it.'

I could see two red lips in the darkness when he sang '*Labe yaar.*' I lost sight of everything when he sang '*Bosaye talabam*'; I could only feel the same paradox of hope and desperation in my heart and finally that firm belief.

Then, in a booming voice, he sang,

Jawan shawam.

I will be young again,

I will regain my youth if only I get a kiss.

The room was filled with mad dancing – I could see Shiva dancing with Parvati, breaking his meditation. One boom after another – '*Jawan shawam, jawan shawam.*' That was not the old man with his sitar, it was like the Mongol dancers who were jumping, drawing lines in the air with their legs, thrusting out their chests, creating a whirlpool with their long hair.

I saw Shah Jahan coming out of the Taj Mahal with Mumtaz Mahal, holding hands. They were young again, ending their centuries of separation.

But the maestro? He had regained his youth, he had got the kiss from his lover's lips, he reached the climax, yet the song was progressing—

Shabi agar, aaz labe yaar boseyee talabam
Jawan shawam.

If I get a kiss from my lover's lips only for one night
I will become young again.
What next? What?
I heard the breathtaking oath—
Zindagi dubara kunam.

'I am ready to live this life twice. If you give me a kiss, I will get the strength to make a journey across the endless desert with bloodied feet forgetting the long separation. Let me face the separation again, and let me burn in your indifference.

'I am ready, I am taking an oath – *Zindagi dubara kunam.* I am ready to live my life again.'

I was apologising with my head bowed, 'Forgive me, oh maestro, forgive me, oh poet. I had the audacity to ask where it was going? I never imagined that you could lift me up to the sky, the spirit of your song could take me to the clouds.'

Wrenching his heart, the maestro was repeating, '*Shabi agar*' – if only for one night – and that firm oath '*Zindagi dubara kunam*' – the rest of the song was playing itself out only in these two lines. Sometime I would hear '*Shabi agar*' and sometimes '*dubara kunam*' – '*Shabi agar, dubara kunam.*'

The eastern sky stays red long after sunset – I could not say when the song ended. Suddenly we heard the morning azaan, '*Allah hu Akbar*' – Allah is great. No need to worry, all your wishes will be fulfilled.

'*Wa lal akhiratu khairun laka minal ula*' (The future will be better than the past).[*]

Opening my eyes I saw that the singer was no longer there. Mullah Mir Aslam was sitting like a statue carved of stone and Dost Muhammad had covered his face with the palms of his hands.

---

[*] Koran 93, 4.

TWENTY

The room was completely empty. I stopped for a minute after entering. The furniture had disappeared. Dost Muhammad was lying on the carpet with his attaché case under his head. Seeing me, he shouted, '*Boro, ghumsho!*' (Leave! Get lost!).

By then I was quite accustomed to Dost Muhammad's eccentricities and his various ways of greeting. Coming close to him I asked, 'What happened? I could never imagine that Agha Ahmad would steal your sofa, table, chairs, couch, all that heavy furniture.'

Dost Muhammad was muttering, 'Everyone is a thief, all robbers, you can't trust anyone from Kabul to Paris.' I said, 'That is unfair. Agha Ahmad stole your belongings and you're blaming the Parisians?'

He said, 'What nonsense. I would have gone after Agha Ahmad with my rifle had he been the thief. Or else how would I be able to show my face in Afridi society? He didn't take anything, it was that chap Laffont.'

'Who is he?'

'He arrived here the day before yesterday, a professor of French. His house is in Lab-e-Dariya. A fine house. The Afghan government makes the best arrangements for all these foreigners.'

I said, 'When you know the culprit and his address, then what's the problem with recovering the furniture?'

He said, 'The law will not apply – he was lamenting that he had no furniture. So I said I had too much – you know French, right – *book de mueble, full de mueble, ta de mueble* – I described to him, in French, everything I possessed. After listening to me he was floored like the dead English soldiers in the second Anglo-Afghan war.'

I said, with annoyance, 'Floored? I don't believe it. I can see that he came and took everything with him.'

Dost Muhammad protested, '*Tauba, tauba.* Would he have taken everything in the room if he came himself? Can't you see that it's looking like razed ground? I sent everything to him.'

I said angrily, 'Go to hell then. Now die on the cold floor—'

Dost Muhammad jumped up and embraced me, 'Didn't I tell you? Didn't I? That you won't be able to talk to me so formally for long. Didn't I say that? But brother, you made a record – for a full fifteen days you talked to me in the most formal manner.'

I said, 'That's all fine. But why were you abusing the whole world when you yourself have donated everything to that Laffont chap?'

'You won't tell anyone? Just forget what I'm going to say to you now. When you entered the room, I noticed that you had a grim look on your face. Maybe you were thinking of home, or maybe the hangover from last night's music session wasn't gone – I don't really know why mad people produce such supernatural music. But let that be. Seeing your face I thought you were too sad. So I made up all that nonsense to distract you. See my trick?'

I said, 'Yes, nice trick. Agha Ahmad befools you and now you have fooled me. It's nothing new. In our country there's a rhyme:

Shaman-daman Ravana aar Ravana-daman Ram
Shashur-daman shashuri aar shashuri-saman hum.

Ravana defeats death and Ram defeats Ravana
Ma-in-law defeats pa-in-law and I defeat her.'

Not a very clever joke and not nicely told either; yet Dost Muhammad was like the good boy who eats everything without making any fuss; he always had a smile on his face.

I said, 'Okay, okay, I understand everything. But at least buy a bed or a cot. Or else you will be sleeping on the floor.'

Dost Muhammad said, 'Let me tell you a secret. Listen carefully. I was never comfortable with this foreign furniture – couldn't get used to it in ten years. But I had paid for it, so I didn't really want to throw it away. Now that I have got this opportunity, why should I fill my house with junk again? No chance of breaking my hip falling from the bed.'

I said, '*Kamarat na shikanad* – hope your hip doesn't break in two.'

The plan was that Dost Muhammad and I would visit Bogdanov together. I mentioned earlier that Bogdanov's living room was the central attraction for all foreigners. We got some indication of the size of the crowd inside from the garden and found ourselves in the midst of a pack of white men and women as soon as we entered the room.

Bogdanov took me to the middle of the room and said in chaste French, 'May I have the pleasure of introducing . . .'

He then kept using one epithet after another to introduce me. I said 'How do you do', some of them said, '*enchante*', some said '*chermer*', and some said, '*ravissant*'. They were 'enchanted', or 'charmed' or 'ravished' meeting me. This was French etiquette. I could not imagine their expression if they were truly 'enchanted' after meeting Greta Garbo or Marlene Dietrich.

Monsieur Laffont, the French professor to whom Dost Muhammad had donated all his furniture, picked up the thread of the story he was narrating, 'Then the king asked me, "It shouldn't take me more than six months to learn French." I said, "No Your Highness, it would take at least two years." '

Bogdanov exclaimed, 'What have you done? Are you supposed to say no to the king? In the middle of the day the king may say, "Look, isn't it lovely to see the moon shining in the blue sky?" At that first you have to say, "I am ready to sacrifice my life for a touch of Your Highness' sacred feet that are resting on the gem-and-diamond studded throne." Then you will say—'

Madame Laffont interjected, 'What if one makes a mistake? That is quite a long introduction.'

Bogdanov said, with a kind smile, 'No harm with minor changes. You can say pearl instead of diamond or you can say the dust of your feet in place of feet.

'Then you'll say, "Your Highness has such keen observation. The moon has taken such a lovely shape and the stars are beautiful too." '

Senora Digoda from Italy asked, 'Is there no way of saying the truth without breaching the etiquette? What should Laffont say if he wanted to tell the king that it took two years to learn French?'

Bogdanov said, 'Surely there is. When the king talks about six months, you will then say, "Sure Your Highness, you can certainly learn in six months. But it will be better if you spend two years." His Highness has common sense. He will get the message.'

Monsieur Laffont said, 'This is too much to handle.'

Bogdanov said, 'Certainly. The other term for "too much" is superfluity. Poet Tagore – he's our guru, teacher—' he bowed, looking at Professor Benoit and me – 'he says, art is born out of superfluity.' He then turned to me and asked, 'Didn't he give a fine example while explaining the theory to Shastri?'* I said, 'The difference between the gardener Radhu bringing water in tin cannisters hanging from a bamboo stick and Nandalal's painting of a slender sixteen-year-old beauty carrying water in a painted earthen pitcher is superfluity. And that, is art.'

Bogdanov said thoughtfully, 'Is it only art? Philosophy, science, everything – everything we mean by culture, flourishes out of superfluity.'

Professor Vinsin joined the debate, 'But this culture reaches its extreme when the gap between the upper and the lower classes becomes so great that the country can't even stand as one in spite of facing invasion. And they lose their independence – like Iran.'

I said, 'India.'

Madame Vorvechievichi from Poland said, 'But the English? They also have the aristocrats and the commoners. The gulf between the rich and the poor is not a small one either. But they can always fight as one nation.'

Bogdanov asked, 'Who did you mention?'

'The English.'

'Oh, those who live on a small island west of Europe?'

There was no Englishman present in our midst. So nobody was offended and everyone enjoyed the comment.

Professor Vinsin said, 'Bogdanov has rightly showed his contempt. There are many aristocrats in England but they don't have the erudition that creates the gap between the rich and the poor. What do they have? Only literature. No music, no fine art, no

* Sanskirt scholar and Indologist Bidhu Shekhar Shastri who taught at Visva-Bharati University.

sculpture, no architecture. The elements that fuel the gap – the finer sensibilities – where are they? We have them in abundance in France; hence we French people don't know how to fight as one. Even in the time of peace, we can't run the country properly. I shouldn't be critical of the country where I'm living now. But see, even this tiny country is independent.'

Madame Vorvechievichi argued, 'But there are mullahs in this country.'

Dost Muhammad said reassuringly, 'No need to worry, Madame. I know these mullahs very well. Their knowledge of religion is very little and I can teach you all of it in three days. However, a woman can't be a mullah.'

Madame Vorvechievichi said angrily, 'Why not?'

With a deep sigh Dost Muhammad said, 'Because she can't grow a beard.'

Vinsin consoled her, 'Mullah or not, you would have spent your life behind the veil if you were born in this country. Consider how much we would have missed.'

Everyone chorused, '*Oui, Madame, si, si, Madame, certainement, Madame.*'

When the refrain ended, Dost Muhammad said, 'But the system of the veil is good.'

Eight invisible sabres were unleashed from their sheaths; I closed my eyes and saw Dost Muhammad's head rolling towards the mountains of the Afridis.

No! My imagination. I heard Dost Muhammad talking, 'Tell me honestly, with your hand on your heart, how many women can you find who are as beautiful as Madame Vorvechievichi, Madame Laffont and Senora Digoda? Most of them are ugly. So there is no harm if you introduce the veil wholesale.'

The women were mildly pleased.

But Madame Vorvechievichi had hot Polish blood – she asked, 'And you think, all men are as handsome as Adonis? Why don't they also put on the veil?'

Dost Muhammad replied, 'Hence it's forbidden for women to look at them.'

The room erupted into a babble of voices. It was not clear if the women were pleased or angry. After they had calmed down, Senora Digoda asked Dost Muhammad, 'Why haven't you married yet – lack of beautiful women?'

Dost Muhammad said while scratching his right cheek with his left hand, 'It's not like that. You see, marrying one woman will mean that I consider the rest of them ugly. I don't want to insult the entire women's race for only one woman.'

Everyone was very pleased, especially me. The Afghan from the mountains defeated the erudition of Vinsin with his chivalry.

Agha Adib from the Iranian embassy had been listening all along. Now he opened his mouth. He said, 'Afghanistan should be careful. It will be in trouble if it decides to ape Iran. Iran has meanwhile become cleverer. Bogdanov learned the decorum of how to address the king ten years ago when he lived there. It is not the same now. There are strong movements against such customs. Now poems are being written caricaturing the politeness that people show to others while entering a room. I have listened to one of them so many times that I know it by heart. I can recite it if you would like.'

Everyone showed a lot of interest.

Agha Adib recited it with relish—

'Lord, you have given us a lot of knowledge,
So I bring this final mystery for you to unpackage.
The folks of Iran, I guarantee,

They are not so very batty.
They have education, got brains, they're no cowards,
They lock horns with the British, and fight 'em afterwards.
Yet, why do they, as a room they are about to enter,
Push so hard and squeeze everyone asunder?
They stop at the door, even as they look inside,
"You go in", "You enter", as they stand still aside.
All joy and laughter disappear, all stories expire,
Amidst all the push and shove everyone perspires.
Astonished, I wonder why everyone goes this way,
In broad midday?
Is there a ghost at the centre of the chamber?
Or, could it be Death's messenger?
Solomon's genie carousing?

Perhaps, a guillotine blade rising,
Will take my neck as soon as I walk in . . .
Is that why, at the door, they all keep freezin'?'

TWENTY-ONE

I could build relationships and establish contacts with the bazaars, the streets, the ministers and other dignitaries, the rich and the poor of Kabul. But I sensed that the chance of seeing and bonding with the rest of the country was very slim. I figured that it would be almost impossible to fathom the social forces that moved at a slow pace in times of peace and ran like a wild horse in times of turbulence.

The backbone of Afghanistan was built on its far-flung villages and various tribes, but until now not a single book had been written on their economic conditions, their traditional systems of administration and their customs. I did not come across a single pundit in Kabul who could give me a decent description, let alone talk at length on such matters. While talking about history, the Kabulis would often say, 'Then the Shinwaris rebelled'; if you asked them, 'Why did they rebel', they would say, 'The mullahs incited them.' After that if you asked what the socio-economic sparks were, to which the mullahs could add fuel to create a countrywide wildfire, you would not get any answer. Only one – that too an Indian – had said to me, 'The crux is that the poor people can't survive without looting the foreign caravans. So, like the trade-cycles of advanced countries, there is a cycle of peace and upheaval in Afghanistan. This is their life.'

From the little information I gathered of village life, I could make out that in times of peace, the only connection between the villages and the towns was confined to villagers coming to town to sell their sheep, vegetables and other produce very cheaply. They bought their bare essentials with some of that money at a much higher price. The towns, in return, built a few roads, schools or hospitals in the villages. There was practically no government institution in any village of Afghanistan. A few boys gathered at the local mosque and recited the Ampara[*] at the tops of their voices – that was all the education they had. The village mullah was the village doctor too. He doled out amulets for illnesses. If one was seriously ill, he gave you holy water, and he was the one who arranged the funeral if one died. The whole village paid for the mullah.

They paid their taxes very unwillingly as they got precious little in return. Some of my acquaintances had explained this to me, though there was no need.

Afghan villages seldom suffered at a time of upheaval – rather it was beneficial for them. The young people would go out looting with their rifles slung from their shoulders. In 'God's Gift' Afghanistan, God had gifted them trouble in abundance – so why not profit from it? When France and Germany fought battles, the Germans would march shouting, '*Nach Paris, nach Paris*' (To Paris, to Paris). Similarly, with the scent of any trouble Afghans said, '*Bia ba Kabul, ba rowom ba Kabul*' (To Kabul, to Kabul).

The king ruled from the city. His main task was to keep the various tribes from looting. He needed soldiers to accomplish that task, and money to pay for the soldiers. In addition, there was the

---

[*] The last chapter of the Koran.

cost of arms and ammunitions. The city people paid for it partly, but the bulk of it came from the rural areas.

Thus, there was a strange vicious cycle in place. You needed soldiers to collect taxes, and used the same taxes to pay for the soldiers. The person who could break the cycle would be the revered one – the King of Afghanistan. The money to buy the hammer that he used to break the teeth of the Afghans, came from the Afghans themselves.

Whatever oil the press produced, went in to keep the press oiled.

The little left over was used to make Kabul beautiful.

That was so little that you could not build new industries or institutions for mass education. So there was practically no educated class in Kabul.

However, it would be wrong to presume that Kabul was a city of illiterate barbarians. The mullahs were the last vestiges of the links between India and Afghanistan.

That might need a bit of explanation.

Kabul's official language was Farsi; hence most foreigners thought that Kabul was culturally linked with Iran. But when Iran went the Shia way, Sunni Afghanistan severed all its ties with Iran. Afghan youth could no longer travel to Iran for studies. Since the country was poor, it did not have the means to build its own schools and colleges.

Meanwhile during the Pathan times, and especially the Mughal period, India's wealth had established many centres of Sunni teaching in Delhi and Lahore. The medium of instruction was Farsi. So it was only to be expected that students of religion from Kabul and Kandahar would come in large numbers to join these schools. In the Buddhist period, Afghans went to Taxila to study. The frescos of ancient Afghanistan contained the influence of Ajanta rather than the Iranian or Chinese styles.

This tradition had continued into the twentieth century. Every well-educated maulvi of Kabul had studied in India. Even though they were taught in Farsi, they came back speaking the Urdu language. They had immense influence over the half-educated and semi-literate rural mullahs, and these mullahs were the driving force of the daily life of Afghanistan.

The educated people of the twentieth century always criticised the mullahs, saying that they were anti-modern and obstacles to progress; they were steeped in the past. But not the past where one learned how societies struggled and developed. Their past was confined within the dark walls of the rigid interpretation of religion, dogma and blind faith.

I did not sit down to write a book on comparative religion, so I do not intend to criticise or eulogise the clerics of all faiths. But I would do a great injustice if I did not praise the Afghan mullahs on one count.

It would be better to explain with an example.

The Hindu Brahmin priests and mullah-maulvis of India had a stranglehold on Indian rural society until the mid-nineteenth century. They could never organise the populace against British rule in India; the Afghan mullahs on the contrary had played a key role in sending the English packing three times.

In light of that, could one not afford to forgive all the shortcomings of the Afghan mullahs? My weak pen fails to appreciate them enough.

There were hardly two dozen people in Kabul who had a Western education. In times of peace, they would pretend as if they ran the country; you would not be able to trace them anywhere during times of crises. I had made acquaintance with them, and figured out that though they had spent three years in Paris, they had never read Marcel Proust or André Gide; the Berlin-returnees had not heard the name of Durar, nor read the poems of Rilke. Michael Madhusudan[*] produced superlative poetry mixing Milton and Valmiki[†] but there was no one in Kabul who would be able to write fine verses taking elements from Goethe and Firdausi.[‡]

So the crux was this – the city-folk were delicate and had no clue about the pulse of the country. On the other hand, the mullahs were half-educated. Even if you forgave the better educated ones, the question remained as to whether or not it was the ultimate responsibility of Afghanistan to fight the Russians and the British? Would the mullah society ever take part in the economic advancement of the country by better educating the people? Possibly not. Would they oppose it? One could not say.

Every nation believed that it was the best country on earth. The poor ones also believed that they would never be able to prosper by mining the hidden mineral resources underground, as they did not have the means to do so. It was difficult to say objectively, but there was little chance that this country would be able to progress if it was not able to tap into its underground resources.

In ancient times the prophets used to predict the future. Currently, soothsayers did so. I did not have the courage to predict the future, but I could guess that the old and special relationship between Afghanistan and India would be re-established soon after India's independence. The students of the author of the *Shahnameh*.

[*] Nineteenth-century Bengali poet and dramatist.
[†] The first poet – writer of the Sanskrit epic the *Ramayana*.
[‡] Famous Iranian poet from the tenth and eleventh century – the wealthy of Kabul and Kandahar would once again go to Delhi and Lahore to study.

Proof? What proof did you need? Parisians did not speak English, the residents of Vienna did not speak French, but the educated people of Budapest still spoke German and went to Vienna to enhance their knowledge – the cultural continuity did not disappear with the formation of a new state. Kabul's maulvis spoke in Urdu, it was not possible for them to shun India.

One day I got proof of the extent to which the Urdu language had spread in this country.

TWENTY-TWO

I had mentioned earlier that my house was two and a half miles away from the city – a new township was being built a further two miles down the road. The newly built road passed before my house. It was beautifully planned – lined with cypress trees on either side, a canal of fresh water, a footpath for the pedestrians and a separate path for the horse-riders.

This road was the boulevard for the Kabulis. Every evening the city-folk used to go for an outing to the new city in motor cars or horse carriages, on horseback or on bicycles. Kabulis did not like walking. One doctor had advised a patient to take a daily walk to improve his digestion. The Kabuli apparently asked how his digestion would improve by tiring his leg muscles?

Some evenings, when I did not go to Kabul, I took a stroll on this road. As the area was not very safe in the evenings, it would be quite deserted by sunset.

One day I was coming back home when a large, expensive car stopped in front of me. A big-bodied bulky Afghan gentleman was at the steering wheel and a woman clad in Western dress was sitting next to him. Through the veil of fine net hanging from her hat, I could see that she was no ordinary beauty.

Without any greeting or preamble, he asked me, 'Do you speak Farsi?'

I said, 'A little.'

'Where are you from?'

'India.'

Now the gentleman started talking in not-so-correct yet fluent Urdu, 'Often we see you here. You're a foreigner, you may not know that this place is not very safe to take a stroll in the evening.'

I said, 'I live here.'

He asked, 'How come? This is a village full of peasants.'

I said, 'The king has opened an agricultural department here. We, three foreigners, live here, sharing a house. As I spoke, I saw that he was translating everything into Farsi for his wife who did not say a word.

He then asked, 'Don't you have any friends in Kabul? Don't you feel lonely taking a stroll alone? My wife was saying "*Bacha gum mekhurd*" (The boy is unhappy). Hence I stopped to talk to you.' I understood her beauty was that of a mother's. I bowed to her.

The gentleman asked, 'Can you play tennis?'

'Yes.'

'Then you should come and play with me whenever you visit Kabul.'

I replied, 'Thank you very much – but where is your tennis court? Besides, I still haven't got your name.'

The gentleman looked slightly surprised. Then he said, 'Me? Oh, I'm Moin-us-Sultana. My tennis court is close to the foreign ministry's office. Come by tomorrow.' Saying that, he left in a jiffy, without giving me a chance to thank him properly.

I had not noticed until then that Abdur Rahman was standing twenty yards behind the car and gesticulating madly with his hands, which were moving like the propeller of an aircraft. After the motor car left, he rushed over to me like a steam engine and said, 'Moin-us-Sultana, Moin-us-Sultana!'

I said casually, 'Who is this chap anyway?'

Abdur Rahman was about to explode in excitement. In response to my queries, he kept saying like a hymn, 'Moin-us-Sultana, Moin-us-Sultana.' Finally he said helplessly and with a hint of rebuke, 'You don't know him? *Baradare-ala-Hazrat* – the king's brother – elder brother. What have you done? You must kiss the hands of royalty.'

I said, 'I couldn't risk wearing out my lips by kissing hands before knowing how many there are in the royal family.'

Abdur Rahman continued his lament, 'Oh, God, by the name of the Prophet, what have you done? What have you done?'

I asked, 'If he is the elder brother of the king then why didn't he get the throne?'

Abdur Rahman put his hands to his mouth, and then whispered, 'I'm a poor man. How should I know all that? But it's best not to ask such questions.'

After dinner, when Abdur Rahman sat in his usual corner of the room breaking walnuts, he kept saying, 'Oh, Moin-us-Sultana, Moin-us-Sultana.' I gave up after scolding him a couple of times. Abdur Rahman was a simple man and as Afghanistan was a country full of nepotism, he was surely thinking that I would soon become a minister or attain a powerful position by getting into the good books of the high and mighty. Surely I would.

By then, I had looked it up in the dictionary; the meaning of Moin-us-Sultana was crown prince.

The crown prince did not become the king, his younger brother did. I had to solve this puzzle.

TWENTY-THREE

I would take my readers towards the beginning of the century to solve the puzzle of why the younger son of the ruler had become the king and not the crown prince, 'Moin-us-Sultana'.

At that time, Habibullah was the Amir, the ruler, of Afghanistan. The mullahs of the country were so fond of the Amir's younger brother Nasrullah that Habibullah was in a quandary after proclaiming his elder son Enayatullah as the crown prince. So the two brothers made a pact that Nasrullah would succeed Habibullah after his death, while Enayatullah would continue to be the crown prince, the Moin-us-Sultana. To make the pact even stronger, they made a decision that Moin-us-Sultana would marry the daughter of Nasrullah. Habibullah probably thought that Nasrullah would at least not kill his own son-in-law and be branded as 'damadkush' – killer of his son-in-law. This was the fate that befell the king of Jodhpur, Ajit Singh, when he joined the conspiracy of the Syed brothers and had his son-in-law, Farukhsiar, killed. The entire city of Delhi shamed him by calling him 'damad-kush'. Street kids would run alongside his carriage shouting 'damad-kush', 'damad-kush', disregarding the threats of his guards. He finally had to leave the city in order to avoid such public humiliation.

Habibullah, Nasrullah and Moin-us-Sultana – everyone was more or less happy with this arrangement; everyone except one person – the stepmother of the motherless Moin-us-Sultana, second wife of Habibullah, and the mother of his youngest son, Amanullah. She was known to the Afghans as the Ulia Hazrat or the Queen Mother. She was so domineering, that Habibullah was terrified of her. Once, in a fit of anger she left the palace and camped on the other side of the river. Habibullah tried his best to placate her and bring her back to the palace without any success. Her heart of stone melted only when Habibullah sat in the mud and dust like a madman on this side of the river.

The Queen Mother thought that if life was indeed a game of chess, as Omar Khayyam had described it, might it not be possible for a small pawn like her own son, Amanullah, to checkmate big shots such as Habibullah and Nasrullah? Why could he not become the king? At that time one of the most famous aristocrats of Kabul, Mahmud Tarzi, came back from exile in Syria. His three most beautiful daughters, Kaokab, Soraya and Bibi Khurd also returned with him. They dazzled the high society of Kabul with their accomplishments, foreign education, ravishing beauty and the use of make-up. All the other women of Kabul looked drab compared to them.

Habibullah was not in the capital. Amanullah's mother – though she was his second wife – had assumed the role of the queen after the death of the Moin-us-Sultana's mother. She organised a big feast in the palace. She had instructed everyone in the household to make arrangements in such a way that Moin-us-Sultana was drawn to Kaokab. A couple of rooms in the palace were kept specially prepared and vacant for them.

The feast was in full swing with food and music. The Queen Mother introduced Moin-us-Sultana to Kaokab and whispered in Kaokab's ears, 'He is Moin-us-Sultana, he will sit on the throne of Afghanistan someday.' Kaokab was an intelligent woman; she understood what that meant. Besides, the laws of natural attraction among the youth were applicable to royal palaces too.

The plan worked. While taking a stroll inside the colossal palace with Kaokab, Moin-us-Sultana entered an empty room and engaged in intimate conversation with her. Moin-us-Sultana thought that he had entered the room of his own free will, but little did he know that it was his planned destiny. The Queen Mother knew the prey was trapped.

According to the plan, the Queen Mother suddenly entered the room. The young couple stood up shyly. The Queen Mother, putting on a display of love, told her stepson, 'Bacha, son, you don't have your own mother. But I'm here. You will open your heart to me. The responsibility of your marriage is on my shoulders. Why are you feeling shy if you like Kaokab so much? Who in Kabul can compete with Tarzi's daughter? What does your heart say?'

What could Moin-us-Sultana say? He was facing a double-edged sword.

Nobody knew what his heart said. There were many variations among the storytellers of Kabul, regarding what he actually said. Some said he gave a silent consent, some said he objected feebly as he was engaged to Nasrullah's daughter, and some said that he had said yes because moments earlier he had professed his love to Kaokab. Possibly he had thought that expressing love and agreeing to marriage were two different matters – but how could he avoid the dilemma now? Some said he simply uttered a 'hmmm' from which it was impossible to make out if he was saying 'Baley' – yes, or 'Ne' – no. And some said, the Queen Mother left the room even before he could say anything.

So five versions of the same story.

The crux of it was, in that situation Moin-us-Sultana did exactly what all others, a king or a commoner, a rich man or poor one, a dove or a pigeon – were supposed to do.

It was not important to know what he said, it was far more important what the Queen Mother made of it and presented in public. Not university textbooks, ordinary guidebooks carried more weight for the ordinary people.

Even though the Queen Mother stayed behind purdah, the whole country could hear her voice when she spoke. So no wonder that her voice rose above the noise of the feast and the music in the palace. The Queen Mother said, 'It's a day of great joy. The light of my eyes – Noor-e-Chashm – Moin-us-Sultana, Enayatullah Khan has decided to marry Tarzi's daughter Kaokab. The party is supposed to end at two. In this joyous moment, it will go on until daybreak. I'm sending the marriage proposal to the girl's family.'

The palace lights lit up with double their brightness. There were encores and merriment. The palace staff ran helter skelter to make arrangements to send the proposal of marriage to the girl's house. Of course, the Queen Mother had arranged everything beforehand, so there was no difficulty in sending the proposal without delay. Tarzi was overjoyed. Kaokab had heaven in her heart.

The Queen Mother sent a messenger to Habibullah with the news right away. As the mother and the Queen Mother she understood the direction of the heart of Moin-us-Sultana and thus had arranged his marriage. A 'progressive' Afghanistan needed an educated queen. There was no girl in Kabul who could compete with Kaokab. The initial ceremony of the proposal was over. The king should now return to Kabul soon and complete the wedding rituals to make his subjects happy.

Habibullah was very angry but kept calm. He understood that the fool Moin-us-Sultana, by falling in love with Kaokab, had not only lost Nasrullah's daughter but was also about to lose his throne. Though Habibullah was normally busy with wine and women, he understood that the hand of the Queen Mother was at play. A stepmother's love could never be genuine.

The stepmother's words?
Are in honey smattered;
She cuts the stem below,
Even as the top she waters.

Controlling his anger, Habibullah sent her a nicely worded reply – 'By the grace of God, the Queen had the right instinct to arrange the marriage. It is true that Tarzi's daughter Kaokab is the right match for Moin-us-Sultana in terms of her beauty and education. But not only Kaokab, Tarzi's second daughter Soraya is equally beautiful, cultured and amply educated. Why should my second son Amanullah marry an ordinary uncultured Kabuli woman? So following the Queen's steps, I am sending a marriage proposal between Amanullah and Soraya instantly, along with this letter. Upon my return to the capital very soon . . .'

Habibullah had fathomed that by fixing Moin-us-Sultana up with Kaokab, the Queen Mother was plotting to get Amanullah married to Nasrullah's daughter. Then the prospect of Amanullah becoming the Amir after Nasrullah's death would increase. In order to counter that move, Habibullah tied the knot between Amanullah and Soraya. The manner in which the Queen Mother praised Kaokab so much for her beauty and foreign education, there was no way she could resist this wedding. Especially when the whole country – from Chihalstun to Bagh-e-Bala – knew that Soraya was more beautiful and more educated than Kaokab.

It was as if the Queen Mother was hit by lightning. By trying to make a checkmate with a pawn, she had found herself in a counter checkmate position. She cursed Habibullah to her heart's content, 'You didn't get Nasrullah's daughter, neither did I. So we are at least even. Both Moin-us-Sultana and Amanullah are now in the same boat – at least in Nasrullah's eyes.'

The Queen Mother now adopted the 'waiting move' of chess.

TWENTY-FOUR

The next chapter began with Raja Mahendra Pratap.

In 1915, on the advice of Raja Mahendra, the German foreign ministry decided that Britain's one wing could be injured badly if they could entice Amir Habibullah to declare war against the British. Britain would have to keep one entire army in the Punjab to fight Habibullah – and the Turks would then be able to gain the upper hand in the Middle East. That would throw up the possibility of closing down the Suez Canal, clipping Britain's other wing.

Mahendra Pratap hoped that through this manoeuvre India might be able to gain independence. That was his sole objective.

The Kaiser received Raja Mahendra with great pomp, conferred on him the Golden Eagle medal and sent him to Kabul with a team of German diplomats. En route, Raja Mahendra got a cordial reception from the Emperor of Turkey too.

Before they could reach Kabul, Raja Mahendra and the Germans had to negotiate the incredible hostility and obstacles in eastern Iran and western Afghanistan. Britain and Russia both found out about Raja Mahendra's mission and they attacked him from both sides. After a perilous journey, Raja Mahendra and his German advisors reached Kabul in the winter of 1915, leaving behind most of their belongings along the way.

Amir Habibullah gave Raja Mahendra and his entourage a royal welcome. The whole of Kabul had lined up on both sides of the streets to greet him. Raja Mahendra was housed in one of Habibullah's own palaces, close to Babur's tomb.

The people of Kabul normally did not accord anyone such a public welcome. They had come out on the streets for two reasons. First, they were getting impatient with Amir Habibullah's appeasement policy towards the British and were craving for independence. Besides, the message of nationalism from the new Egypt and the young Turks was already seeping into the country. Secondly, the Afghans might not have been sure about the motives of the Germans, but they did not doubt the intention of the Indians for a minute. From his vantage point in Berlin, the Kaiser had guessed that correctly. Hence he had sent Raja Mahendra as the leader of the German delegation.

Britain had ordered Habibullah to expel Raja Mahendra and the Germans instantly. But clever Habibullah kept them at bay by dilly-dallying on some pretext or another. He also knew that Britain's hands were full and they did not have enough troops to fight another battle.

Habibullah did not act according to Raja Mahendra's plan either. I heard many different views about why he did not do so and whether he was right or wrong. It was difficult to decipher the truth, but everyone agreed on one point, that the whole of Afghanistan would have supported him had he decided to fight the British at that time. Habibullah ignored the public opinion of Afghanistan and disappointed Germany, Turkey and the Indians.

The Germans tried their best for a year and finally left. On the other hand, though Raja Mahendra Pratap had given up all hopes for the time being, yet he tried to prepare the ground for the future. Raja Mahendra knew that either Nasrullah or Moin-us-Sultana would become ruler after Habibullah's death. While lobbying with them, Raja understood that they too did not have any mettle – both were fakes. Nobody had counted Amanullah in the equation of the power struggle at that point in time, but everyone in Kabul knew that Raja Mahendra had spent some time with him too. It was not known what mantra Raja Mahendra gave Amanullah, and neither did the former make that clear. After the revolution in Russia in 1917, Raja Mahendra left Kabul. The Great War had come to an end.

The progressive elements in Kabul had gradually given up their battle for a revolutionary change in society. At that point one invisible hand started playing chess from behind the purdah. She was Ulia Hazrat, the Queen Mother.

The Queen Mother had been waiting for such a moment for many years. She knew that the progressive elements of Kabul would not think about Amanullah until they became completely disillusioned with Habibullah, Nasrullah and Moin-us-Sultana. From behind her veil she started to convince the enlightened youth of Kabul that Habibullah was like a stone – not even Raja Mahendra could instil life in him. So what were they waiting for? Nasrullah and Moin-us-Sultana – both were assuming that the throne was theirs. But they were not ready to pay any price for it.

Yet Amanullah was ready. How? He was ready to shed his own blood to fight the British for the independence of Afghanistan.

So how could they succeed in making Amanullah the Amir? The Queen Mother brought out the blueprint from behind her burqa. The following winter, when Habibullah would go to Jalalabad with Nasrullah and Moin-us-Sultana, Amanullah would become the governor of Kabul. If Habibullah were to die in Jalalabad, it would be possible for Amanullah to get hold of the armoury and the treasury of Kabul. One needed both to become a king.

But a man dies only at the wish of God. Would God's wishes match the Queen Mother's blueprint? The impatient Queen Mother explained that God normally had his work done through the hands of men – especially if that hand held a small pistol.

Plotting to kill her husband? What? Yes. Any personal relationship was irrelevant – when we are talking about the future of the country, its hopes and disappointments, it is only self-determination that prevails. Then, husband-wife or father-son relationships do not matter.

Shankaracharya[*] had said, '*Ka taba kanta*' – who is your wife – but I understood the meaning of his theory of '*samsar ateeba vichitra*' – life is mysterious.

Some of the greenhorns asked, 'But wouldn't Amir Habibullah's army and the people of Jalalabad side with Nasrullah?'

Apparently the Queen Mother became speechless with anger. She said, 'You fools! Wouldn't we spread the word that the vulture Nasrullah had killed the Amir for the throne?' These 'fools' now understood that the Queen Mother was actually the mother of all plotters.

Listening to these stories, I could not say for sure how much of it was accurate and how much concocted. But most storytellers of Kabul agreed that this was how it happened.

The story of the children's fable was wrong – someone was indeed found to bell the cat.

Habibullah died because of his own laziness. In Jalalabad, one of his spies sought his audience in private one evening, soon after

---

[*] The Hindu religious leader who led the resurgence of Hinduism in north India between the eighth and ninth century after the decline of the Buddhist period.

he came back from his hunting trip. Apparently the spy had smelled the conspiracy being hatched by the Queen Mother. Habibullah brushed him aside, saying, 'Tomorrow morning.' The spy could not say anything in front of the rest of the hunting party – the Amir said only 'tomorrow'.

That 'tomorrow' never came. That night Habibullah died at the hand of the assassin.

As expected there was much hullaballoo in Jalalabad the following morning. Some asked, 'Who killed the Amir?' Some asked, 'Who will be the Amir?' Some said, 'The wishes of the old Amir were not binding, Moin-us-Sultana should be the Amir, only he has the right to the throne.'

Most people had gone to Moin-us-Sultana, Enayatullah Khan. His eyes were red with weeping; he only said, '*Ba kakayem boro*', (Go and ask uncle). It was difficult to say why he did not show any interest in taking over the throne. He might have been too stunned at the assassination of his father. It was also possible that he wanted to honour his father's wishes. Or perhaps he thought that the people who had had his father killed, would eventually seize power and would not hesitate to remove him if he stood in their way. Thus, Nasrullah became the Amir.

Meanwhile the Queen Mother spread the word in Kabul, Kandahar, Herat and Jalalabad that greedy Nasrullah had killed the Amir to take over the throne. He never had the right to be the Amir, there was no way he could be the ruler under the circumstances. The only person who had the legitimate right over the throne, Moin-us-Sultana, had surrendered to Nasrullah; he too had lost the moral right to be the Amir. So only Amanullah could be the next ruler.

The logic was solid but Kabul said only feebly, 'Long live Amanullah.'

The Queen Mother instantly announced a substantial bonus for the troops. Amanullah announced that the salary of the soldiers was 'too little'; he doubled their wages. All the money came from the state treasury. Kabul now thundered, 'Long live Amanullah.'

Someone once asked Voltaire if it was possible to kill a herd of sheep with a curse. Voltaire had said, 'It is possible, but only if you give them a strong dose of poison before cursing.'

For the Afghan troops, political logic was the curse, and money was the poison.

Amanullah mourned his father's death standing in the middle of the bazaar in Kabul. With tears in his eyes, he took an oath in a powerful voice, 'Until I avenge the killing of my dearest father, drinking water will be sacrilege for me, touching any food will be like eating non-kosher meat.'

Amanullah's enemies said that he could have had a good career in theatre; his friends said that the Queen Mother had masterminded the entire plot with the help of the chieftains of the court, keeping Amanullah out of it. After all, people might not have liked the idea of kissing the hands of the 'pidar-kush' – the 'patricidal' Amir. Besides, when the Queen Mother could manage everything, what was the point of dragging young Amanullah into the play? He would have remained behind the scenes all his life, had Afghan customs allowed a woman to become the ruler.

Amanullah's troops reached Jalalabad. Both Nasrullah and Moin-us-Sultana surrendered without a fight. Nasrullah was like the minarets of a mosque for the clergy or the mullahs. Why they did not try to mobilise the army in his favour would remain a mystery.

It seemed, on the way to Kabul, Moin-us-Sultana had broken down in tears thinking about his future. The troops who wanted to put him on the throne a few days earlier had by then switched sides to Amanullah. Apparently they taunted him by saying, '*Ba kakayem boro*,' meaning, now go to your uncle and ask him to save your neck.

Both were interned in the Arg Fort in Kabul. After a few days, Nasrullah died of 'cholera'. Some said he got 'cholera' from drinking coffee. Did anyone put anything in the coffee he drank? I realised that the storytellers of Kabul largely had amnesia in that regard.

A weakling Bengali such as myself could not even imagine what was going on in the mind of Moin-us-Sultana. There was no comparison to the fear of death.

Disregarding all his failings, here the whole world should bow down to show their deepest respect to Amanullah. He did what had never happened in the history of the Orient. With the power he had gained by the mercy of his mother, he freed his half-brother Moin-us-Sultana against the advice of all his counsellors.

People who had read the history of the Mughal and Pathan periods would understand how much courage he had shown. There was no other such example of valour and generosity in the history of Afghanistan.

TWENTY-FIVE

Raja Mahendra Pratrap had given him the inspiration to do so, but after fighting with the British, Amanullah understood well that an honest man got only one chance as opposed to the three that a thief received. He gained his chance by winning the battle against the British; now he had to tackle his enemies. Amanullah started to get ready.

On opening his account books, he saw that the credit column said – Amanullah has won the hearts and minds of his people by winning independence from the British. He was no more the Amir, he was now the Gazi – the victor, King Amanullah.

The debit column noted that even though the gang of mullahs behind Nasrullah had exited the scene, there was no way he could trust them.

Amanullah knew that it would be impossible to run the motor car in top gear if he had to always be fearful of the ditches that the mullahs might have dug in the middle of the highway to reform. Yet there was no option but to drive the car at full speed because the honest man had only one chance.

After reaching Kabul, I saw that hundreds of youngsters were moving about in uniforms. On enquiring, I found out that some of the uniforms were French, some German, some English and some military. Not only uniforms, village students who came to town to further their studies were provided with free schooling, boarding, lodging, books, dictionaries, instruments and even the cost of hiring donkeys to visit home in the holidays – to put it simply, 'all found'.

On behalf of India I said, 'Nothing lost.'

Paris-returnee Saiful Alam said, 'You thought "all found" automatically meant learning? No sir. The boys often flee from the hostels.'

I asked, 'Isn't there any system of getting them back?'

Saiful Alam said, 'The village boys are hardy; they can live anywhere under any circumstance. Amanullah has found a way to track them. Soon after a boy flees the hostel, we inform the government. At the order of the government, two policemen will go and park themselves at the boy's home. Contrary to their orders, they will beat up the father with the butt of their rifles if they do not get good pulao and kebab there. The father then goes out in search of his son. The son finally turns up at the school, a letter confirming his return goes to the department, then the policemen will return to Kabul after enjoying the farewell feast at the boy's home. They will not object if the whole saga is repeated again.'

I asked, 'But what if someone is really a dull student?'

'The head teacher would consider dismissal if he failed three times in a row. If one is intelligent yet refusing to study, then there's no respite.'

What else can a king do to lead his country to the path of progress? The responsibility of running the military school lay with the Turks. The tradition of Turk generals was linked to the military colleges of Berlin and Potsdam; so this school was built in German style. But nobody could tell me what progress it was making. Professor Benoit said, 'Afghanistan will not lose anything if they close it down.'

King Amanullah and his wife Soraya had taken an extra inter-est in educating the girls of the country. In Kabul about two thou-sand girls were attending schools wearing the burqa. They played basketball and volleyball in the school grounds surrounded by high walls. Saiful Alam said, 'They are learning to write and do maths. I don't mind if they don't learn anything; at least they have come out of the closed confines of the harem into the open air and are running around joyfully. Isn't that enough?'

I agreed with him wholeheartedly. Saiful Alam whispered in my ears, 'But one person is totally against this – the Queen Mother.'

I grew alarmed. The person who removed two obstacles and neutralised the third to make Amanullah the king, had to have some weight in this matter. In her opinion, Afghanistan was not ready for so much education. There had been a serious difference of opinion between mother and son regarding this – by all accounts, the mother was so hurt, that she had stopped giving advice to her son. Apparently Soraya too was ignoring her mother-in-law.

But the city of Kabul was then trotting like a mad horse wear-ing 'dereshi'. The word 'dereshi' came from the English word 'dress', meaning hat, tie and trousers. I was told that one had to wear dereshi if you were in government service – be it a lowly clerk's job or a constable's. Not only that, one could not enter public parks if one was not in dereshi. First, the pressure from the government; secondly, an attraction towards the culture of advanced societies and thirdly, images from the movies – Kabul was mesmerised by dereshi.

Even Abdur Rahman was infected with it. He used to nag me if I sat at home in my shalwar. He insisted that I wore my best blue suit if I went out wearing informal dress.

Women were also keeping pace with time. Habibullah used to make the women in his harem wear frocks and blouses. In Amanullah's time upper-class women moved about in high-heels, knee-length frocks, full-sleeved tight blouses, gloves and hat. Their faces were not fully visible as they were covered by a thin net veil hanging from their hats. The bolder the woman, the thinner the net.

In French, 'figure' meant the shape of one's face. Professor Benoit used to say that it was possible to make out the figure of Kabuli women but not their 'figure'.

But it was not possible to open schools or colleges every day, buy new dereshi or show your figure without increasing the income of the exchequer. You needed to have factories and production lines to achieve that. Afghanistan did not have its own resources, and the king was not keen to invite foreign investment. Amanullah's grandfather Amir Abdur Rahman used to say, 'Afghanistan will have railways on the day that it is able to build engines.' His father Habibullah did not abide by the same principle entirely; he bought the equipment for supplying electricity in Kabul. Amanullah could not make up his mind – some had advised him to raise the national loan debt, but that meant returning it with interest and the system of interest was prohibited in Islam.

Amanullah probably thought it would be easier to lead the country towards the path of progress if he shared the heavy burden of running the government with others. So he announced, 'We will have a parliament.'

I saw the face of that parliament in Paghman.

Paghman was twenty kilometres west of Kabul. The whole town had been built on steps cut into a mountainside. From a distance it looked as if a conch-shell had been placed upside down and small villas, like the ones in Italy, had been constructed on its curves. Apple and pear trees surrounded the villas all over the town. Water from the melting icecaps of the mountain peaks flowed down into the roadside stream sparkling on the steps. I climbed up the newly tarred road, absorbing the silence of the dark green woods on both sides. There were no signs of hurry anywhere, no wall of naked mountain on either side, no boring yellow houses. It did not feel as though I was walking through dry and rough Afghanistan. I had the illusion that I would bump into the women from the Khasi hills* coming down with their baskets full of oranges on their backs.

The king spent the summer in Paghman with his council of ministers and other civil servants. The whole of Afghanistan came there for a week to celebrate 'Jashan' – Independence Day. They came in groups and pitched their tents by the side of the road. They spent the whole day shooting at targets, watching the Mongols dance and the army parade, or chitchatting at the cobbler's. In the evening they had their own musical gatherings. No classical song like 'If I get a kiss from my lover's lips only for one night/I will become young again', the main tone of those songs was to express their love for the likes of 'Fatu Jan'. Sometimes someone would jump up and break into a whirling dance. Keeping the beat of the song, everyone would clap and encourage the dancer, saying, 'well done, well done'.

It was difficult to sit in such gatherings for long – the way it was difficult for a smoker to sit in a closed room where everyone was smoking. His insides would crave a puff and his throat would itch. Likewise, you had to paint a picture of your 'Fatu Jan' in your mind; if not, you needed to sing at full blast with them, or else

---

* Hills in north-east India, now in the state of Meghalaya. The author was born and raised close to those hills.

your ears would get blocked by all the noise. There was some similarity between such music and playing rugby – it was good to
enjoy from a distance.

But I felt Paghman was not a place for noise. The streams
murmured as they flowed, the leaves were humming in the light
breeze, birds were singing and the intoxicating smell of damp pine
leaves beneath one's feet would make one's eyelids heavy in the middle
of the day. It was the middle of summer, and yet one could still feel
the chill – making one want to lift the collar of one's coat. There was
no need for a glass of wine or having your lover or a book of poetry
beside you; all one needed was a warm coverlet before dozing off.

I dozed off. I woke up to see a fantastic figure staring at me
with a broad smile showing his yellow teeth – an Afghan with a
long grey beard, drenched in sweat, unclean and unwashed. I had
seen such Afghan men before but this one was wearing brand-new
well-creased black trousers, a black waistcoat, starched white shirt
with stiff collar, black tie, a double-buttoned fashionable jacket
and a tall shiny silk top hat on his long-haired head. It seemed like
he had jumped right out of a tailor's cardboard box. Not any
dereshi, but a genuine morning suit. On the day of the military
parade in India, the Viceroy and the governors made their salutes
wearing such a dress.

In the absence of a belt, he had used a piece of pyjama string to
hold his trousers in place. An inch of white shirt was visible
between the trousers and the waist-coat, the tie too was hanging
over the waist-coat.

In his left hand he was carrying a bundle made from his turban.
A pair of shoes tied by the laces was hanging from his right hand.
I looked down – he had no shoes or socks on his feet.

After greeting me in Pashto he left, taking long strides, the
bundle on his shoulder and the shoes hanging from his hand.

I could not fathom how this Afghan man could lay his hands on such a suit and why he was wearing it. But he was not alone. Before leaving the woods I bumped into another similar figure. I saw a third one sitting by the roadside chatting with a cobbler while the cobbler was hammering some nails onto his unworn shoes.

Amanullah's speech was to take place the following day. On the way to the celebration ground, I met a few dozen such men. After reaching the ground, I saw some one hundred and fifty men clad in morning suits sitting right in front of the podium. They were the members of the Afghan Parliament.

The Tajiks, the Hazaras, the Mongols and the Pathans had moved about comfortably in their traditional dresses for ages attracting appreciation from foreigners. Yet this lot was sitting stiff as logs in the meeting ground, wearing such out-of-place clothing.

Amanullah talked at length about the past and the future of the country. People from Kabul applauded his speech. It was not clear if they had been trained, but the members of parliament also clapped in the wrong places and then looked around in embarrassment. Foreign diplomats kept looking at Amanullah without batting an eyelid – that day I realised how much discipline and self-control one needed to be a diplomat.

I knew that it did not really matter if one could wear a suit properly; but the question was, what was the point of embarrassing those hundred and fifty village elders in full public view in order to establish a false sense of modernity?

I did not know if they made any sense of Amanullah's speech – you could speak the same language yet you might not be able to communicate.

TWENTY-SIX

I spent the whole summer observing the Kabuli farmers at work. We had no such advantage in our country; you needed to negotiate the blistering sun, heavy rain and knee-deep mud full of leeches if you really wanted to observe farming in progress. In this country, farming took place in dry weather. The farmer tilled the land well at the onset of winter hoping that there would be enough snowfall all through the season. If he were lucky, there would be a few heavy snowfalls, which would then melt, keeping the soil damp and soft. There would be a few showers at the beginning of spring, but not enough to flood the fields. The farmer would begin his work on that semi-damp and semi-dry land. It was pleasant to watch the farmers toiling sitting under a tree by the stream. In the summer, the melting icecaps of the high mountains filled the canals and streams of the Kabul valley with water. The Kabuli farmers would then build little dams in them to hold the water and irrigate the fields. They did not need to flood the fields like in paddy cultivation. There were strict rules regarding the sharing of the canal water. They knew which farmer had the right to build dams on the stream. Not only that, but there were written diktats from the government regarding how the water was to be shared by the villages upstream and downstream. Sometimes there would be fights over the sharing of the water, but I saw that Afghan farmers were like the mild Bengali farmers who liked to fight verbally rather than becoming physical. The possible reason was that the Kabul valley was as fertile as Bengal. If it snowed a lot in the winter, covering their land, or enough water came down from the melting icecaps, then they would not wait for the rains. Hence the people of Kabul said, '*Kabul be zar bashad, lakin be-barf na bashad*' (No problem if Kabul was devoid of gold but it should never be snowless).

There was a small stream just opposite my house. A path lined by tall chinar trees ran alongside the path. I often took a walk along that path and relaxed under the shade of a cluster of trees at the turn. One farmer upstream used to irrigate his land by constructing a dam in the canal. Sitting on the other side, I used to chat with another farmer who told me his life stories. Both farmers' ears were tuned to the afternoon prayer call from the local mosque. The moment the call was heard, my farmer-friend would get busy; he would break the upstream-dam by removing the rock and mud. The water would then flow downstream in the bund, which he had already built. He would then move on like a busy beaver, making the dam stronger by putting more rocks onto it or creating a channel through it by removing mud from one side so that water could flow into his land. His shalwar would be folded up to his knees. He would take his shirt off and keep it on the ground next me. Often he would wipe the sweat off his forehead with the tail of his turban. I used to take care of his hookah while he was busy. He would come round once or twice to take a few puffs while fanning his face with the tail of the turban. The gamchha of Bengali farmers and the turban of the Afghan farmer were quite similar – they had multiple uses. There was nothing that you could not do with a gamchha and a turban – even catching fish in shallow water. But there was hardly any fish in our canal.

Village women would gather by the stream before sundown to collect water in containers. Initially they were shy at seeing me there, like our farmer women who felt shy in the presence of a 'gentleman'. But this lot was less shy. They did not run like Arab horses on seeing me, drawing their head-cover up to their chests. Soon they got used to my presence and sat down to chat with my farmer-friend.

But my friendship with the farmer did not last long. Moin-us-Sultana was entirely responsible for that. My farmer-friend told me that he did not believe his eyes when he saw that his Agha-friend was playing 'top-bazi' or tennis with Moin-us-Sultana. I tried to explain to him that nothing changed because of that. He appeared to agree but he would not let me prepare the hookah for him any more, he stopped opening his heart out to me, and started to address me with respect. He would often lose the thread of his stories while trying to be extra careful with his language. He could not forget that I played 'top-bazi' with Moin-us-Sultana. Our flourishing friendship somehow dried up.

But our business did not stop. As long as I lived in that village, he regularly brought me chicken and eggs. He refused to take money for it, and eventually accepted a small payment very reluctantly, fearing Abdur Rahman's gigantic presence.

The farmer turned into a woodcutter after the harvest at the end of autumn. He had told me beforehand – one day he came around with a five-donkey-load of wood for the winter. Even a picky man like Abdur Rahman had to admit that it was the best wood – 'nim-tar-nim-khushk' – semi-damp-semi-dry. Abdur Rahman explained that a very dry wood would burn quickly making the house very hot; hence it was a waste. Damp wood would last long but would create more smoke than fire. So the best wood was the semi-damp-semi-dry type.

We almost had a fight when I tried to pay him. He refused to take the market price, saying that he did not make that much money at the market. After a lot of debate I realised he had to give a cut from his income to the local police and other officials as a bribe. Finally Madame Girard came down to settle the price.

Our friendship nearly ended when he heard that I was a 'Syed'.* After that day, every time we met, he would put his turban on his head properly and kiss my hands. If I tried to stop him, he would look at me with saddened face, unwind his turban and retie it.

I sighed deeply remembering the good old days of sharing the same hookah.

Democracy is indeed a fragile concept.

---

* It is believed that Syeds are the direct descendants of Prophet Mohammed.

TWENTY-SEVEN

Maulana Ziauddin arrived in Kabul from Shantiniketan towards the end of autumn. Bogdanov, Benoit, Maulana and I made a wholesome quartet.

Maulana Ziauddin was a native of Amritsar. He had quit college in 1921 after joining the Khilafat movement. In 1922 he came to Shantiniketan to be a student under Rabindranath Tagore. He soon became fluent in Bengali. He sang well too. He translated some of the songs written by Tagore into Punjabi and used to sing them well keeping to their original rhythm. The songs came in very handy here; the Punjabi community in Kabul made him a part of them very quickly. He also gained respect from the Kabulis because of his proficiency in Farsi.

But our gang of four broke up when Bogdanov went back to Shantiniketan; he was not keeping in good health in Kabul. Benoit became rather morose after his departure. He was a true and ardent follower of Tagore; under the circumstances, he became more and more aloof, thinking about Shantiniketan all the time. He never liked Kabul; his criticism of the city grew all the more.

It was around that time that Benoit took me to the Russian embassy for the first time.

I took a liking to Tavarish Demidov from our first meeting. He was slim, of average height, with blond hair, even his eyebrows were blond, a skeletal face with bright intense blue eyes. It felt as though he was welcoming me with his eyes when Benoit introduced me to him. He bowed more than the usual Continental way while shaking my hand. When he pressed my hand, I felt a warm and heartfelt welcome.

His wife was blonde too. She was quite plump and had an ever-smiling face. There was no sign of any jewellery on her body, nor any make-up. Her hands carried signs that she did much of the household chores herself. Unlike Bengali women, her forehead was wide; she did up her hair in the most casual manner with a parting in the middle.

Demidov spoke in English but Madame Demidov spoke French.

After the introduction and initial greetings were over, Demidov asked, 'Tell me, what would you like to drink? Tea or something else?'

Meanwhile he had already offered me a papirosi – a Russian cigarette.

I was a Bengali and Benoit had become a half-Bengali by spending so many years in Shantiniketan. So we were aware that the Russians could beat us in a contest of tea-drinking.

But they drank tea in a different manner. Water would be boiling in the samovar kept on the table. Some dark, strong tea liquor would have been prepared with plenty of tea leaves and hot water and kept in a teapot. As the water in the samovar boiled, the liquor in the teapot turned cold. With the teapot in her hand Madame asked everyone, 'How much?' A quarter cup was enough. Then you needed to fill the cup with boiling water by opening the tap on the samovar to make it look like Bengali black tea. You could make strong as well as light tea with the same liquor. There was no tradition of adding milk, so no hassle of heating up the milk. Some liquor made in the morning was enough to last through the day.

I was attracted by the samovar. Made of silver – the whole body including the handles on both sides, the legs, the top, the nozzle, was covered with an intricate handcrafted design.

I said admiringly, 'Your silver Taj Mahal is very pretty.'

A shy smile floated on Demidov's face – like a young child who had been praised for something he had accomplished. Madame told Benoit garrulously, 'Your Indian friend knows how to compliment well.' Turning towards me she said, 'But, Monsieur, no comparison other than the Taj Mahal would have worked on us as that is the only Indian monument that we are aware of. I have seen its photo too.'

Demidov said, referring to the samovar, 'It was made in Tula.'

In a flash I remembered something. I told them, 'I read in some Russian text, either Chekhov or Gorky, that there is a Russian proverb, "Taking a samovar to Tula". We have a similar one, "Putting oil in oily hair".'

This led to a discussion of similar proverbs, 'Carrying coals to Newcastle', '*Barelli me baans le jana*'* and a few others. I did remember the French one, 'Taking your wife to Paris'. Considering the current company, I decided to keep my mouth shut.

Hafiz had said, 'I'm neither a Qazi nor a mullah, then why should I say *tauba tauba* or shame.' I thought, 'I'm not French. Why do I need to utter this steamy proverb?'

Demidov asked if Indians read Russian literature.

I replied, 'I can't say for the whole of India, but I can certainly talk about Bengal. Once upon a time, French literature used to have a special place in Bengal. Now it is losing that place to

---

* Hindi proverb – 'Carrying bamboo to Barelli'.

Russian literature. Many leading critics now say that Chekhov is superior to Maupassant – far more creative.'

Benoit then talked at length about why the whole of India would gradually get attracted towards Russian literature. Very objectively he explained where the Indian sensibility resonated with Russian sensibilities, the likeness of the mindset and social environment. He did not forget to mention that the library in Shantiniketan had a steady supply of Russian novels and short stories.

Demidov observed, 'It hasn't been decided yet whether the Russians are people of the West or the Orient. A true Westerner will tuck his shirt in but the people from the east don't. The Russians are somewhere in the middle – they will tuck their shirts in, but not when wearing a Russian shirt – and that shirt looks Oriental too, intricately embroidered and saturated with colours.'

I had rarely seen anyone who was as gentle as Demidov. He spoke slowly as he did not know English very well but he used his repertoire of English words thoughtfully and carefully.

Realising my interest in Russian literature, he described to us the discussions that Tolstoy, Gorky and Chekhov had in Yasnaya Poliyana,[*] telling us, 'Most of it could not come out in public during the Tsar's times – now much of it has been published and is being analysed.'

I said, 'But we hear that you are not keen on pre-Bolshevik literature.'

Madame's face grew red. She said agitatedly, 'It must be a British propaganda!'

I hurriedly apologised and said, 'We don't know Russian, we read Chekhov in English and we read the criticism of Red Russia in English too.'

---

* Tolstoy's country house and estate.

Demidov did not say anything. His attitude was that he did not care what the British said. It was apparent from what he was saying that he believed in lifting the fog of misinformation only by presenting his own case with clarity and evidence.

We had come at four and it was already seven. Amidst the flow of stories and conversation, I could not keep track of the number of papirosis we smoked and cups of tea we drank. Madame kept cleaning up the cups with hot water and filling them again with liquor and hot water. She had figured out how light I wanted my tea. So she did not even ask me after a few rounds. I thanked her a few times and apologised at times for not noticing in the middle of our deep discussions on Gorky and Chekhov that she had refilled my cup.

As we continued to talk, Madame suddenly said, 'Why don't you have dinner with us.' Benoit stood up instantly and said, 'Many, many thanks but we'll go now. Sorry for staying so late.'

I was slightly confused. It took me a while to understand how Benoit had interpreted the offer of dinner. It became apparent that Madame too had understood. Blushing, she said, 'No, Monsieur, I didn't mean it in that sense; I was very glad that you were enjoying this session so much. I simply wanted it to continue.'

Demidov said, in a bid to clear the air, 'In Western etiquette, this may mean that it's getting late, so you'd better leave. But my wife didn't mean it in that sense. You know, in the matter of food, we're Oriental, we don't tuck our shirts in.'

The cloud was lifted. But we did not eat dinner there that night. While coming down the stairs Demidov asked, 'Why don't you learn Russian?'

I asked, 'Will you teach me?'

He replied, 'With pleasure.'

Benoit said, 'No, not with pleasure,' and he winked at me.

Madame asked him what he meant.

Benoit said, 'One Frenchman had gone to a restaurant in London and said, "Waiter, please bring me a cotlette." The waiter answered, "With pleasure, sir." The Frenchman said hurriedly, "No, not with pleasure, with potatoes please!"'

Benoit was a learned man. He lifted the last bit of cloud with a subtle joke.

But Madame was no less witty, she had the final word, 'But I shall give you cotlette both with pleasure and potatoes.'

I thanked Benoit after coming out on the street, 'Both are really genuine souls.'

TWENTY-EIGHT

Kabul showed the signs of middle-age spread at the end of autumn, its belly grew fatter and it seemed as though it was walking with a certain gravitas.

The wheat and maize grains swelled, the apples were about to burst, even the leaves of the trees had become thick by sucking in air, sunlight and rain during the summer months. They would not sway in the breeze; they would either tremble lightly or simply leave the branches and land on the ground all of a sudden. Harvesting was over, and the farmers had put on some weight. Some people had started to add a few layers of warm clothing on top of their normal ones, the donkeys had become fatter by eating grass and the hay was bulging from the carriages.

The real display of wealth could be seen in the morning dew. The dewdrops would dazzle the Kabul valley in the morning sun as if a shameless rich man was showing off his diamond-studded ring under the spotlight.

Such displays were happening at the expense of the Kabul river – by sucking its water. The river lay like a discarded snakeskin and the sand from its drying bed blew in the wind. Marx had rightly said, 'The oppressors get fat by sucking the oppressed.'

The source of all the wealth of Kabul – the blue peaks of the Paghman mountains that supplied water to the valley – had shed their white icecaps one by one. It seemed that the sky had become older compared to the earth – there was a whitish layer of cataracts in its blue eyes. The smell of overripe and decomposed fruit was intoxicating. The way the age-old stink could not get out of an Afghan inn, likewise this smell of overripe fruit could not leave the valley as it was surrounded by high mountains all around. Sometimes a strong wind would try to sweep away the dry leaves and sand but failing to find a way out would soon be back, depositing them at the same spots.

One evening there was a fierce storm. I had to close my eyes at its onset, but later when I opened them, I saw that Shelley's 'West Wind' was chasing away Keats' 'Autumn', even 'Borshosesh' – 'Year-end' by Tagore. Hay and twigs, fallen leaves, discarded baskets – everything was leaving the country like people migrating to a new land. Some were turning summersaults like circus clowns, some were jumping around like monkeys and then taking off like unicorns and the rest were moving in a group – as if a group of rich people was being chased away by proletarians.

In half an hour all the trees had been shorn clean of their leaves.

What a horrible sight!

In our country we often witnessed such scenes – following a big flood, trees would stand pale, like patients of leprosy, with rotten barks.

It was like that here – the trees were standing naked and bare.

Every few days I saw dead bodies being carried away for burial. I asked Abdur Rahman if there was any epidemic in the vicinity.

Abdur Rahman said, 'No, Sahib, old people fall with the falling of the leaves. This is the time most old people die.'

On further enquiry I learned that not only Abdur Rahman, most Kabulis believed in this theory.

Meanwhile I had formed a strong bond with Abdur Rahman for which he was responsible.

After supervising my dinner, he would sit in the corner of my bedroom every night with some work or the other – sometimes he would break nuts, sometimes he would make pickles or pick out dirt from grains. In the absence of any other work he would sit there with all my shoes and polish them.

Abdur Rahman's shoe polishing was no simple science but high art. I always thought one could paint the *Mona Lisa* with half that effort.

First he would spread out a newspaper, keep every pair on it and observe them very carefully. He would then clean dried mud with a matchstick. Polishing with a brush at the speed of an engine piston would follow the cleaning of the mud. After that he would take off old polish very delicately with a piece of cloth soaked in methylated spirit. Cleaning with a cloth moistened with soap water would follow this. He would then let them dry for half an hour – just as a watercolour artist waited for the canvas to dry. The ladies of Paris did not put on lipstick as carefully as the way in which he applied cream and polish on the shoes next – that was the most critical moment for Abdur Rahman. You would not get any answers if you asked him a question at that point in time. Then putting his left hand inside the shoe, he would start brushing, holding it close to his ear like a concert violinist who was totally submerged in his music. There was no question of making any sound at that moment; the maestro would frown if you said, 'Bravo.'

At the end of this performance he would give his final touch with a soft piece of silk like a lover caressing his long-lost woman's hair, face, cheeks and forehead.

I said, 'Bravo' on the first day.

Once, some of us had been appreciating the beauty of a little girl of eight or nine. She sat listening to us quietly. After we were finished, she said softly, 'But I'm yet to shampoo today.'

Abdur Rahman's face looked the same.

Initially I thought of telling him that I felt uncomfortable if he sat in my bedroom. But his simplicity prevented me from saying it. After a while I thought that I ought to be able to cope with his presence in my room. There was a Farsi saying that this life was nothing but a journey, so there should be no difference between my bedroom and an Afghan inn. Afghan inns could beat Paris with their concept of 'Liberté, Egalité, Fraternité'; so how could I keep Abdur Rahman away from my bedroom? If he could break nuts completely ignoring my presence, then why could I not study Russian grammar without taking notice of him?

Sitting in my room one night, Abdur Rahman said, in a tone that suggested complaint, that I was not doing the right thing by going to the Russian embassy so often, while not playing tennis with Moin-us-Sultana as frequently.

I explained to him that in that court, the tennis ball, as well as the hearts of everyone except Moin-us-Sultana were really hard. On the other hand, the ball in the Russian embassy was soft, as were their hearts.

Abdur Rahman whispered, 'You don't know, Sahib, they are all, *bedeen, bemazhab.*' Meaning without religion, faithless.

I scolded him, 'Who has given you all these nonsensical thoughts?'

He said, 'But, Sahib, everyone knows that. The women there have no modesty; they have even done away with the system of marriage.'

I said, 'Is that so? Then why has King Amanullah invited them to this country?' I thought this question would impress him.

Abdur Rahman said, 'But King Amanullah is—' he stopped abruptly.

Next day, while playing tennis, I told Demidov what opinion the proletarian Abdur Rahman held about the USSR. Demidov said,

'We are not particularly worried about Afghanistan. But we are having to advance slowly and carefully in Turkistan. So a murky image of our ideology is reaching this place from there. We don't want to impose programmes of reform onto Turkistan, we want them to reform on their own and integrate with the rest of the state.'

Madame Demidov said, 'Bukhara's Amir and his followers have fled the country after the establishment of the Bolshevik state. They have now taken shelter here and are out on a propaganda mission against us.'

I did not know anything about communism, but I was impressed with their conviction in the ideology, ways of explaining and patience towards the ignorant.

What impressed me most was their social life. In other embassies, the difference in status between the bosses and the others was like the Himalayas and molehills. I do not want to say that there were no differences in the Russian embassy, but these differences were never as jarring.

I spent many afternoons and evenings in Demidov's living room. Many people from the embassy visited us regularly, smoked papirosi and chatted for hours. Some of them were secretaries, some doctors, some clerks, some pilots in the Afghan air force and Demidov himself was the Head of Chancery. Everyone was equally welcomed; there was no way of telling who was the secretary and who the clerk.

Even the ambassador, the representative of the Russian state, Tavarish Streng, came a few times. During the first introduction, I bowed like Demidov to shake his hand and said most formally, 'I'm honoured to meet Your Excellency!' But His Excellency was not at all concerned with my display of etiquette. He shook my hand hard with both hands in such a way that all my show of etiquette evaporated instantly.

Madame Demidov said, 'He is an ardent fan of Russian literature.'

Hearing this, a British big shot like the ambassador would have said dismissively, 'How interesting.'

Streng, however, said, 'Is that so? Then let's sit together; we can talk literature.' Others were busy in their own conversations. Streng first tested my depth of knowledge by asking a few pointed questions; then he recited from Pushkin's ballads for me. The poem he chose was very delicate. Onegin had come back to his first lover after going through a series of upheavals and suffering in life and he was offering his love to her again; she, in reply, was saying, thinking about the lost years of their youth, 'Onegin, O my friend, when I was young, I was possibly good-looking too . . .'

From our country, Radha had also said in similar vein, 'Why didn't I meet you O Shyam,[*] in my budding youth.'

I was mesmerised. After the recitation was over, I thought that however improbable it might be, I could perhaps one day hear that Churchill was sneezing, sitting with a runny nose by Hedua Square[†] after eating spicy peanuts, but that it was not possible for the British ambassador to recite Keats's 'Isabella' to a stranger. It would be more believable if one said, 'Monkeys are singing and rocks are floating in water.'

I had always seen the Minister of the British Legation in striped trousers and tail-suit – his demeanour suggested that he was the first cousin of George the Fifth. Only by bad luck was he spending time in this god-forsaken place. 'Who is Keats? Or who are – since the tail has the "s" of the plural form? Do they want passports? Nothing doing, see them off.'

[*] Another name of Lord Krishna.
[†] A park and public swimming square in Calcutta.

I never saw the French ambassador in Bogdanov's house either. Whenever we talked about him, Benoit said, 'Who? The Minister of the French Legation in Kabul? Mon dieu. He is the Minister of French Negation in Mabul.'

My eyeballs nearly came out of their sockets when Streng said that he had read an article on Chekhov at the literary gathering of the embassy. I knew of another legation where they might discuss sparrow hunting; but Chekhov? 'By God, Sir!'

I said, 'I would most certainly like to read your article after learning Russian.' Streng said, 'Sure. I will send you a copy – no rights reserved.'

When we were talking nobody tried to hang around the boss to try to catch his attention. They were all dispersed in small groups and chatting in their own way. I could not tell what they were discussing but I could say for sure that they were not talking about their laundry bills, the laziness of their servants or scarcity of butter in Kabul.

Such a lowly race that they did away with class divides. Not only that – they were so shameless that they were not even trying to hide that fact!

No wonder they did not even catch a glimpse of the British. Meanwhile Britain was training its binoculars on Moscow to observe the bullfight between the followers of Stalin and Trotsky and counting down the final hours of the USSR.

It was 1927.

TWENTY-NINE

The poet had said, 'The poor man follows the king to the pilgrimage.' Amanullah left for Europe and I too took off during the two months of winter vacation. As it was not the ancient golden age, only half of the proverb came true – I went home, instead of to Europe.

Nothing really happened but I saw that my entire homeland was excited about Amanullah's visit to Europe. The Oriental Indians were proud of the honour bestowed upon Amanullah.

Seeing my Kabuli attire and the ticket from Peshawar, the police stopped me at Howrah station – possibly they were informed by their agents in Landikotal. They searched me for hours, as if I was a counterfeit coin. But I had been trained at the customs house of Kabul – no Bengali officer could dent my patience. After they let me go, I said involuntarily, in Bengali, 'What nuisance.' The Bengali officer was alarmed. He said, 'A Bengali? Wait, I need to search you again.'

I said, 'Go on. Try my patience.'

I gave my mother a suitcase-load of almonds, walnuts, pistachios – all bought for half a rupee in Kabul. She happily distributed all of it to relatives and neighbours. Even my little sister who was married off to a man in a remote village did not miss her share.

So much for this chapter. After spending seven months in Kabul I had realised that Bengalis were far more cautious than the Kabulis. I did not hold very high hopes that they would bring out their wallets to buy this book. So I was thinking of publishing the stories of these past months in Farsi – that way, I might earn some money. If not, the Kabulis would appreciate the effort at least. A Farsi proverb said,

> *Khar baash O khuk baash O ya sagey murdar baash*
> *Harche baashi baash amma andaki zardar baash.*
> Be ye a donkey, or a swine, or a dead canine;
> Be ye this or be ye that, keep your gold in line.

THIRTY

There was a snow everywhere when I returned to Kabul. Abdur Rahman was waiting for me at the door while a fire blazing in the fireplace kept the rooms warm. I was, by then, nearly frozen.

Abdur Rahman kissed my hands, a broad smile on his face, but his smile evaporated when he looked at my face.

'Wait, Sahib', he said, practically lifting me in his arms as he moved swiftly to the courtyard. Taking a handful of snow he started to rub it on my nose and earlobes. While rubbing, he kept asking in a fearful tone, 'Do you feel anything?' I thought it was some strange kind of welcome custom of Panjshir. I said irritably, 'Okay, okay, let's go inside, I'm frozen to my bones.' But Abdur Rahman had gripped me like a vice with his long arms; even the famous wrestler Kikkar Singh would not be able to break that grip. He kept rubbing ice on my earlobes and repeating his question like a hymn, 'Do you feel anything?' Finally I felt pinpricks on my earlobes and the tip of my nose. As soon as I gave that news to Abdur Rahman, he leapt inside the room, carrying me with him. But he kept me away from the fireplace, in the other corner of the room. I tried going close to the fire the way a sun-scorched buffalo rushed to the cool water of the pond, but Abdur Rahman stopped me saying, 'Let the blood circulation begin properly, then Sahib can move close to the fire to warm himself.'

Meanwhile he had taken off my shoes and inspected my toes – checking if they were blue. It seemed he had a deep hatred for that colour. He turned my toes purple by rubbing them. Finally he placed me on a chair close to the fire. While trying to take my gloves off I realised that my fingers had grown to the size of bananas. I kept the information away from Abdur Rahman like a naughty boy who would not tell his mother that he had a stomach ache. While Abdur Rahman was taking care of my toes, I stretched my hands towards the fire in order to warm them. By then, my fingers had become even fatter, like branches of a tree. Abdur Rahman finally noticed that I was still wearing my gloves. His face turned red and he said angrily, 'Why didn't you tell me that your fingers were also frozen?'

I saw him angry for the first time. He spoke with the tone of Amir Abdur Rahman, not the servant Abdur Rahman. I tried feebly to give an excuse. Without taking notice of it, he said, 'If they don't come off by the time you finish drinking tea, I will cut them off with scissors.'

I asked, 'What? The gloves or my hands?'

Abdur Rahman lacked a sense of humour. I got even more worried.

Not only me, even the pair of gloves could figure out that an angry Abdur Rahman was not good news for anyone. Before I touched the teacup, the gloves came off.

That night Abdur Rahman served me dinner early and tucked me in bed under the blankets. He had already kept a hot water bottle wrapped in flannel in the bed. Touching that bottle was the most satisfying experience one could have. A stomach full of thick gravy, the warmth of the hot water bottle and Abdur Rahman's massage – all of them put me to sleep in no time.

The only reason I am giving details of this episode is that I am sure that this book will be of no use to anybody. The budding communists of India are also of the opinion that an art is no art if it has no use.

If you ever get frostbite then you should use the technique of the proletarian witchdoctor Abdur Rahman. You will surely be cured. All gratitude should then be directed to Abdur Rahman. I would not want to be branded as the 'bourgeois' and the 'oppressor' by taking his credit.

Next morning, old man Mir Aslam showed up trekking through three miles of snow. He said, 'I heard from strangers that you came back last evening. Give me your news. Hope you did not suffer much in this cold and snow.'

After I gave him the full account of Abdur Rahman's treatment, Mir Aslam said, 'On short winter days, riders of open horse carriages get frostbitten. Your servant did a very good job by saving you from frostbite. Have you not noticed that in your country a mother does not give water to her son when he comes back home after being out in the sun for a long time to avoid sunstroke? She does not even open the windows for fresh air. The principle is the same in both cases.'

Very true.

I briefed him, 'Both the Hindus and the Muslims are proud of Amanullah's successful visit to Europe.'

Mir Aslam said, 'The king loses gravitas if he gets too much honour in foreign lands.'

It sounded like the third rule of Chanakya. I was tempted to ask him what he had studied in India – Hinduism or Islamic studies. Instead, I asked, 'But with these honours from foreign lands, won't it be easy for him to go ahead with his reforms?'

Mir Aslam said, 'The king is already overburdened with the

weight of reforms. He will further be drowned in the bog with the extra weight of all the foreign honours.'

I said, 'The whole of Paris had lined up for hours to see Queen Soraya.'

Mir Aslam responded, 'Mister, people will gather in great numbers for hours if a little-known person like you stands on your head instead of your feet.'

I protested, 'It is a wrong analogy. The queen didn't do any such mad thing.'

Mir Aslam said, 'What more do you expect from a Muslim woman? Which Muslim woman can do such an irreligious act in broad daylight on the open streets?'

I countered, 'You have read the Koran and the Hadith more than I have done. They don't say that Muslim women can't show their face in public.'

Mir Aslam said, 'It's irrelevant what I know or what I believe. In this country what is most relevant is the tribal law and custom, which you are aware of.'

In an attempt to lighten the discussion I said, 'You know that in French "*sourire*" means "smile". The name of Queen Soraya has brought a smile on the faces of Parisians.'

Mir Aslam said, 'The meaning of the name of Amir Habibullah is "dearest friend". The British made him take an oath on that name hundreds of times. But when the bullet was about to enter his temple, which of his Habibs came to his rescue? On the contrary, the Habibs of Habibullah sent him to his death without any reason and much ahead of his time.'

I said, 'That is old wine. But don't you support the reform programmes of Amanullah?'

He replied, 'My dearest, I took lessons sitting at the feet of my gurus. Why should I oppose education? But I have no respect for the kind of Western education Amanullah is trying to introduce. I have seen enough of that while living in India. But, brother, why are you engaging in such dry and bitter subjects instead of serving your famous tea. I can smell the aroma that I used to get in my guru's house.'

I said, 'I have a packet for you too.'

Looking at me suspiciously Mir Aslam asked, 'Hope you have paid the customs duty on it.'

I was not offended by his question, and said reassuringly, 'No worries. I don't have the talent to hoodwink the customs house of Kabul. Even the bedbugs have to show a passport and pay tax there. I have given every penny I owed them as I don't have any intention of going to purgatory by giving you something illegal.'

Mir Aslam left after giving me a great deal of advice on how to cope in this cold and snow and enquiring about our stocks of oil-salt-butter-cereal-firewood etc. from Abdur Rahman.

Maulana came too. I told him Mir Aslam's opinions about Amanullah's honours in Europe. Maulana said, 'Amanullah's advisors think that these are their honours and not Amanullah's. They are telling him, "If Mustafa Kemal in Turkey and Reza Shah in Iran can bring their countries onto the path of modernity then why can't Amanullah?" This is what they have in their minds; but they are not being explicit. Because nobody is objecting to it.'

I asked, 'But Maulana, I can't fathom the meaning of some of the reforms at all. Take for example the weekly holiday – why did he have to move it to Thursday from Friday?'

Maulana said, 'On Friday, half the day is lost because of prayer. People don't get time to get their weekly work done. So Amanullah has made Thursday the weekly off day and given one hour of extra time for the Friday prayer. But I have worked out another advantage. Say if you start from Shantiniketan on a Wednesday, which is a holiday there, on an aeroplane you will reach here on Thursday – an off day. Then you go to Iraq the next day – Friday, holiday there. Next go to Palestine on Saturday – Sabbath for the Jews. Sunday will be weekend in Europe. Then you can go to the South-Sea Islands – a whole week of off days.'

I said, 'Good discovery, but have you come here taking leave from work? How will you go back to Kabul in this snow?'

Maulana said, 'In a day or two there'll be a track on the snow. Then it won't be difficult to walk on it. But I'm going home to bring my wife. Benoit has given permission. What do you say?'

I asked, 'Does your wife agree?' Maulana told me that she did.

I said, 'Then why are you taking a plebiscite everywhere? Don't you have this in your language—

> *Mian Bibi razi*
> *To kiya karega Qazi.*
> If the man and woman agree
> What can the judge do.'

I told myself, 'Bogdanov has already left. I am not going to see the trace of your beard for some while after your wife arrives. Newly-wed after all. It will take you at least six months to come out of the house.'

After Maulana left, I asked Abdur Rahman, 'Put the chair next to the window. I will spend the winter looking at the snowfall.'

It snowed matching the description given by Abdur Rahman. Sometimes in flakes; sometimes in piles; sometimes it whirled in strong wind making it dark on all sides; sometimes it made a translucent screen creating an outline of the mountainous horizon; sometimes it fell by my window and sometimes far – kissing the peaks. Gradually everything was covered in snow except the row of leafless chinar trees, which created an impression that an old grandmother was sleeping, spreading her tufts of white hair all around leaving her old broken comb by the wall.

But Abdur Rahman was heartbroken. While serving tea he looked outside and lamented, 'No Sahib, this is not real snow. This is the snow of the city, gentleman's snow. Real snowfall can only be seen in Panjshir. See, the gate is not yet blocked in the pile of snow. People are still walking on the streets and not getting stuck.'

Abdur Rahman was afraid that the Kabul valley would dump some fake snowfall for a naïve person like myself. If I had to buy some, I ought to buy the real stuff – 'Made in Panjshir'.

THIRTY-ONE

I spent the winter and spring inside the house – hibernating.

The spring in this country could be compared with our monsoon. There, the parched earth waited eagerly to flourish into a new life with the touch of early monsoon clouds and rains. Here the earth went into deep slumber in winter and opened her eyes with the first sun of spring. The first glimpses of this awakening were already visible on the trees.

From a distance it seemed that there were thousands of green insects on the pale and bare branches of the trees. On closer inspection I saw that they were actually the innumerable buds of early leaves – like the closed eyes of newborn puppies. I did not take notice for a few days. Suddenly one morning I saw they were budding, a pair of leaves coming out – as if the trees were attempting to take off like cranes that had been standing on one leg for a long stretch of time. Thousands upon thousands of green leaves gave wings to millions of trees.

The chained prisoner had been unshackled.

The trees were showing off, the leaves were competing – as if trying to overtake each other. Some did not wake up on time; but they saw, after opening their eyes late that the others had gone forward; they would then race very fast to beat them and would sway their heads proudly wearing the ivy laurel as the first prize.

Some trees simply put on a green hat over a bare body and some applied spots of green balm all over themselves. For the past few months the wind had raced through the branches without stopping, now it would pass leisurely, caressing the leaves.

The rock-solid ice cover of the Kabul river cracked into a thousand pieces. Hundreds of streams came down from the mountains with tremendous noise, carrying with them millions of boulders and chunks of ice. The wooden bridges on the river trembled. Right from the time of Alexander, no one had been able to keep count of just how many times they had been washed away after collapsing on their knees, only to stand up again.

Looking up I could see that the young blue sky had spread a canopy with milky white buntings of clouds. Looking at the valley I saw the towns and the forests were submerged in green floods.

How did the valley obtain such a green hue?
O my love, what forest-drenched green waters
Have you bathed in, to get the queen of all colours?
The blue of the sky and the yellow of the young sun.

But there was an essential difference between the monsoon of our land and the spring in this place. In the monsoon, our souls would crave for home, while here in spring nobody could wait to go out. One also felt the rush of life in the trees and plants; hence the poet said,

I pledged by night: never would my mind ever
traipse down the path of sin,

At dawn's door I met the Pledge-Killer Spring, who royally did me in.

Only Omar Khayyam did not like this tension. He thundered,

The Winter wears of orthodoxy
Burn it in the fire of Spring;
Bird of Life has spanned its wing,
O Saki, hold the cup up to my chin.

The Kabulis were all out on the streets. There was no other option but to go out – the stocks of firewood for the winter and the fodder of the sheep and lambs were dwindling and the dry meat was rotting. One could warm oneself in the spring sun, one could graze the sheep in the newly grown grass and one could hunt some of the migratory birds coming back in small numbers. Abdur Rahman said people caught some kind of fish from under the broken ice in Panjshir. I guessed it would be spring trout.

Some experts said that there was a deep reason for Kuber to banish the Yaksha for six seasons. Apparently the full extent of the pain and agony of separation could only be felt through six seasons of separation from one's lover.[*]

The Afghan government relieved me from my banishment after exactly six seasons and gave me a job in the city. This time they gave me a house in Lab-e-Dariya – the promenade on the Kabul river, next to the Russian embassy. I shared the house with Benoit.

---

[*] Reference to the ballad of *Meghdūta* or the 'Messenger Cloud' in Sanskrit by the sixth-century poet Kalidasa. The demi-god or Yaksha was banished by King Kuber from the Himalayas to central India for failing in his duty. In severe pain of separation from his wife, the banished Yaksha sent his message of love to her through the monsoon clouds floating over the hills towards the Himalayas where she lived. The Yaksha had to live through all six seasons – summer, monsoon, autumn, late autumn, winter, spring – to complete his period of banishment and separation from his wife.

It was a big building – almost a small fort – surrounded by high walls. There were twenty-six rooms spread over two floors around the courtyard, which housed a garden including a fountain. A rich man had given the house on rent to the government – Benoit had manipulated it our way.

I took four rooms in one corner and Benoit took four on the other side. The rest of the house was empty – the house was so big that even Abdur Rahman's singing reached the other end after a delay.

I started enjoying the company of my friends after moving to town. I visited the Russian embassy every day while Demidov turned up if there was a gap of two days and Saiful Alam came round regularly. Even though his young wife had arrived, I could see Maulana's beard once in a while. Dost Muhammad came round like a whirlwind and inevitably gave a gift of something or other before leaving and the erudite scholar Mir Aslam often dropped by to drink the famous Indian tea. A few other acquaintances came by too. My last resort was Benoit himself who was already behaving like the Yaksha suffering from the pangs of separation though not from his wife but from Shantiniketan. I made friends with a few more people in the Russian embassy. Besides Demidov, I need to mention just one name – Bolshov. His stature matched the meaning of his name. While introducing Abdur Rahman, I had mentioned earlier that I would talk about another giant. Bolshov was that horror. It would be an understatement to say that if I called Abdur Rahman a giant with his bull-like shoulders and knee-long arms, Bolshov could have eaten that description easily and asked for a second helping.

I had taken walks on the streets with him several times. In the league of nations in the bazaars of Kabul, I had not seen one person who was not startled by his presence.

A careful rider would pull the reins of his horse – I had seen many horses jumping nervously when Bolshov drew near.

At the tennis court the opponent would stand ten paces behind the baseline if Bolshov stood at the net. His partners refused to stand at the net if he took position at the base line. The normal strings of his racket broke so frequently that he used some kind of aluminium strings. He could simply walk over the net instead of jumping.

Apparently under-sixteens are not allowed to watch some films in the West – for their adult content. Similarly people weighing under one hundred pounds were not allowed to shake hands with Bolshov for fear of dislocating their shoulders. There was a different custom for women.

Bolshov was known as a hero in the Russian embassy. After taking part in the Bolshevik revolution in 1917, he had fought in many other countries. Bolshov was a young cavalry soldier during the battles against Poland in 1916–17 when the Russian army had to flee after their defeat. While fleeing on horseback, he had received fourteen injuries on his back. Once, after a lot of coaxing, he had shown us his scars – some of them were half-inch-deep.

Nobody had ever seen him angry. After listening to the Indian code of chivalry and heroism of giving one's life on the battlefield instead of fleeing, he had said, 'It was good that I fled that day. Or else I would have missed the fun of beating the Poles during Trotsky's time. So what do you say to that?'

His only quirk was that he could never sit still. He did not know what to do with his hands. He always fiddled with things and often broke them absent-mindedly. We removed every breakable object from the range of his long arms whenever he entered the room. I used to keep a bowl of whole walnuts right in front of him.

He ate only a few but used to shell the rest without a hammer before he left.

He was one person who had no enemy in Kabul. We were discussing this in Demidov's living room once when his closest friend, tiny Snieshkov said, 'Everyone becomes his friend fearing his strength and power.'

What Snieshkov said could be expressed by our Bengali love-poems from the Middle Ages:

> Ah Beloved, proud am I in your pride,
> Made beautiful by your beauty—

Bolshov countered, 'Then you should have the most enemies. This is the bad habit of weaklings. They talk too much – self-contradictory, superfluous rubbish talks.'

I have spoken so much about Bolshov because he was by then a leading pilot in Amanullah's air force. After the Bolshevik revolution was over, danger-seeking Bolshov came to work for Amanullah in search of new adventure.

He served Amanullah till his last day.

THIRTY-TWO

Amanullah came back from Europe with a large amount of expensive furniture, a number of motor cars and the bad habit of giving speeches. In the Orient, we reclined, burping, after meals. In the West there were speeches after dinner and oratory after lunch – on too difficult political topics that gave you a headache.

The Europeans had given the intoxicating taste of post-lunch-dinner-speeches to Amanullah but he became totally drunk on it only after coming back to Kabul. Apparently he had given thirty hours of speeches in three consecutive days.

But speeches do not burn one's skin. So some slept during his speech, some listened and some silently calculated the money wasted on his European trip.

Then the season of reforms started. One morning, on my way to Maulana's house, I saw that ninety per cent of the shops had their shutters down. Among the big ones only the record and gramophone shop was open. The owner was a Punjabi, from Amritsar; I knew him.

I could not believe my ears when I heard what it was all about. Amanullah had ordered, 'The system of doing business sitting on the floor, on the carpet, is hereby forbidden. Every shop has to have chairs and tables like the way it is in the West.'

SYED MUJTABA ALI

I asked, 'What? Even the carpenters, artisans, blacksmiths, cobblers?'
'Everyone, everyone.'
'How can they put tables and chairs inside their tiny kiosks?'
No reply.
'People who are wealthy and have space in their shops?'
'Where will they get tables and chairs overnight? The carpenter's shop is closed too. He hasn't learned to work with hammer and chisel sitting on a chair.'
'Didn't they give any notice?'
'No. You know how it is. Amanullah is very prompt in his actions.'

Most shops remained closed for a full three weeks. The grocery business continued through the back door, and the policemen made some extra income.

I never found out if Amanullah accepted defeat but the shops gradually opened up as before, without tables and chairs. I was sure that the Kabulis were angry but they did not express it because they were used to the king's whims. I could never fathom this particular aspect of the Kabulis; in India, we were accustomed to oppressions and repressions by our rulers, not so much their whims.

I started to have doubts. I remembered the madness of Paghman when Amanullah had made the village elders wear morning suits. It was a repeat show; but more painful, meaningless, only blind aping of European ways.

Mir Aslam did not try to give a detailed analysis. If I had to turn what he said into verse it would sound a bit like this—

> Friendship with the coal-man? Never!
> No respite from dirt
> Perfumer's box is closed
> Yet you get the scent.
> I said, 'That is the clue; now expand.'

214

Mir Aslam replied, 'Rubbing his skin against that of the French and the British, Amanullah's body is full of dirt – he's now attempting to spread that dirt all over Kabul.

'The people of this land would have accepted that if he brought some coal with him. At least the poor people of this cold country could have burned it to keep themselves warm.'

I said, 'If the introduction of chairs and table is like spreading dirt, then that can't be too bad.'

Mir Aslam said cryptically, 'Unnecessary wastage of energy. Humiliation of the king. Future is dark.'

By talking with others, I realised that not everyone was predicting as bleak a future for the country, wearing tinted glasses like Mir Aslam. The youth were wearing pink glasses, no, it would be wrong to call them pink – their glasses were red, bloodshot red. They said, 'People who are still doing business sitting on the floor, should be tied to a cannon and blown into a thousand pieces. Amanullah is a gentle king, hence he's forgiven all.'

I decided to wear pink glasses after giving it some thought.

Maulana brought the next news of reform. Afghan soldiers had been banned from accepting mullahs as murshid – gurus.

There was no provision for the system of gurus in orthodox Islam. The pundits said, 'The Koran is *kitabum mumeen*.' Meaning 'The open book'; it explained very simply how to lead one's life and the measures of sins and piety – all that one needed to know. So there was no need to be a guru's disciple.

The other camp said, 'This may be applicable for the Arabs as they can read the Koran in Arabic but the Iranians and Afghans don't know Arabic. So what's their way out except for taking a murshid?'

This debate was unending.

But Amanullah would not have banned the system if it remained within the confines of religion. People took a guru for religious reasons but often the guru would advise his disciple on all worldly matters and his advice became like the Bible.

So the implication was that the soldiers would be obliged to obey the mullahs if they asked them to disobey the orders of Amanullah.

The Church versus the State.

Lifting my pink glasses on my forehead, I started to look for writings on the wall – why had Amanullah issued such an order? Any sign of disobedience, or revolt or—? But you would shiver even to think about such things in Kabul, let alone talk.

My last resort was Mir Aslam. I saw that he was looking at the political sky of the country wearing even darker glasses. He had heard the news long before. Responding to my question he said, 'There is no necessity to have a guru in this world or the next. But it is equally unnecessary to stop someone from looking for one.'

I said, 'But your words of praise don't stop when you talk about your Indian guru.'

Mir Aslam said, 'There are two kinds of gurus. That guru is the true guru if he makes you think at first that you won't be able to move a step without his help. But he'll ultimately give you the confidence to think that you won't need him any longer when you finally leave his shelter. The second category of gurus makes you more and more dependent on them. Eventually you wouldn't even be able to breathe without their assistance. My guru fell into the first category but the Afghan soldiers' gurus belong to the second one.'

I said, 'Meaning your guru made you independent and the Afghan soldiers' gurus make them servile? Dependence is not good but why do you say that a guru is not necessary? You can say that taking a particular guru is a mistake.'

Mir Aslam responded, 'My man, what you say is true. But how many people in this world would like or could manage to be independent? What's the way out for people who can't?'

I said, 'God knows. But tell me, is there any possibility of a revolt?'

Mir Aslam said, 'Troops close to the throne never revolt until a competitor arrives on the scene.'

Before taking leave of him I said to him, 'I've noticed that recently you're using fewer complex Arabic words in our conversation. Are you doing so deliberately?'

Nodding his head with satisfaction Mir Aslam said in colloquial Farsi, 'You finally understood that, brother? Then listen to my strategy. When you arrived here last year, your Farsi knowledge was very limited. In an attempt to train you, I created a barrier of Arabic words in our conversations so that you had to jump over them. I remember, at the beginning you used to injure your legs frequently. Now I can see that you're jumping over the fence with ease, like an Arab stallion. So I've eased it because there's no need. Has it entered your thick skull now?'

On my way back, I thought, 'That man is a real scholar. He proved with example how a good teacher makes himself redundant.'

Not very long after that, I received an invitation for an event. A group of Afghan girls were being sent to Turkey for higher education, and the king himself would be there at a ceremony to see them off.

I did not go. I heard the details from a high-ranking Indian official from the British Legation. He said, 'After arriving at the event we saw that about twenty Afghan girls were standing there in girl-guide dress. Amanullah was present with many government officials, diplomats from various embassies and legations and women on one side. Queen Soraya was there too, wearing a hat that had a thin net covering her face.'

Amanullah ended the preamble of his speech on higher education with some predictable and some new lines, saying, 'I'm not in favour of the purdah system; hence I'm sending these girls without any veil. I'm a supporter of independence. So I'm ready to help any woman who wants to come out on the streets of Kabul without the veil. But I don't want to force anyone. I won't object if the queen wants to wear the burqa.'

The official said, 'So far so good. But soon after Amanullah ended his speech, Queen Soraya walked up and very dramatically tore away the net hanging from her hat. The people of Kabul saw the queen's face in public.'

The official had little sense for aesthetics – thus his description was rather dry. But there was no way I could ask for details. It might be that he was here to prepare a secret report – to find out how the Indian community reacted to the incident. I sat there with a poker face.

Before leaving he said, 'What was the point of taking her veil off so dramatically? She could have done it slowly.'

I told myself, 'Typical British way. Everything to be done on the sly – be that the introduction of English education or the destruction of the muslin industry. They enter as a needle and come out as a scabbard!'

But I had to say something to him. 'Once upon a time the Indians gave their opinion on such matters. At that time Afghanistan used to take its cue from India. But Amanullah has been to the West and seen things with his own eyes. He now knows his way; we will now watch from the sidelines and appreciate what happens. That is all.'

I gave it a lot of thought after he left.

But I want to make one thing clear to my readers that like the Kabulis I was not at all bothered about Amanullah's reform programmes. Normal human instinct was to think about oneself – to think about one's own problems and personal gains. Besides, these reform programmes did not touch my life. We had brought suits with us to Kabul; so why should the diktat on wearing suits bother us at all? We were not in the business of selling veils either. So the queen's rejection of the veil could not pose any threat to our livelihood. But the main point was that in Iran and Afghanistan, the king was the owner of all the properties and lives of his subjects. And everyone knew that both were mortal and human. Nothing would last forever – the king's whim was just a pretext. The king was not a mule that he would carry the burden of the country on his shoulder. He was like a racehorse. He would run fast taking the country towards the path of modernisation. In that race he might kick the rider and the onlookers a few times. But you could not stop his fodder for doing that.

So the people of Kabul were going about their own business.

At that juncture, Amanullah's promise to help women to come out without the veil took on different interpretations. Some said the king had ordered that the husband could not object if a woman wanted to come out in the open without the veil. Men who had an objection, could divorce their wives. Amanullah would take steps against those who were in government service. What step would he take? Nobody made it clear but the insinuation was that he would lose his job, along with his wife. In Bengali we said, 'Bibi goes, leaving me starving.' But why should a healthy man starve if his wife left him? He would only starve if he lost his job.

Mir Aslam came to say, 'I told my wife, "This is your chance to go out with kohl in your eyes and make a round of the streets of Kabul without the veil." But brother, you wouldn't believe it! She threw the big metal pot at me. You know I wear this big mullah turban. So the pot got a dent in it and I took off.'

I said sympathetically, 'Yes, yes, I know, a turban is extremely useful and it has multiple purposes.'

He said, 'You know nothing. You would have known if you were married. You don't have to keep your wife tied down at home.'

I said, 'Rubbish. Amanullah has done the right thing by cutting the shackles. A wife is to be tied down with love and heart.'

Mir Aslam said, 'The purpose of the heart and love is a matter for the youth. Can a sixty-year-old tie a sixteen-year-old with his love and his heart? For them there's only the nikahnamah,* the burqa and the tail of the turban.'

I admitted, 'That is correct.'

Mir Aslam said, 'The youth are not bothered about Amanullah's attempt to break down the system of purdah. The problem is not there. It is the old chieftains who are now worried about their young wives.'

I asked, 'Are the young women making waves by coming out on the street without their veils?'

Mir Aslam said, 'How would I know? I don't have a daughter. No daughter-in-law either. My wife says she is fifty but I'm sure she's much older.'

I asked, 'Why are the old chiefs afraid?'

Mir Aslam sighed, 'Listen. Let me explain. If the young women came out of their homes in droves following Amanullah's speech, then the old guard would have found a way to counter it. What will you do if someone attacks you with a sword? You'll either fight if you are a brave person or you'll show your tail if you are a coward. But it's not like that. It's like an open sword hanging over your head. The young women are sitting still – you can't see them in great numbers out on the streets – but the few who are out, are hanging like a thousand open swords over their heads. Close your eyes and imagine.'

I shuddered.

---

* The *nikahnamah* is an Islamic marriage contract.

THIRTY-THREE

One morning after waking up, I saw a unique figure standing in front of my bed. It seemed I knew him but not quite. The tray he was carrying looked very familiar. Bread, butter, omelette, the kebab from the previous night – everything was on it as normal. As smoke indicates the presence of fire, this tray could not have simply walked into my bedroom, Abdur Rahman had to be present there too.

But what was he wearing! No shalwar, he was wearing trousers. Like those of prisoners, they only covered three-quarters of his legs. They were so tight on his thigh that they looked like the satin breeches of French gentlemen from the seventeenth century. His shirt was without a collar. There was a tie on his open neck. The jacket was so small that there was no question of buttoning it – the shirt and tie could be seen through it. The hat came down to his eyebrows as if it were on display in a shop.

Afghan shoes on his feet and a broad smile on his face.

I had been living with Abdur Rahman for more than a year now. Sometimes in a fit of anger I had compared him to an elephant but I never doubted his sanity. Closing my eyes I said, 'Explain.'

He was aware that I would be shocked, so he had his answer ready, '*Dereshi pushidam*' (I am wearing a suit).

I asked, 'People wear dereshi when they work for the government; are you leaving my employment?'

He replied, '*Tauba, tauba*. You are my government, you give me bread.'

'Then?'

'The police caught me when I went out to buy bread in the morning. They said, "By the king's order it is forbidden to come out on the streets in traditional shalwar, kurta and robe – everyone has to wear dereshi from today." They fined me one penny too. On the way back I was stopped again by another group of policemen. I somehow dodged them by dropping your name. I met our neighbour, the colonel, in front of the house. He gave me the dereshi. He likes me – I run some errands for him too sometimes.'

I heard everything silently. Finally I said to him, 'The tailor's shop will be crowded now. So get a proper dereshi made after a couple of days.'

Abdur Rahman was an economical man; he responded, 'What's wrong with this one?'

I said, 'Silence. And buy a pair of shoes in the afternoon.'

Abdur Rahman protested again, 'No Sahib, there is no need for that. The police said nothing about the shoes.'

I was surprised at first but then thought it might be true because the royals never looked at the feet of their subjects.

I said, 'Shut up. Buy a pair in the afternoon. And please take off the hat now.'

Turning pale, Abdur Rahman said feebly, 'In front of you, Sahib?' I suddenly remembered that in northern Afghanistan and Turkistan, people take off their turbans to scare away Satan. They believed that Satan fled seeing a bare head. Hence Abdur Rahman was caught in a dilemma. I also remembered that one was not allowed to speak in the House of Commons if one had no hat on. So I said, 'Okay, keep your hat on.'

The city looked emptier than usual. Most men could not come out on the streets, as they did not have the dereshi. The streets were supposed to be full of women after the abolition of the purdah system. Instead the 'dereshi law' had now sent the menfolk inside the harem.

I was incapable of describing the dereshis worn by the people on the streets. Kabul city teemed with men wearing all manner of torn, dirty, oversized and small jackets, trousers, plus-fours and breeches. The effect would have been less dramatic if you had let loose the inmates of ten mental hospitals in the green room of a Hollywood studio.

The Europeans were out to see the fun. I was so ashamed to witness that; I had never considered Afghanistan a foreign country.

I had to go to the city's fringes for work. The scene there was even more surreal. The village woodcutters, poultrymen, vegetable vendors were being fined by hoards of policemen the moment they set foot within the city limits. No one gave them any receipt. So they had barely gone a few yards when another group of policemen would stop them and extort another fine. All the cops from the police force had gathered on the city's outskirts. I heard that even those who were not on duty were out in uniform just to make some extra bucks. Meanwhile, there was no system of depositing the fines in the government treasury.

The Kabuli policemen, who could easily fall asleep while standing on their feet, looked so busy that day that it seemed there was a big fire somewhere close by.

I could not tell how long this torture continued.

*   *   *

I did not receive any letters or newspapers from home for more than two weeks. I heard that the Jalalabad-Kabul road was blocked with snow and hence the mail bus could not travel. Some people whispered that there was looting going on, on that road. Mir Aslam came and cautioned me that I should not ask too many questions on the streets.

At the end of my daily work, I used to give English lessons to the headmistress and the second teacher of the girls' school. Afghan women were clever; they knew that it was difficult to extract money from a rich man but a poor man was generally very generous. Possibly they had chosen me thinking the same rule applied in the field of knowledge. The headmistress was above fifty; she was learning a language other than her mother tongue for the first time. I used to sweat in the freezing cold of Kabul trying to teach her. She was learning English, yet she was curious about everything except the English language. She was especially undeterred in asking her teacher's age, where his country was, if he felt homesick and many such questions. Except for the size of my appendix and why I was born in this world, she had found out everything about me. My answers were also very strange. 'Where is my country? My country is Bengal – now learn how it's spelt – B-e-n-g-a-l. Learn the pronunciation too – some people say Bengole, some say Bangol. Similarly France is spelt as F-r—.'

She interrupted, 'I've understood. Now tell me what do Bengali women look like? I've heard that they have long hair. We get some hair oil here called "Zulf-e-Bangal" meaning Bengali hair. Do you apply oil in your hair?' Our lesson could not progress much in the middle of such questions and answers, especially when she asked me about my mother. It was not possible for me to teach a language in the guise of talking about my mother.

The second teacher was younger – hardly thirty. A mother of two, flabby, flat nose, an everlasting smile on her face, always wearing a long slipover, a long-sleeved blouse and navy blue skirt. She was the wife of a colonel and was clever too. She used to laugh when I tried to negotiate the barrage of questions from the headmistress. She often rescued me when I struggled to respond.

It was winter yet there was no snow. One day when I went to teach them, I entered the room and found that the second teacher was sitting at the desk with her face buried in her books while the headmistress was trying to console her by patting her back. Hearing my footsteps, the colonel's wife sat up hurriedly. I saw that there was no welcoming smile on her face. Her eyes were red and the tip of her nose was flushed too.

One should not take notice of such situations. I opened the book and started my lessons. Within two minutes, in the middle of our lesson, the colonel's wife covered her face with her hands and started to cry loudly. I was startled. The headmistress quietly patted her back saying, 'Don't be worried, not to worry. God is merciful. Don't lose heart, be calm.'

Indicating with my eyes I asked the headmistress, 'Shall I go now?'

She asked me not to by shaking her head. But I had barely resumed my lesson when there was another bout of crying and consoling. I could not figure out what I should do. I could make out from what the colonel's wife was saying through her sobbing, that she was worried sick about her husband. Whenever she tried to say more, the headmistress prevented her. I understood that her worries about her husband were not unfounded and there was possibly more that one should not discuss in public.

But she had lost self-control and it was difficult to stop her. Sometimes she said, 'The Shinwaris are barbarians'; sometimes she said, 'There was no official news for seven days'; or, 'The families of officers will not survive if the Shinwaris reach the city.'

I had heard rumours that there was looting going on in the Jalalabad region. By adding these bits and pieces from her outbursts, I could construct the situation; the Shinwaris of the region had taken up arms and were marching towards Kabul. Amanullah had sent one army to fight them and there was no credible news for seven days and the rumour in the army circle was that the officers had been captured by the Shinwaris.

There was no point in trying to carry on with our lessons in the midst of such a crisis. Besides, the headmistress did not like the fact that I had heard what the colonel's wife had said, but she could not control her either. Finally when I tried to leave, the colonel's wife sat up and said, 'No, Muallim* sahib, don't leave. I'll try to study.'

I wished that I would never have to teach in such a situation again. This time when she broke down again, she said through her sobs, 'They are cutting the upper lips of those who have a moustache like Amanullah.' Amanullah had a toothbrush moustache and hence it had become a fashion among the officers in the army.

Now I had a chance to console her. I said, 'Normally there are so many rumours at the time of war. One should not believe all of them. You are worried, so you're believing every bit of rumour.'

She sat up again wiping her eyes. She held my hand completely forgetting that I was a man not related to her, 'Muallim sahib, tell me honestly, on your honour, for how long have you not received any letters from home?'

Mails from India came through the Shinwari region. The mail had not arrived for three weeks.

---

* Farsi word for teacher.

I stood up. Looking into her eyes I said, 'I have got letters from home early this week.'

I saw that she was slightly reassured. I said, 'You don't get the chance to talk to men outside, so you don't get the accurate information. Women are more fearful and hence they add to the rumour-mongering. That is the reason King Amanullah doesn't like the purdah system.'

Accompanying me to the door, the headmistress said, 'Whatever you have heard here, keep it to yourself. Don't tell anyone.'

I said, 'These things are not news, they are rumours. I'm a foreigner. I have to be extra careful.'

Coming out onto the street I realised the difficulty of giving false consolation! I entered the gramophone shop to divert my mind and thoughts. I did not own a gramophone, but as a fellow Indian, the shopkeeper always welcomed me. I asked him, 'Have you got the supply of Bengali records from Calcutta for Maulana?'

He said, 'No.' It was clear he would tell me the reason if I pressed him. But I chose not to and left after listening to a few records.

But I did not have to probe. With the snow came waves of rumours; Kabul's bazaar was filled with them. That bazaar sold rice for a price but doled out rumours free. It was no wonder that things that came free would be cheap and useless. So there were yet more rumours and less information.

But it was clear that Amanullah could not put down the rebellion with arms. Now he had no option but to quell it with money.

I mentioned earlier that Afghan tribes fought with each other all the time. At times they would withdraw arms because of a truce but they would never become friends. So the first rule of Afghan diplomacy was: if one tribe rebelled against the king then the king would bribe the opposing tribe to fight the rebel group.

If money did not work, he would then give them rifles. Afghans would very happily attack their enemy if they got rifles. Cynics said the main reason was they wanted to do target practice with their new rifles.

In this case, the blueprint of the rebellion had been hatched by the mullahs. They had convinced all the tribes that the rebellion against 'kafir' Amanullah amounted to saving Islam. If any group opposed the rebellion for money, rifle or inter-tribal enmity, then they would be considered 'kafir', like Amanullah. They would not only go to hell, but their descendants would not see the door of heaven for fourteen generations.

It was the most serious curse. Holding rifles close to the chest in this life and the virgins of heaven in the afterlife had been the two basic pillars of the Afghan male psyche. No one could tamper with either of them. But the question remained, was Amanullah really an infidel – a kafir?

The mullahs came up with irrefutable evidence. The Shinwaris or Khugianis could not say one word against it. The mullahs said, 'Didn't you see that Amanullah sent twenty young girls as a gift to Mustafa Kemal in Turkey? Didn't you see that they came in a motor car and shamelessly walked the streets of Jalalabad without the veil?'

It was true that the Shinwaris and the Khugianis had come to Jalalabad on a market-day and had seen the Kabuli-girls-without-veils with their own eyes. And it was also true that Mustafa Kemal Pasha never got the certificate of good conduct from the Afghan mullahs.

Yet some 'fools' tried to say, 'The girls were going to Turkey to be doctors.' The Shinwaris apparently roared with laughter, 'Women doctors! Who has heard that women can be doctors? It'll be more convincing to say that the girls are going to Turkey to grow beards.'

Who would then try to show them that the Shinwari women worked in the fields without the purdah? Why could women not become doctors when their old grannies made poultice with herbs for various ailments and did the leech treatment for high blood pressure? These were all false debates. Some people had mentioned a real reason. I investigated but could not establish whether or not it was true. Apparently Amanullah had imposed an extra tax of five rupees on every Afghan in order to increase the state revenue.

Amanullah gradually learned of every twist and turn of events. But he knew the Farsi proverb, like many others, that people adored a dead dog if it had some gold in its name. Amanullah gathered all his ministers to ask, 'Who knows how to bribe the tribes?'

My neurotic friend Dost Muhammad was not wrong; the reality was that the ministers had knowledge of many things except for the intricacies of tribal rivalries – who the main leaders were and through whom they could send bribes to a tribal chief. In short, they did not know anything of the real world.

Then the ignored and abandoned old traditionalist elders were brought in but they said that for a decade they had not been involved with the government and hence they had lost contact with the tribes. The channels through which the king's generosity flew to the tribal chiefs via them had been blocked due to lack of maintenance. Now there was no other way but to flood these channels.

After a great deal of thought Amanullah sent his brother-in-law Ali Ahmad Khan to Jalalabad. He was given money, some said a million, some said two, to flood the Shinwaris.

Omar Khayyam used to pick up his earthen drinking pot when he felt confused with philosophical discussions. The earthen goblet apparently led him to the truth.

My earthen goblet was Abdur Rahman. Giving every detail to him, I wanted to know his opinion. Initially he used to ask me not to talk politics. But when the news of the Shinwari rebellion reached the bazaars of Kabul, it became the mainstay of all gossip and discussions. Abdur Rahman was a jeweller of snow. Snow was his yardstick. He said, 'So many people are saying so many things. What do I know? But, Sahib, don't forget one point, the Shinwaris won't be able to reach Kabul in this snow as they don't have enough winter clothing. Let the snow melt, then we shall see what happens.' I observed, 'Is this why there's this saying, let Kabul be empty of gold but not snow?'

I was convinced. I remembered that in my land, all rebels in Bengal would go to slumber blissfully during the monsoon months.

THIRTY-FOUR

At that point something happened for which no one was prepared. I did not get any indication of it, neither from the older generation nor the youth.

It was four in the evening. Soon after coming out of Dost Muhammad's house I saw that there was a big pandemonium on the streets. Shopkeepers were closing their shops and putting down their shutters in a hurry, there was noise all around, people were running in complete panic shouting, 'Oh, uncle, come quickly', 'Oh, brother, where are you?' The horse carriage drivers were driving their carriages through the crowd of people, almost trampling them. In front of my eyes one carriage lost control and collapsed on the ice of the Kabul river but nobody paid any attention.

Over the noise, you could hear the shout that 'Bacha-e-Saqao is coming, Bacha-e-Saqao has arrived.' Then we heard the bang of a rifle and the crowd lost all sense of reason. Throwing aside everything they were carrying, people started running for their lives, some landed in the roadside ditch, some slipped time and again while trying to run over the ice on the Kabul river. The blind beggar who used to sit by the road stood up trying to find his way with his hands in the air.

I somehow managed to leave the road, crossed the ditch and stood on the front porch of a shop. I decided that I would rather die from the bullet on which my name was written rather than be trampled by mad horses or in the stampede of the crowd.

Within a minute another man appeared and stood next to me. An Italian colonello or colonel, aged about sixty, with a long corrugated beard.

He was the first person whom I could ask something cogently. I said to him, 'I heard that the bandit leader Bacha-e-Saqao was coming to fight for Amanullah. But what is really happening?'

The colonello said, 'Seems like wrong news. He's coming to take over the city.'

If that was the case, then why were Amanullah's soldiers not going to the north of the city to fight him? How did Bacha-e-Saqao arrive in Kabul so suddenly? How many men did he have? Were they carrying only rifles or did they have cannons? The colonello could not answer these questions; he only kept saying, 'What an odd experience!'

I said, 'I can understand why the ordinary Kabulis are afraid, but why have the foreigners joined them? Where are they going?'

The colonello replied, 'To their own embassies or legations – for shelter.'

The sound of rifle shots was drawing closer. By then the crowd was moving in waves rather than in a stream. In between two such waves I told the colonello, 'Let's go home.' He said he would not leave without seeing the last act. Military whim – there was no point in arguing.

Abdur Rahman was waiting for me at the door. His worries disappeared at the sight of me. As soon as I entered the house, he closed the door and started to fortify it with heavy rocks. Intelligent man. He had made all the arrangements for fortification when I was out. I asked, 'Where is Benoit?' Abdur Rahman informed me that Benoit had left for the French Legation in a tonga carrying only one suitcase.

By that time the sound of the gunfire had been overpowered by the heavy sound of machine guns. Abdur Rahman brought tea. Listening to the sounds carefully, he said, 'The king's soldiers have now attacked. From where would Bacha have gotten hold of machine guns?'

I asked him, 'The king's soldiers are facing Bacha this late? How could he reach Kabul so easily?'

Abdur Rahman said, 'I asked many people while waiting for you at the door, but nobody could say anything clearly. It seems he has arrived without any resistance. He comes from the north of the country; my place is also in the north – Panjshir. I would have got some news of troop mobilisation in that region from my fellow Panjshiris in the bazaar, but there was none. The king's troops have gone to the east under the command of Ali Ahmad Khan to fight the Shinwaris.'

The exchange of fire continued. Abdur Rahman served me dinner early that evening and then he sat down to tend to the fire in the fireplace. From our chat I could make out that he was worried about my well-being in case Bacha won, which would be followed by anarchy and looting. But clearly he was highly excited and curious – much like a small child when the circus came to town.

But who was this Bacha-e-Saqao? I did not have to ask Abdur Rahman, he told me many stories about him of his own accord. I realised that Abdur Rahman had many qualities – a jeweller of snow, a doctor of frostbite, chef-de-cuisine – but he certainly was no Boswell. You could have constructed an image of a Robin Hood from what he said about Bacha, but much of it was certainly a figment of imagination and myth.

After filtering through all the stories carefully, I had a glimpse of the life of Bacha; he was the leader of a gang of about three hundred bandits; lived in Kohistan, north of Kabul; he looted the rich and distributed a portion of his booty to the poor. When Amanullah was away in Europe, he became so powerful that he started to collect tax from the traders of Kohistan. After coming back, Amanullah proclaimed a price on his head, 'Five hundred rupees reward on the head of bandit Bacha-e-Saqao.' Bacha removed all the posters and put up his own proclamation, 'One thousand rupees reward on the head of Kafir Amanullah.'

Abdur Rahman asked me, 'But, Sahib, help me solve a riddle. The colonel's son asked me, if I cut off Bacha's head and my brother cuts off Amanullah's, then how much money would we make together? I said, one and a half thousand. He nearly rolled on the floor with laughter; he said, "You won't get a penny." Please, Sahib, explain why wouldn't we get any money?'

I consoled him, 'Because neither of them will be alive to give you the rewards. But you can tell the colonel's son that the throne of Afghanistan will then be bestowed upon your family.'

I had also heard that only a few days earlier Bacha suddenly turned up in front of some high-ranking officials and swore his allegiance to the king in the fights against the Shinwaris by touching the Koran. By doing so he managed to get hold of about a hundred rifles and then disappeared.

Did he turn those rifles against Amanullah? That should not be a surprise. If Amanullah could tax the tribes to pay for his troops and then deploy the same army against the same tribes, then why could Bacha not use the guns given to him by Amanullah against him?

It was midnight. Abdur Rahman said, 'Tonight I want to sleep in your living room.'

I said to him, 'I know that you can't sleep unless your room is cold. You don't have to worry about my safety.'

He said, 'But how will you know if I was in danger? Didn't my father give you the responsibility to look after me?'

That was true. After he started working for me, his old man came down from the village once and made me responsible for his son's life and character. He had even given me the right to shoot him if he ever misbehaved.

His cunning greatly surprised me. It was like Newton – on the one hand he made two holes in a box for two kittens to breathe, while on the other he discovered the laws of gravity. Abdur Rahman was foxed by the simple riddle of the colonel's son but he could easily outwit a Bengali with his logic.

Lying down in my room he explained what 'qatle-aam' – mass killing – meant along with various descriptions of looting and ransacking. I could understand that all of it would take place if Bacha-e-Saqao captured the city. Zhenghis and Nadir could do so as emperors; so why could Bacha not repeat the act being a bandit leader?

On opening the door in the morning, I saw that the city was full of strangers. They had gathered from surrounding villages to take part in looting in case it got to that. Some of them were carrying guns. It was clear that many had knives and pistols hidden under their heavy winter coats. I went out to investigate the situation despite Abdur Rahman's resistance.

Arg is the big citadel in the middle of the city – Humayun was born there. One wide road connected the citadel with the promenade by the river. I came across a big gathering there. Approaching the crowd, I saw one high-ranking official requesting the citizens to fight against Bacha-e-Saqao.

It was by no means the inspiring oratory of the French

Revolution – with a pale face he was talking so feebly that one could not hear him from ten paces away.

The way a team captain distributed hockey sticks before the game, he also distributed brand-new rifles. Without saying anything, people were walking away with the rifles slung on their shoulders. I observed nobody went north – the fighting was taking place there.

The officer left promptly after distributing rifles – the way one would leave a dangerous place after completing some essential work. At that point I noticed that he was wearing the Afghan shalwar, kurta and robe – he was not wearing dereshi. Then I realised that others were in their traditional dress too, including the turban. I was the odd one out there in a suit and hat – I felt uneasy.

At that moment I saw Mir Aslam walking through the crowd at a brisk pace. Without saying a word he simply wrapped his arm around my shoulder and steered me towards my house. Abdur Rahman opened the door immediately on seeing both of us.

Mir Aslam started scolding me. Was this the time to have fun out on the streets? That too, in dereshi?

I only said, 'How would I know that the dereshi law has been lifted?'

Mir Aslam said, 'Who's asking if the law has been lifted or not? Bacha can enter the city any moment, so the Kabulis have become proper Muslims again by shedding their dereshi. Didn't you see that the sardar who distributed rifles was wearing a robe?'

I asked in surprise, 'What? The king's family too have discarded the dereshi?'

Mir Aslam said, 'There was no other way. The soldiers in the king's army have fled. Now Amanullah's only hope is if the citizens of Kabul fight against Bacha. He has discarded the dereshi in order to appease them.'

I asked, 'But didn't you say that the soldiers in the capital never revolted?'

'They haven't revolted. They have fled. Some, whose homes are far away, who can't reach their homes through this snow and ice, are hiding somewhere in the city. Some, who can't find shelter, have gone to fight – at least that's what the king thinks. Actually they are firing in the air sitting on the slopes of the hill in Deh Afghanan. Only the palace bodyguards are fighting Bacha.'

I said anxiously, 'Maulana's house is in Deh Afghanan. Let's go and check how they are doing.'

Mir Aslam said, 'Calm down. I tried to reach his house in the morning but couldn't. There's a gunfight going on there. I'm an Islamic scholar – the whole city of Kabul knows me. How would you go there when I couldn't?'

All my questions dissipated after hearing that news. I sat quiet, trying to think if anything could be done. Mir Aslam left after warning me repeatedly not to venture out again.

Meanwhile Abdur Rahman returned with a new rifle. He was brimming with happiness. He said, 'Sahib, why don't you write a note saying that you don't have a rifle? I can go and get another one quickly.' I was deep in thought about Maulana – Abdur Rahman left after getting no response from me.

It was true that looting had not yet started. But it might not be long before it did. When I went out in the morning, I had not seen any policemen on the streets. The royal bodyguards had gone to stop Bacha's advance. Who would now protect the city? Such a situation was not new in Afghanistan's history, even Babur had written in his autobiography that bandits and robbers always gathered in Kabul whenever they sniffed trouble. Mir Aslam gave a bit more good news that Babur's time was a lot safer as he used to deploy guards on the streets at the hint of any trouble. I could see for myself that Amanullah failed to do that.

But one consolation was that it was not easy to rob Kabul's houses. They had been built like little forts with high walls on all sides. Towards the top the walls slanted inwards, so it was not easy to use ladders to climb and jump in. On the top of the wall, there were holes through which one could safely fire guns from inside. The doors had been constructed with hard wood and riveted with sheets of iron and long nails.

A very secure arrangement. With two rifles one could fight fifty bandits for hours. The bandits did not have any cover outside so that they could try to burn down the door or break the wall.

But the question was, who would stay up on the roof all night as the sentry in this December winter? It could be managed if it was a big family – people could take turns. But we had a problem – 'Uncle and I are alone but the thief and his stick are a team of two!' And the people we were talking about were not small-time thieves, they were bandits carrying rifles and possibly many in number.

In this situation how could I even think of sheltering Maulana and his young wife in our house? But they had been caught in the middle – under fire of two forces. So I decided not to think too much. We would try to go to their neighbourhood at the first opportunity and after explaining the situation would leave the decision of moving in with us to him.

Abdur Rahman brought news that apparently Bacha's bandits had taken over the aerodrome and hence the king's planes were not being able to fly.

I asked, 'But what happened to the tanks and armoured cars that the king had brought from Europe?'

No answer.

'Aren't the citizens of Kabul fighting with the new rifles given to them?'

Abdur Rahman's answer was akin to a Bengali proverb[*] – but here it meant that the water-reeds were not ready to die by remaining in the middle. I asked, 'Very strange, Abdur Rahman, since when did Bacha-e-Saqao become king?' The gist of what Abdur Rahman said was that the previous Friday Bacha received the crown from the mullahs. In the religious edict – khutba – his name had been pronounced as the king and Amanullah was termed as the 'kafir'. Bacha-e-Saqao had taken a new name – Amir Habibullah – and he had proclaimed a jihad – a holy war to evict 'kafir' Amanullah .

What irony! Amanullah's father's name was Habibullah. Was the spirit of assassinated Habibullah trying to avenge his death in this cruel manner?

Abdur Rahman brought the last evening bulletin; Amanullah's pilots could manage to fly a few sorties to bomb Bacha's positions. He had now retreated and camped out a few miles away.

---

[*] *'Rajai rajai ladai hoi/Ulukhoder pran jai'* meaning the water-reeds die being caught in the fights between two kings.

THIRTY-FIVE

The road was completely empty – not a soul to be seen anywhere. Normally this road was full of life and activity. I began getting goosebumps all over my body.

Shops on both sides of the road were closed. The front doors of the houses were bolted from inside. There was no way to figure out if people inside had fled or if they were hiding like flies on the wall. Where did the stray dogs and cats go? I peeped at both sides of the main road from the side lane. The same silence there too. These lanes that were always so noisy with the sound of children playing were now eerily silent. The lanes were normally very dirty; in the absence of the cover of passersby, the ugly patches and the dirt on the walls became visible like a naked body full of open wounds and boils.

The northern end of the city. The foothills of the mountain. Maulana's house was still far. A group of Bacha's bandits had attacked that part of the city. Had they retreated or were they lying in wait for their prey?

Suddenly I saw a man with a rifle in the distance, walking towards me. No lane on either side of the street to take cover. There was no point standing there or turning round – I would be a sitting duck either way. It seemed the man with the rifle had seen me too, but seeing me unarmed he did not feel the need to lift his weapon. We faced each other. Lost in deep thought, he did not cast his eyes on me. Was he out to look for someone too and going back without finding him? Who could tell?

Maulana's house was in a side street. I did not meet a second person during my entire journey to his house. But now there was another problem – my hands started to ache from knocking on the door, but there was no response. Did that mean that Maulana and his wife were not there? All the windows were closed too, so my shouting did not enter the rooms. I could not tell for how long I knocked and shouted. A new thought started to cloud my mind. Was it possible that Maulana had been taken away and his wife was waiting inside, having bolted the doors? She was not likely to open the door without hearing her husband's voice. Or was she unconscious inside the house? I kept on shouting, saying my name – it did not sound like my own voice, it did not sound like my own name.

Suddenly I heard a meow – Maulana Ziauddin's cat. The door opened slowly. Maulana. His eyes were puffed, his voice had cracked – he had aged by ten years in these two days.

He said that he had sent his servant to get a carriage when the troubles began two days ago, but he never came back. Everyone in the neighbourhood had fled. Bacha's troops had come down that street twice and retreated. Taking the name of Allah, the husband and wife were waiting to be attacked by the bandits.

That was all fine. Now we had to make a move. It would be inadvisable to stay in that ghostly neighbourhood any longer. At that point I realised that we had a serious problem. Maulana's wife was in an advanced stage of pregnancy. They would have walked to my house on the first day if they could.

I told him, 'I am going right away to look for a tonga.'

I searched every street corner, every stable, every tonga stand for two hours. But I could not find one single horse; I was told that the owners had taken them away leaving the carriages behind.

So what was our way out? The only option was the Herculean strength of Abdur Rahman. He could easily carry Maulana's wife on his shoulder, but . . . There was no point wasting time with ifs and buts. We would have to make her agree.

I had never seen such a pleasant sight in my life when I returned home. My courtyard was looking like the front lawn of the library in Shantiniketan where Maulana and Benoit stood talking to each other. By clearing his throat Abdur Rahman indicated that there was a woman inside the house. Maulana said that his servant had come back with a carriage an hour after I left. I was so overjoyed that I forgot to ask him how he managed to get hold of a carriage in the middle of all this trouble. Benoit looked unwashed, with an unshaven face and crumpled clothes. He was French, he liked to stay clean and well-dressed all the time – even in Shantiniketan everybody knew that among the foreigners he would always be dressed in a freshly starched dhoti like a Bengali and wore it confidently. He told us that when he had tried to flee two days ago, his tonga could not reach the French Legation. As the legation was at the northern end of the city, the driver could not plough his way through the stream of traffic coming from there. Finally without paying any heed to Benoit, the driver took him to his village three miles east of the city. Benoit had spent these two days hiding in the stable of a poor farmer. Apparently every few hours, the driver and his brethren tried to tell him, through sign language – by showing their throat – that foreigners in Kabul were being slaughtered. Benoit was a good writer, so he gave a captivating description while trying not to talk too much of his own worries. But his appearance clearly indicated that he did not underestimate the gravity of his recent experience.

Maulana said, 'You had a lucky escape; it's our good fortune that the villagers did not succumb to the temptation of becoming gazis – victors, by killing a white man.'

Benoit said, 'I couldn't tell if they didn't contemplate it. Whenever I saw a few of them whispering among themselves, I thought they were talking about me. But I think the farmer who gave me shelter thought it was his duty to save me as a guest and thus kept the murderous lot at bay.'

I said, 'I lived in a village for one year and I think Kabuli farmers are peace-loving gentle souls and they don't like bloodshed or killing.'

Benoit left for his legation after changing his clothes.

I said to Maulana, 'You see, everyone – the French, the Germans, the Russians, the Turkish, the Iranians, and even the Italians are taking shelter in their respective legations. Only you and I have no place to go to.'

Maulana said, 'Technically the British Legation is meant for the British people. But the fact remains that the legation has been built with money from India, it's run with our money. Even the minister, Sir Francis Humphrys, buys his bread with our tax.'

I said, 'Lots of bread – at least three to four thousand loaves a month.'

Both of us agreed that the humiliation of a colonised country could not be felt fully until you went abroad.

The German poet Goethe had rightly said that one would not understand the true nature of his own country unless he went to a foreign land.

THIRTY-SIX

The anarchy went on for four days. Confucius said, 'A country in anarchy is more dangerous than a tiger.' I told myself, 'It's even worse if a bandit sits on the throne.'

Amanullah was confined inside the Arg Fort. His confidants from his inner circle were going around the city pleading with the citizens to fight against Bacha. Nobody paid them any heed. The city was full of thieves and robbers. Even the houses of the not so well-off were being looted. One could not walk safely on a deserted road – poorly dressed small-time thieves would do anything for a heavy winter coat. The robbers had their eyes on goods like that more than cash because one could not buy anything with money at that time. As the markets were shut, one could not purchase milk, meat, potatoes or onions. The grocers were hoarding wheat and lentils hoping the price would shoot up – Kabul city apparently had been totally cut off from the rest of the world.

The white folk were not coming out on the streets, all except the Russian pilots who walked bravely through the crowd to the aerodrome. They were not even carrying rifles, only small pistols tucked in their belts.

I was surprised to see the behaviour of Kabul's citizens. They were wearing weapons as if they were ornaments; some slung over the shoulder with the bullet belts around the waist; some were

244

wearing them as cross-belts; some had them strapped onto their arms and some on their legs.

These weapons had been bought with the hard-earned money of poor Afghanistan to fight the murderous marauders. Today they were being worn as ornaments.

But why were they not interested in saving the city? Were they not afraid of being looted if the bandit won? Why were they not bothered about the lives of their near and dear ones? Were they not worried about the all-round uncertainty?

Mir Aslam whispered in my ears that he had heard that there had been a pact between Bacha and the city elders. Bacha had assured them that he would spare the city if they did not fight for Amanullah.

This bit of news made me draw a parallel between what was happening and what Jesus' touch did to the blind. The philosophical attitude of the Kabulis could be explained with the information that Mir Aslam had just brought. But the people had rejected that king who won independence by defeating the mighty British empire; abandoned that king who tried to drive the country along the path of modernity, sacrificing his own luxury; turned against that king who gave his country an identity on the world stage and accepted a lowly bandit as their leader? Was this not called treachery?

Was Amanullah really a 'kafir', a godless man?

Mir Aslam roared, 'Never. It is a sin to rebel against a king who never stopped people from practising their religion, offering their prayers or carrying on with their fasting. It is a bigger sin to side with the enemy of that king who never taxed people for going on their annual Hajj or pilgrimage. On the contrary Bacha-e-Saqao is a murderous bandit – he's *wajib-ul-qatl* – one to be killed. He can never become Amir-ul-Moomineen or the king.'

Mir Aslam was a scholar of many disciplines. My common sense supported his views. I still said, 'Since when did you become a big fan of Amanullah?'

Mir Aslam roared even more, 'What I am saying is negation. I'm saying Amanullah is not a kafir – it's a sin to rebel against him – it's not in the religion.'

I heard the same in the atheist Russian embassy. I told Demidov, 'So the revolution has started.'

He said, 'It's not revolution, it's rebellion.'

I asked, 'What's the difference?'

He said, 'Revolution is progress, rebellion is regress.'

I thought Mir Aslam would be happy to hear this view. The old man said angrily, 'The Muslims of Samarkand and Bukhara should rebel against the Soviets. Soviet Russia doesn't let them go on Hajj.'

Maulana and I were both in the same state as the village head who loses his wits with the news of the unannounced visit of the governor. We had no clue how to receive the governor who had been invited by Maulana's wife. We did not know where to seat him or what to feed him. Maulana's wife had no experience either – this was the first time she was giving birth. I had heard that Afghan women took a little break while working in the fields to give birth under a tree. The Afghan trade caravan would not wait for the woman about to give birth. The woman normally caught up with them carrying the newborn in her arms. Maulana's wife was a middle-class woman; it would be unjustified to expect such feats from her. We became quite nervous seeing her symptoms. She could not eat anything, could not sleep at night, remained drowsy all day and would not let Maulana out of her sight for a minute.

It is easy to find people who can take another's life but difficult to spot someone who will be ready to stake his own life for others. The doctor simply refused to come out on the street. I could have moved a mountain that day with half the effort I had put into pleading with him to come to our house. On my way back I promised that if Maulana had a boy, I would make him a doctor.

The civil surgeon in our country would often write a long prescription without taking into account the financial condition of the patient. Likewise the Kabuli doctor gave us a diet chart. For four days we had been eating only bread, lentils and black tea. Even Amanullah would not be able to organise such a fancy diet in these troubled times. Milk! Grapes! Eggs! What was he saying? Was he mad?

Abdur Rahman said he could give it a try if he got a rifle and a break of a couple of hours. I had no moral objection to robbery. But sometimes the robber did not come back home. What would happen to us if Abdur Rahman did not come back?

I started having dreams that Bacha-e-Saqao was standing before me holding an unsheathed sword, dressed in the attire of a doctor, and saying to me, 'Give me grapes or I'll take your head.'

THIRTY-SEVEN

On the fourth day after the troubles began, Abdur Rahman brought a special edition of his daily bulletins. Bacha had been pushed back by ten miles or so. Schools, colleges, offices, courts all opened after ten days. Amanullah too found some breathing space.

Even though he could force away Bacha for the time being, he was defeated from within. The dereshi law had been abandoned, girls' schools had been closed and frocks and skirts had vanished from the streets. The women who were out on the streets were under the cover of tent-like burqas. No man or woman had the courage to put on hats – they had put on either turbans or woollen hats. Nobody tried to get the school and college students who had fled in this chaos back from their homes – because the police force was still on the run, who would catch the criminals?

Maulana said, 'In a way the outcome is good. If he survives this round, Amanullah will understand that for this backward and poor country there is no need to impose unnecessary reforms like dereshi, making Thursday the weekly holiday or banning the burqa. That leaves only education, trade and commerce. No one was objecting to reforms in these areas. After saving his crown Amanullah can carry on with these two programmes and the rest will happen automatically.'

Mir Aslam came round to say, 'I don't see much hope. The Shinwaris are still not ready to put down their arms. Apparently a talk of truce is going on between them and Amanullah. There are two conditions – he has to bring back the girls from Turkey and he has to divorce the queen. Apparently the queen lost her honour by mixing with men when she was abroad.'

We said, 'What nonsense! Nobody in this world has said anything like that – not even in India where people follow the purdah system. They praised her instead. From where did the Shinwaris get this information and why are they spreading this rumour?'

Mir Aslam said, 'Shinwari women work in the fields without the veil but they know what will happen to them if they look at other men – Amanullah knows that too. Tell me why did he then take the queen to the ball? Some foreign newspapers do reach a backward town like Jalalabad – there are photos in those papers in which the queen was embracing other men. Amanullah still hasn't understood how serious the matter is, but his mother has. She too is insisting that he should divorce her.'

I had huge faith in the Queen Mother. I said jubilantly, 'The Queen Mother has appeared on the scene? Then there's no fear. She will make pickles of the Shinwaris, Khugianis, Bacha – everybody.'

Mir Aslam said, 'But Amanullah does not pay any heed to his mother.'

I became despondent. Before leaving, Mir Aslam said, 'Let me teach you an old Farsi proverb. Running a country is like riding a lion for life – meaning you can't get down for a minute. It is fine as long as you're riding the lion but you have to be alert all the time. Amanullah is talking truce with the Shinwaris but he can't afford to step down for a minute – the Shinwari lion will eat him.'

At that point Abdur Rahman brought the news that our neighbour, the colonel, had come to meet us. Even though we had been neighbours for some time, we had never met him before. We welcomed him with due respect, but he said he had come to ask for our good wishes before going to join the war. Mir Aslam instantly started praying and we also raised our hands saying 'Amen, Amen'. Abdur Rahman brought the hookah, and he too squatted on the floor to join the prayer.

The colonel left. Mir Aslam said, 'It's a custom for the Afghans to ask for forgiveness and good wishes from neighbours and relatives before going to war.'

In his first push Bacha reached the Shahr-Ara area on the northern outskirts of the city. The Habibia School was located there. The vanguard of the bandits spent the first night in that school. Most of the boys from the hostel had fled except the ones from Kohistan who were waiting there for their brethren. The bandits cooked pulao with the rice and spices in the school kitchen. They used the wood from the tables and chairs, fat volumes of Steingass and Volastone dictionaries, textbooks and notebooks to fire the oven. They apparently liked the roll of maps made with wood and felt the most.

Amanullah was 'kafir', books were 'kafiri', chairs, tables were 'kafiri' – they proved their piety by burning them.

But the bandits did after all have some sense of right and wrong. Even though the students had become 'kafir' by taking lessons from schools set up by 'kafir' Amanullah, they did not deny them food. They had given them a few slaps. Some distant cousin of Bacha was a boarder in the hostel; he apparently became the local leader. But when Bacha retreated, he too fled with him, discarding his 'kafiri' reincarnation. On my way back home, I saw the kids collecting empty bullet shells.

I heard that Sir Francis Humphrys was of the opinion that it was no longer safe for foreigners to stay in Kabul. Amanullah also agreed to the evacuation plan, as he did not want the outsiders to get caught in Afghanistan's internal matters. Kabul was cut off from the rest of the world, and hence aeroplanes were arranged.

The aeroplanes arrived. Women went first. The French left; then the Germans; the Italians; the Poles; in brief, women of all nationalities left but no one asked about the Indian women. The planes had been bought with India's money; the pilots got their salary from India's money too. The Indian women were the most vulnerable – at least the other women got shelter in their respective legations but who was going to look after the poor Indian women? But then, how could Sir Francis show his face in his high society if he took the wives of Indian professors, shopkeepers and drivers into the exalted premises of the British Legation? The Hindu Brahmin could redeem himself if he lost his purity; the Muslims had no such problem as they had no caste system. But the class division of the English was a very serious matter. It was a country where there was no written constitution. Similarly the rules of the class system had never been engraved in any book of faith. You could be a well-known philosopher, a famous mathematician, a renowned political scientist or an ordinary miner of a coalmine; but you would not be accepted in their high society unless you reached the House of Lords. Until then, your expertise in philosophy or the honours given to you by the trade unions would be deemed as useless. One who defied this was branded an eccentric, like George Bernard Shaw.

Was I crossing the line? Was I diverging from the main story? Never. We had been talking about revolution, war, bloodshed – all these were the mainstay of our narration but we also had some side stories.

You could not explain the attitude of the British minister without mentioning this sense of 'snobbery' and the idea of 'nobility'. The British Legation was so big that all the foreign legations in Kabul could fit into its premises. It was like a mini town with its own water supply, electrical power station, and even its own fire brigade. All the Indian women could easily have been accommodated inside the winter gymnasium for the white people. Food? When the embassy people fled Kabul they left behind vast amounts of tinned food with which they could have fed the women for six months.

Even the Minister of the French Legation, who Benoit sarcastically called 'the 'Minister of the French Negation' had opened up the wine cellar to the French people sheltered there, to keep them happy.

The doctor was refusing to visit us, there was no food, no midwife, a heavily pregnant woman was not getting any shelter. Leaving her behind, the Indian aeroplanes were transporting the French, the German and the British women. We could only pray, 'Oh Lord, save our woman, she is pregnant.'

To attack the city from the north one needed to occupy one mile of empty space after passing the British Legation. Bacha reached the hostel in Shahr-Ara by that route. The whole of Afghanistan knew that for four days the legation and Sir Francis were at the mercy of Bacha. Bacha could have massacred everybody in the legation – if he turned his eyes away, his keen followers could have looted the place as they wished. The son of a water-carrier, a bandit, had spared their lives but they had no empathy for a pregnant woman who was about to give birth.

Demidov sent a memo asking me to go to his house. I had never received such a note from him; normally he came over if he needed anything. Looking at his face I could sense something serious had happened. I asked him at the door, 'What's happened? Tell me?' Without saying anything he took me to the living room and made me sit on a chair. He sat down facing me. Looking straight at me, he said, 'Bolshov is dead.'

I exclaimed, 'What?'

Demidov said, 'You know after the trouble started, Bolshov went to Amanullah with the proposal of bombing Bacha's position. Yesterday evening—'

I was thinking, Bolshov could never die, it was unbelievable.

'– yesterday evening, after coming back from his bombing sortie, he was playing chess at the embassy club. He had his small pistol in the pocket of his breeches. You knew his habit – he was fiddling with the pistol inside the pocket and accidentally pressed the trigger. The bullet reached his heart through his stomach. He lived for six hours, the doctors could do nothing.'

I could still not believe that a giant tree like Bolshov could fall in the absence of a storm. After so many wars, after so many injuries, finally by his own hand . . .

Demidov said, 'I knew you would be hurt, so I told you in brief. If you want to know more—'

I said, 'No.'

'Let's go, let's see him.'

I said, 'No.' I got up. Madame blocked my way, said, 'Please have dinner with us.'

I said, 'No.'

While passing the tennis court, I could hear Bolshov's voice as if he was asking, 'Yes, my friend, how are you?' I shuddered. I still could not believe that Bolshov was no more. I had met him for the first time at this tennis court. I had met him so many times at this gate.

That night I went to bed without eating anything. Waking up in the morning, I realised that the whole night I subconsciously thought about Bolshov. I remembered our last conversation. I joked, 'Bolshov, you are fighting for Amanullah? Amanullah is a king and Bacha is a proletarian of the proletariat. You should join Bacha.'

Bolshov had said, 'How did Bacha become a proletarian? He is here to put on the king's crown. One king is progressive and the other is the enemy of progress. I fought all my life on the side of progress; I fought under Trotsky, and here I am fighting under Amanullah.'

In these dark times, under Bolshov's leadership only the Russian pilots had fought for Amanullah without thinking much about what would happen to them if Amanullah were to lose the war.

After fifteen days, I heard that all the foreign women and children had been evacuated. The only foreigners left were the Indians. I ran to the British Legation and pleaded for Maulana's wife. The British were kind enough. They gave her a seat on the first flight that was to take the Indians out. I ran back home and started shouting from the courtyard, 'Maulana, I have got a seat for her. Ask your wife to get ready. We have to take her to get weighed. They want to know her weight.' Maulana was silent. I was puzzled. Finally he said that his wife was refusing to go. She would rather die with her husband in this country. I asked, 'What did you say?' Maulana remained silent. I said, 'Maulana, you are a Punjabi, but you have become soft and sentimental like the Bengalis after living in Shantiniketan for years and singing Bengali songs composed by Gurudev. It is not the time of "holding your hands".' Maulana still had no answer. I said angrily, 'You have become a Hindu – that too of 1810 – when they practised sati. You are a great disciple of Gurudev. Did you know that his grandfather Dwarkanath fought against that system?' No response from Maulana. I said, 'Jokes apart, look at the practical side. You didn't keep any count. There is no way to know when the baby will be born. Suppose we manage to get a doctor and a midwife. But after the baby is born, if your wife – ' I cleared my throat thrice, '– where will I get milk? Who knows when we will get milk in the market.'

Maulana went to talk to his wife. Standing outside I could hear her sobbing. He came out and said, 'She won't agree.'

Finally I had to go in. I told her, 'It's not as if I don't understand why you are refusing to go. But think for a moment, aren't you becoming a problem by staying here? He can go to a safer place very easily if you are not here. Not only that, he may have to leave the country if the situation becomes worse. All that will become much easier if you leave now. He is not thinking about himself at all. He's only concerned about your well-being. Likewise, as a wife, shouldn't you think about the well-being of your husband?'

I was thinking, while pleading with her, if she gave birth to a boy, I would make him a barrister and if a girl I would send her to be trained by the Queen Mother.

The medicine worked. Her husband's well-being was the best ploy to convince any Indian woman to move from her position.

Next morning Maulana took her to the aerodrome. Abdur Rahman went with them in case of any emergency. I stayed back to guard the house. The day was clear, I was standing on the roof. I could see the Victor bomber plane flying in, landing and again flying back to the east. It waited on the ground for hardly half an hour, as Kabul was not safe.

After returning, Maulana went to his room with a long face. Abdur Rahman said, 'Seeing her clothes, the pilot said that her legs would freeze at the higher altitudes. They had brought straw. So Maulana wrapped her legs like a vinegar bottle. Almost every woman's feet had to be wrapped like that.'

We were talking standing at the door. Suddenly we saw some people carrying a dead body down our street. Abdur Rahman joined the procession. The pall-bearers stopped in front of our neighbour, the colonel's house. Abdur Rahman knocked on the door, and the shrill cry of a woman came out like an arrow as soon as the door opened. As the body was being carried inside the house, more and more voices joined the wailing.

It seemed as if someone had throttled the voices. The dead body was inside the house and they had shut the door. The sudden silence rather than the wailing affected me more. I ran into Maulana's room. Abdur Rahman came with the news, 'The colonel died in the fighting.'

Maulana started to pray lifting both his hands. Abdur Rahman and I joined him too. After finishing Maulana said, 'Before going to war, he had come to seek our good wishes. He now has a right over us.' After performing his ablutions he sat down to read the Koran.

Entering his room in the afternoon I saw that he had regained his calm after reading the Koran. The pain of separation from his pregnant wife and the worries about her were not visible any more.

I had respect for the colonel. It was strange to see how one man's death could have a calming effect on another.

I felt a sense of loss too. I had met him only for five minutes, but at his death it felt as though a five-year-old child had passed away. Our acquaintance never got the chance to flourish.

THIRTY-EIGHT

An Afghan proverb says, 'When the parents so happily say that their child is "growing", they don't think that he is also "nearing his grave".' Amanullah was only thinking about his reforms, but he did not notice that his reign was nearing its end. But it would be unfair to blame only Amanullah – his ministers and close confidants were trying to get back to their routine like ordinary people on the streets.

Exactly a month after the attack by Bacha, on a terrible cold day in mid-January, one Punjabi professor came to see us. The city had returned somewhat to normal; it was safe to be out during the day.

He asked, 'Have you got the news?

I replied, 'What news?'

He said, 'So you don't know. Okay, listen. You don't get such news every day, even in a country like Afghanistan.

'My servant told me early this morning that something was happening at the royal palace, many were going in that direction. I too ventured out to see what was happening. I saw all the important ministers, their assistants, high-ranking army officers and some elders of the city gathered there. Moin-us-Sultana Enayatullah Khan and his eldest son were standing in their midst. The most surprising part was that there was no sign of Amanullah in that grand gathering.

Before I asked anyone, one important-looking man – possibly the Rais-e-Shura (the President of the Council) started reading a proclamation. I was standing a bit far away – so could not hear everything clearly but he read the ending loudly; and that removed all doubts. Amanullah has abdicated and has requested his elder brother Moin-us-Sultana, Enayatullah, to take over the reign.'

I asked excitedly, 'So sudden? Why? What happened?'

'Listen. After the reading of the proclamation, one elder of Kabul requested Enayatullah to take the throne. The summary of what Enayatullah said in a very controlled and calm voice was that he never wanted the throne. Ten years ago when there was a power struggle between Nasrullah and Amanullah he had given up his right to avoid bloodshed.'

Taking a breath the professor said, 'What he said after that was quite valid. He said, "Considering the welfare of the people, I never took the throne that was rightfully mine. Now I'm ready to take the responsibility if people think that it will do them good."'

I asked, 'But Amanullah?'

The professor said, 'I asked around and heard that Amanullah's troops lost the battle at night. He got the news early in the morning. He immediately called Enayatullah and asked him to take over. Seeing the gravity of the situation, Enayatullah apparently didn't agree – but Amanullah forced him at gunpoint.

'Amanullah had left for Kandahar in his motor car in the morning. Before leaving, he had assured Enayatullah that his ancestral Durrani[*] land would not desert him. He would be back with their assistance very soon.'

Finally Amanullah fled. I was trying to digest the situation silently.

---

[*] A major Pashtun tribe.

The professor said with a laugh, 'You used to be Enayatullah's tennis partner. As he was too fat, you had to cover most of the court for him. Now that he's the king, you should ask him to share with you a bit of the country, if not most.'

I said, 'Very true. But would that mean that I would have to face a few bullets from Bacha?'

The professor said, 'Tut tut. Why should Bacha fight any more? The Hazrat of Shor Bazaar* and Sardar Osman Khan have taken a message from Enayatullah to him. "What is the point of fighting when Kafir Amanullah has abdicated?" So Bacha should go back home – he had no enmity with Enayatullah.'

After the professor left, I took a walk to the Arg Fort.

The city looked strange. Even after Bacha's first attack, at least there was a semblance of a government – people did not know if he was strong or weak but there was a king. But now there was the air of chaos everywhere. People who were walking on the streets were not from the city. They were walking in groups. Greed and the desire to loot were painted on their faces. Nobody would be able to stop them if it started somewhere.

I walked for an hour but did not meet one person I knew. I also noticed that no one was walking alone – everyone was moving in groups except for the beggars and the homeless.

I could not find anyone who could give me the true picture. I got the indication that Enayatullah had taken refuge inside the Arg Fort and sealed it from the outside world. I could not find out how many of Amanullah's soldiers had accepted Enayatullah's leadership and were there inside the fort with him.

* The most important religious leader of Afghanistan of that time – he had a large following.

I knew that Dost Muhammad had left the city to fight for Amanullah, so his house had been empty for a month. I thought he might have come back by now. But I was disappointed when I reached his house. Maulana was still out when I came back home. So I decided to visit Mir Aslam for some authentic news.

The old man started with his same old lines, why was I unnecessarily out and about in these troubled times?

I told him, 'Be careful, sir. You know the king is my partner in tennis. Not a small deal. Just let me know what you want and I shall arrange everything for you.'

Mir Aslam laughed heartily. Then he said, 'There's a Farsi proverb – Whosoever has embraced the Princess/Has the sharpest sword blade kissed.

'But your king is a very strange man! Normally one becomes a king after fighting with guns and troops but your King Enayatullah agreed to take the throne at gunpoint!'

I said, 'But you see, one who had the right over the throne finally became the king. The people of Kabul haven't forgotten that Enayatullah was Habibullah's eldest son.'

Mir Aslam said, 'That is true but it's too late. Five other people have now cast their eyes on what is rightfully his. You must have heard that the Hazrat of Shor Bazaar has gone to Bacha with the message from Enayatullah. What do you make of that?'

I said, 'Enayatullah is not a kafir. So Bacha will now go back.'

Mir Aslam said, 'You don't know Shor Bazaar at all, hence you're saying that. He is the most influential mullah in Afghanistan. Amanullah had put him in prison at the start of the revolution but he didn't dare to hang him. He's now free, but what's his benefit if Enayatullah becomes the king? In this time of crisis Enayatullah has pleaded with him to mediate. But Enayatullah will become stronger if Bacha leaves. After consolidating his reign he will not have time for an audience with Shor Bazaar. After all he is a king's son; he knows how to run a kingdom. He will not need Shor Bazaar any more.

'On the contrary, if Bacha drives Enayatullah out, then it's better for Shor Bazaar. Bacha is a bandit; he doesn't know a thing about running a country. The mullahs who are supporting Bacha zealously until now will be in the driver's seat, should he become the king. The leader of the mullahs, Shor Bazaar, will be running the country.

'But there is a greater reason for Bacha not to retreat from here. How can he send his followers, who have been fighting for more than a month camping in the snow, back home empty-handed? He had lured them with the carrot that was the looting of Kabul.'

I said, 'But you said the other day that there had been some agreement between the neighbourhood elders of Kabul and Bacha that he would not loot Kabul if they did not fight for Amanullah.'

Mir Aslam replied, 'This is called politics. Like the British – during the Great War they convinced the Palestinians that they would give them a homeland and extended the same offer to the Jews.'

After coming back home I saw Maulana had returned along with a group of Punjabi professors. They teased me a lot. Some said, 'Brother, I need six months off', some said, 'I didn't get any promotion for five years. Please put in a word for me to the king.' Maulana responded on my behalf, 'Since you're only making the cake in your dream, don't be a miser, put in generous amounts of butter.'

I realised that they were convinced that Bacha would go back and the city would return to the lawful times of Harun-al-Rashid.

In the evening Abdur Rahman brought the latest bulletin: Bacha was refusing to return. He said, 'I have been crowned by the people, I have to abide by it.' Mir Aslam rightly said, 'Taking the throne is like riding a lion – once you're on it, there's no way to get down.'

That night some thieves tried to rob us. Getting his chance to use the rifle, Abdur Rahman shouted more in elation than he fired it. They must have been small-time robbers, they fled hearing Abdur Rahman's roars and war cries.

Abdur Rahman used to gather the content of his bulletins standing at the door. He asked every passerby detailed questions – his fear was now gone after Amanullah left Kabul. He now called Bacha-e-Saqao 'Amir Habibullah', showing a lot of reverence.

His midday bulletin said, 'Enayatullah Khan is waiting inside the Arg Fort for help from Amanullah. Bacha has ordered him to surrender. Or else he has threatened to ransack the city and kill everyone. Enayatullah has responded, 'Kabulis have enough rifles and stocks of bullets. It's better for the flock of sheep to die if they can't save their own skin.'

Maulana said, 'The city elders are of no use to Bacha any more.' Then like a parliamentary supplementary question he asked Abdur Rahman, 'How much food is in stock in the Arg Fort? For how long can the troops sustain themselves in there?' Abdur Rahman was a novice in diplomacy – he did not talk about the notice period; he responded, 'Up to six months.'

On the third day the bulletin said, 'Bacha has threatened, "If Enayatullah doesn't surrender, he will massacre the families of the ministers, other officials and soldiers who have taken shelter inside the fort".' Enayatullah said, 'Don't care.'

Meaningless question from us, 'Why isn't Bacha attacking the fort?'

Smart answer, 'You can't break walls of stone with rifle rounds.'

That evening one Indian clerk from the British Legation took shelter in my house. He had come to the city for some work but could not go back as Bacha's bandits were marching into the city. We heard from him that the ministers and officials were holed up in the fort while their family members were living out in the city. But Enayatullah's family was inside the fort. So the king's interests and that of the ministers and officials were not the same. The ministers were keen to surrender to save their families.Enayatullah apparently said that he had taken the throne against his own will, at the request of the ministers. So he would not want to save the fort against their wish.

Abdur Rahman was present in the room. He said, 'I have heard that the soldiers are ready to save the fort. They have said, "We didn't join the army thinking about the safety of our families." Actually the ministers and officers have lost their nerve.'

The clerk said, 'I have also heard the same. But there is no way to tell what is true and what isn't. The main point is Enayatullah has agreed to abdicate, but he has one condition: he wants safe passage for himself and his family out of Afghanistan through a third party. Sir Francis has agreed to take the responsibility.'

Very surprised, I asked, 'But who got Sir Francis involved in this matter?'

'Difficult to say. The Hazrat of Shor Bazaar, Enayatullah, Bacha – anyone or all three of them. Now they are working out the details.'

That night there was a hot debate and lots of discussion on Afghan politics between Maulana and the clerk.

Next morning Abdur Rahman brought homemade bread, salt and black tea without sugar for breakfast. We had got used to this basic food. But the clerk could not eat it. There is a saying, 'The maid in a judge's house can write a few lines.' I extended it,

'The clerk in the British Legation eats well – even during this time of trouble.'

Around noon, I went out with the clerk. The city was full of Bacha's troops. I was taking leave of him on the avenue next to the Arg Fort – he would be going to the legation – and I would come back home – when suddenly, without any warning, about a hundred rifles went off all around us. People on the streets started running in all directions, as though they had lost their wits. Surely they were looking for shelter but nobody had any clue where they were heading. Bacha's bandits were everywhere. So they were running in every direction.

It was not comparable with what I had seen on the day Bacha had first attacked the city. That day the Kabulis were afraid on hearing the roar of the tiger, but now the tiger was right in front of them. The clerk was a Pathan from Peshawar. They were brave people, yet he too started running, pulling me with him – who knew where to. One horse ran past us.

While trying to jump over the roadside ditch I saw that the rider was hanging on to one side with his leg caught in the stirrup and his head was banging on the road with every gallop.

By that time the surreal picture of the street started to take a vague shape in my mind. I stopped freeing my hand from the clutches of the clerk. The shape of the picture that my subconscious mind had captured was that the bandits were not firing their guns to massacre the people; it was no *qatle-aam*; they were shooting in the air. I brought that to the notice of the clerk.

By then only the bandits, the clerk and I were standing on the road, the rest were sheltering either in the ditch or on the porches of the shops or on the solid ice of the Kabul river – close to the high banks.

The firing went on for three to four minutes – we stood there blocking our ears with our fingers. Then people came out of their respective shelters.

The bandits were laughing loudly – it was 'shadeeyana' – celebratory shooting – yet the people of Kabul got scared. Shadeeyana for what? 'Haven't you heard the news? Enayatullah has abdicated and left the country for India on an aeroplane. So Bacha – oops – Amir Habibullah has given the order to fire guns in celebration.'

Long live 'Amir' 'Gazi' Habibullah.

There was the ancient system of human sacrifice on the day of the coronation in the lands of barbarians. There was no such system in Afghanistan but on that day a few people lost their lives unnecessarily. The thousands of bullets of the shadeeyana showered down from the air on their heads, killing them – they did not have thick turbans like that which Mir Aslam always wore.

One should not ignore the turban. Amanullah wanted to pull the turban off the poor Afghans and he paid the price by losing his crown.

THIRTY-NINE

The bandit picked it up and put it on his head.

The mullahs blessed him.

A proclamation came the following day. The gist was, Amanullah was kafir, he taught children algebra, geography and said that the earth was round. Nobody could believe that such a proclamation could be issued in the twentieth century. But when a bandit like Bacha could sit on the throne, then everything was possible. That was not all, we saw that it carried signatures of not only the mullahs of the country but also Amanullah's ministers.

Mir Aslam said, 'They got those signatures by holding bayonets on their belly. Or else which madman can sign a proclamation declaring Bacha as the king?' He was livid, his face had become red with anger, his beard was sticking up. He roared, 'Wajib-ul-qatl – the man who every Muslim should kill on sight, has become the king?'

I said, 'What you are saying is true, but I hope you're not saying it in public.'

Mir Aslam said, 'Listen Syed Mujtaba Ali, I criticised Amanullah in front of everyone. I will express my opinion about Bacha exactly the same way. You think the mullahs of Kabul don't know me? Won't they want to put my name on the proclamation? But they know that even if they cut off my left hand, my right hand will not sign this paper. They know very well that I've issued my own fatwa, "Bacha is *wajib-ul-qatl* – one to be killed." '

After he left, Maulana said, 'There is hope for Afghanistan's future as long as there is a man like Mir Aslam alive in this country.'

I said, 'Very true. But won't it be better if we think about our future now?'

Both of us gave it a lot of thought; sometimes silently, sometimes in words. Subject: while pronouncing Amanullah a kafir, Bacha said in his proclamation, '. . . and all the foreign teachers and professors who helped Amanullah in his efforts are hereby dismissed. Schools and colleges are being closed down.'

Finally Maulana said, 'No point thinking too much. Not only us, lots of people have been dismissed. Let's wait to see what they do.' Maulana believed that ten donkeys were equivalent to a horse.

But these were personal stories.

Bacha did not keep the citizens of Kabul in suspense for long. He ordered the arrests of Amanullah's ministers and the looting of their houses.

The looting happened in instalments. First Bacha's bandits swooped on the cash, gold, jewellery and expensive materials. In the second instalment, petty thieves took the furniture, carpets, clothes, crockery and utensils. Finally the rest was washed away in a deluge – ordinary people from the streets took the wood of the doors and windows to light fires at home.

The ministers were made to stand on the snow and ice in their bare feet and tortured in various ways to extract information about 'hidden treasures'. Kabulis shuddered hearing the description of the torture. Maulana and I looked at each other.

Then came the turn of Amanullah's friends and army officers. At night we could hear through the closed doors and windows –

robbery, bandits. Those were government-approved bandits – there was no way to fight them, there was no respite from them.

Gradually we got used to everything – bloodstained snow on the streets; naked dead bodies; cries of scared women and children at night. But strangely I never got used to dry bread, salt and liquor tea without milk and sugar. I remembered my mother said the coolies in tea gardens drank such strong black tea, not to relish but to kill hunger. I realised that it was true but then the body became weak at the same time. Luckily there was no malaria in Kabul, or else I would be down with malaria like the coolies too. After that what? I would not have to explain to the Bengalis. I asked Maulana, 'Which is the best way to die – starvation, a bullet or malaria?'

Maulana recited a verse of another Maulana – poet Sa'di's:

Chu ahangey raftaan kunad jaaney pak
Chi bar takhtmurdan chi bar sarekhak.
When life prepares itself for the great exodus,
It's the same death – be it on a throne or the road's dust.

A week after Bacha's proclamation, the foreign teachers – the Indians, the French and the Germans – held a meeting and decided that they would go to meet Sir Francis to explain their crisis and plead with him to evacuate them in aeroplanes.

The professors said, Kabul was cut off from the world; Sir Francis said, hmm. The professors explained that as there was no bank in Kabul, their money was in Peshawar and there was no way to get it; Sir Francis said, ha. The professors pleaded that they were starving with their families; Sir Francis said, oh. The professors said in desperation, they would soon die if they stayed here any more; Sir Francis said, ah.

On one hand there was the description of life and death, on the other hand there was a list of exclamations. As if a college student and a nursery child were studying in the same room.

After completing the list of exclamations, Sir Francis said, 'The British Legation is representing the British government. It is not our responsibility to look after the Indians. You have no right, I may be able to do something, but only as a favour.'

In our village plays I had seen the role of the greatest of villains – Duryodhana.* I looked at the ambassador – there was some discrepancy – Duryodhana never engaged in a debate of 'right' or 'favour' but here this villain was ready for 'favourable considera- tion'. That was the difference.

I remembered the story of Yudhishtir.† Before going to heaven he caught a glimpse of hell for half-lying only once in his life. I thought I might get a glimpse of heaven for a moment if I spoke the truth for once. I said, 'The aeroplanes have been bought with the money from India, the pilots get their salary from its coffers, the aerodrome in Peshawar is India's property – in this situation we have no right?' As a courtesy, I did not mention that the British Legation had been built with India's money and he earned his bread with our tax too.

He was fuming with anger and I could see that the professors were scared. I understood it was a question of life and death – the Indians were desperate to go home – they did not want to debate on 'right' and 'favour' unnecessarily. So I said, 'What I said just now was my own opinion. I don't want any "favour" but that should not affect others.'

---

* One of the main characters of the *Mahabharata*. Duryodhana was the eldest son of the Kaurava clan.
† From the *Mahabharata* – the eldest son of the Pandava clan; an epitome of honesty and truth.

There was no point getting into further discussion. The minister understood my position and his was nothing new to the Indians – we always saluted these people, asking for favour in the most humiliating manner.

I got the news that evening. A list of Indians to be evacuated had been prepared and the minister had crossed out my name.

Abdur Rahman now only supervised the fireplace. There were no nuts for him to break. There was no polish for him to brush the shoes. It was sad to see how thin he had become on our diet of bread and black tea. Maulana had retired for the night. Abdur Rahman entered my room. I said, 'Abdur Rahman, the bandits have blocked every road out of the city. Is the road to Panjshir open?' Abdur Rahman took my hands, kept on kissing them and placed them on his eyes; he said, 'That's a lot better, Sahib, a lot better. Let's go to my land. At this rate, you won't be able to walk in a few weeks – with only dry bread and salt. My home is well stocked. If nothing else, there are nuts, raisins, pistachios and soft cheese. And, Sahib, I have three sheep. One more month, after that when the ice melts, I will catch fish for you. You can eat it as you like – fried, baked or roasted. You have told me about fish delicacies so many times; I will make everything for you. You will sleep well and look out of the window . . .'

I did not want to stop him. The poor man was talking to his heart's content after a long time; he was dreaming of Panjshir again and trying to mesmerise me with his imagery. It pained me to break his reverie. Yet I somehow said, 'No, Abdur Rahman, I won't come. I'm asking you to leave. You know I have no job; I don't have any means to pay your salary. There's no rice or lentils left. We are only left with some wheat; that too won't last for long. You should go home. If Khuda wants, if the tide turns, if good times return, we will meet again.'

It took Abdur Rahman a while to digest what I was saying. After grasping it, he left the room silently. I felt terrible, but what to do? After spending many evenings talking to him, I realised that if he was not convinced about something he would ignore it completely. I understood that he did not like my proposition. I thought he would object; in that case I would have got the chance to put forward my case. I realised that there were similarities between a simple man and the betel-nut trees; as there were no branches, you would come down straight to the ground if you slipped once.

He returned after a while. Hanging his head, he said, 'You can measure a handful of flour for me every day. I will survive on that.'

How was it possible to make this man understand that I knew how little he was eating for the last month? Besides, food was not the main point – he was pained by my proposal, how could I lessen that? I said before that there was no point trying to make him understand with logic – I thought of calling Maulana. But there was no need. Abdur Rahman said, 'In the good times I ate things that my father never dreamed of having even in his in-law's house.' Then he raised his voice, 'As there is no food now you are trying to dismiss me? Am I that ungrateful?'

He spoke a great deal. Some of it logical, most of it reminiscence, a little scolding but all topped off with the feeling of hurt. Sometimes he said, 'Didn't you have dereshi made for me'; sometimes he said, 'Didn't you have the best quilt made for me', how many rich men in Kabul had such quilts, who would guard the house if he left, I had the right to sack him as he had not been able to serve me properly.

It was like the snowfall in Panjshir. Piles and piles of snow. I lost my way and was covered in it. At our first meeting Abdur Rahman had said that the snow cover made you warm. I too was feeling the warmth.

But Abdur Rahman had lost all his Panjshiri strength without any food. It did not snow for seven days, he stopped within minutes. I said, 'Yes, that's right, I didn't consider who would save me if you left.'

Abdur Rahman was instantly happy. This is the advantage with simple people. He immediately sat down to supervise the fireplace.

I realised that there was no dark cloud in his mind when he came to tuck in my quilt at night. He said, 'You know, Sahib, what my father will do to me if I go back home? He will first recover the price of a bullet from me and then shoot me with it. He had said many times, "He's more useless than you if he has to shoot you with his own bullet."'

I asked, 'Is that why you don't want to go home?'

He was puzzled initially, but then he laughed. I laughed too – I always thought Abdur Rahman was as dry as a log and never imagined that young leaves of humour could grow on it.

Abdur Rahman brought an open letter; it carried the date on which Amanullah fled the city:

'Kamarat be shikanad—

My dream has been fulfilled. I'm off to the Afridi land usurping Agha Ahmad's five years' salary and his brother's rifle. I will join my family business there. I hear that the age-old business of extracting ransom by kidnapping English officers is not doing very well because of lack of proper leadership.

Well, I need an interpreter with a good knowledge of English – you know how weak my English is. If you have some common sense, then come to the Jalalabad market to look for me as soon as you have read this letter. Salary? What I can give you in a month will be more than your one-year's salary in Kabul. It will be better to be my brethren and share our hard-earned money rather than working for a bandit king.

There is no Amanullah – yet Fee Amanullah.* Dost Muhammad

P.S. Agha Ahmad is here with me. There's a fine Mauser rifle distributed by Amanullah slung over his shoulder.'

Stories of what the bandit-king, the son of a water-carrier, did in the royal palace willingly or unwillingly started to percolate in the bazaars. I really liked one of them. Maulana held the copyright. Amanullah used to go to the parades in London with King George the Fifth in a Rolls Royce. King George had gifted the Rolls to Amanullah when he came back to Kabul. As the car used to gobble up oil like a giant, Amanullah had left it behind when he fled the city.

After becoming the king, Bacha sent that Rolls Royce to his village to fetch his wife. When the car reached the village, Bacha's wife was picking nits from the hair of Bacha's bachas,† In the middle of all that excitement Bacha's wife said to the driver, 'Go and tell your boss that he himself should come here to get me on a mule.'

After conquering the world when Buddha came back to Kapilavastu, his wife Yashodhara too had said the same thing.

---

* The word Amanullah means 'Allah's protection'. 'Fee Amanullah' means 'Leaving you in Allah's protection'.
† The Hinglish word bacha means a small child.

FORTY

I am waiting, wearing the finest dhoti, silk kurta and the best scarf. Flower garland in one hand and a touch of perfume behind my ears. The servant has gone to get the taxi – I will go to the cinema.

No, I was not dreaming, I was drawing parallels.

In that situation one could not think of any other mode of transport but the taxi. The only difference was that Sir Francis had an air taxi – but, like the Sikh taxi drivers in Calcutta, their eyes bloodshot after a few drinks, would refuse to go anywhere, Sir Francis too was speaking with his inflated sense of authority – to hell with what he was saying.

By then we had been waiting for a month.

There was no tea left – so we lost our only means to kill our hunger. Now it was only bread and salt. You did not need salt if you added enough of it while making the bread. But Abdur Rahman served it separately as an extra course.

Benoit had left for India on the aeroplane three weeks before. I mentioned earlier that he had practically become a Bengali by living in Shantiniketan. But that did not matter. He had a passport from France and it was inevitably white in colour. So he got a seat on the Indian plane without any effort. I did not mind in his case, but I was sure I would not be that generous with any other French people.

The night before he left Benoit came to give us a can of tinned French food – the size of a sardine tin. For ages our stomachs had not had anything but bread and salt; as a result Maulana and I suffered from loose motions for a week after relishing that small portion of French food. Our condition was like that of the poor peasants who suffered from malaria. They knew that they only needed nourishment for a week rather than quinine to rid themselves of the fever. We also understood that our loose motions would evaporate like Amanullah's troops if we just had some good food for three days.

Both Maulana and I were so cranky with hunger and stomach pains that we would jump at the sound of the cat walking on the carpet. Yet such were the mysteries of the nervous system that we could sleep in the midst of all the gunfire. We started to fight meaninglessly. Looking at him I thought, why did men wear such beards, and while I did not know what he thought of me, we would surely have come to fisticuffs if he had expressed it.

Maulana knew how to engage in unnecessary debates. What I said had been the ultimate truth since the creation of the universe; I said, 'The best meal is fine rice and fried hilsa fish.' The fool said that biryani and qorma were far better! How could I give a better example of the parochial narrow-mindedness of the Punjabis? He had not become civilised even after living in Shantiniketan. One should not look at the face of the lowly man who could insult the hilsa fish, but the generosity of the Bengali was such that I stopped talking to Maulana only for three days.

And it was a killer winter. English cinema was full of elaborate depictions of hot climates, yet there was little on winter. Because films were made in the Western countries where people were used to cold conditions, which would not sell at the box office. The only thing they showed was a blizzard or a snowstorm. In our land a powerful sudden summer storm was dangerous but the killer was the long spell of a hundred and twelve degrees; likewise the blizzard was bad but nothing compared to ten degrees, day after day.

If you put your clothes out to dry after washing, the moisture in the clothes would become ice. The sun could not melt the ice, let alone dry it. The shirt would become so stiff that you could make it stand in one corner of the room. The clothes would become soggy after you brought them inside.

The reader may think that I am making it up but I would swear on all my travels, that if you spat from the roof your saliva would turn into flakes of ice before reaching the ground. Abdur Rahman managed to get a couple of onions one day – only God knew if he stole or robbed them – after cutting one, we saw there was a fine dust of ice in between the layers. We exhausted our stock of firewood.

Abdur Rahman brought the news around midday. Outside, the sun reflecting on the snow was blinding, but we saw darkness around us. The temperature was far below freezing point in spite of the sun.

That night we slept with our thermal inners, flannel shirt, pullover, jacket and even our overcoats. We covered ourselves with two quilts and a carpet. Maulana started singing his most favourite song:

> The heart dies thirsty, pierced
> By the arrows of fire so fierce!

Normally I joined in with him but that night I could not, my teeth were chattering. The curtains swayed in the wind coming in through the windows. The sky was full of stars.

One French poet had created the imagery that the tears from the sky had turned into stars. Some other unknown foreign poet had said that stars were made from the droplets of wax from the candles lit on the coffin.

> My beloved, she parts the clouds for a sight
> Of someone in the evening's starry light,
> Remembering the faded glow of the evening lamp, alas.

Rubbish poetry, rubbish parallels.

Oh god of the sky, your blue quilt had millions of holes in it. Were you also shuddering like me? Could you not warm yourself from the fire that was engulfing Kabul?

For three days and three nights I hardly came out from under my quilt. On the fourth day, Abdur Rahman pleaded, 'You won't be able to get up if you remain like that, Sahib. Please get up and take a walk to get your blood circulating.' It was like the doctor in our country advising the poor peasant to take a morning walk. I said feebly, 'I will then feel hungry – feel less hungry if I stay like this.'

Abdur Rahman knew that I would sack him if he committed a robbery; hence he was not out with his rifle looking for food.

House cats normally did not leave the house. For three days we did not see our two cats. We realised that our neighbours were eating better than us. They were wise, accustomed to rebellions. They had enough stock.

Elephants did not live long in cold climates. Yet Amanullah had a pet elephant. There were no banana or pineapple plants or shrubs in Kabul. So it was literally a white elephant. There was a scarcity of firewood, so the elephant stable did not have any fire to keep it warm. One day Bacha's followers decided to ride the elephant on a whim. In those cold conditions they took it out for a round of the city. I saw long icicles hanging from the poor creature's emaciated body. I knew the elephant was brought from Tripura in eastern India. Tripura and Sylhet in East Bengal were neighbours which had had a link that went back over centuries. Sylhet's criminals used to take refuge in the forests of Tripura. I felt sad for the elephant. I remembered Remarque's story of the farmer who once stood up in the middle of heavy gunfire to shoot an injured horse, thus relieving it of its misery.* One could read the agony on the face of a dog. But no one had ever seen an elephant suffering, so only when its pain became so visible, did one feel sympathy for the creature.

Amanullah owned many cars. Bacha's followers drove them around the city for three days till their fuel tanks became empty. The streets were full of such cars – they had abandoned them wherever they had stopped. They did not even roll up the windows. So the cars were soon filled with snow and rain; the street kids had pushed some into the ditches.

One such car – a brand-new Buick – had been abandoned in front of our courtyard. Abdur Rahman was very keen to pull it inside; he wished to ride in it after the revolution was over.

We could not differentiate two white men by looking at their faces. Similarly for Abdur Rahman, all cars were the same. It was difficult to convince him that after this revolution when the royals would look for their cars, the car would go to the garage and he to prison.

Optimist.

Like in Shillong, earthquakes were common in Kabul. Everyone would run out into the open.

There was a strong quake in the afternoon. Maulana and I were so weak that we did not leave our beds.

---

* Erich Maria Remarque's *All Quiet on the Western Front*.

FORTY-ONE

A speaker, after completing his speech that lasted for hours, apologised to his audience by saying, 'Please forgive me, I wasted your valuable time unknowingly. I could not keep track of time as there was no clock in front of me.' Someone from the audience said angrily, 'But there was a calendar on the wall. Why didn't you look at that?'

Maulana and I had stopped looking at the calendar a long time ago. Yet the chill in our bones reminded us that it was still winter.

Meanwhile the French, the Germans and other foreign men had been airlifted – the women had left a long time ago. Finally I heard that some Indian men could leave too by the 'favour' of Sir Francis. My name had been struck out from the list, so I told Maulana that if his chance came, he should leave without looking back. He should not give up his life in a foreign place instead of going back to his motherland just because his younger follower failed to accompany him. Chanakya had said that a true friend was he who remained with you at all times – during festivities, in times of revolution, and at the graveyard. But I was sure that when he mentioned revolution he meant trouble in your own country, not when you were starving after being trapped like a rat in a foreign land.

In the delirium of fever I saw that a uniformed messenger was entering the room. My body was weak; so too was my mind. I thought he must be the executioner sent by Bacha. Or who else would come now?

No, he was the messenger from the German ambassador. He also insisted that I should visit the ambassador as soon as I got the letter. How could I go and what was the purpose? Why should the German ambassador invite me in these troubled times?

The German Legation was two miles away. How could I go? And what was the point? I was sitting on the last step of the stairs; I would not be able to descend further even if someone kicked me.

Finally I went after a lot of persuasion from Maulana.

The road to the German Legation was a beautiful one – quiet, lined with tall leafy trees. The Kabul river meandered to one side of the road – sipping water from there, young groves and clusters of chinar trees had sprung up here and there. Even the most dry and prosaic man could imagine that it was the most ideal place for a romantic rendezvous or playing hide-and-seek.

But now the road was a haven for robbers and thieves and a slaughterhouse for lone pedestrians.

Abdur Rahman had put a small pistol in my pocket; it might come in handy if I were to face a mugger.

On this road, one should walk briskly, holding his head high, full of confidence – but I did not have the strength to do so, so I walked slowly, whistling. At least people would think that I was a regular on that road.

There was a hill at the end of the road. The German Legation was located on the higher ridges of that hill. I looked like a damp cloth after I walked all the way up to the legation. The ambassador quickly poured me a glass of brandy. I was amused in spite of my misery. A Muslim normally quits drinking before he dies, should I take a drink now? I declined, shaking my head.

Germans are very efficient people. Without any preamble he said, 'Benoit told me that you were working here in order to save money to go to Germany to study. Is that true?'

'Yes.'

'Is it true that all your money was with some Indian business-man and you have lost everything because he has been killed?'

'Yes.'

The ambassador thought for a while, then asked, 'Why have you chosen Germany in particular to study?'

I said, 'After working in the library in Shantiniketan and coming in contact with scholars there, I feel Germany is the best place for me for my higher education.'

There was another reason, I did not tell him that.

Diplomats apparently lost their job if someone could read their minds. So I sat there with a perplexed face, indicating that I could not figure out the meaning of his line of questioning.

He said, 'Don't think that I called you only to find answers to those questions. I wanted to tell you that I would be only too happy to be able to help you in any way I can. Just tell me how.'

I thanked him greatly. The ambassador was waiting to hear from me and I was struggling to come up with an answer. It suddenly occurred to me – there was a God; I had been blessed by my guru. I told him, 'The German government gives a few schol-arships to Indian students every year. If you can arrange one of—'

The ambassador interrupted, 'I am giving you my word, you will get it even if there's only one scholarship.'

After thanking him, I said, 'I studied in the university of the poet Tagore. He will be happy to give me a certificate.'

He said, 'Then why did you go through so much trouble in such a faraway place? Who in Germany doesn't know Tagore?'

I said, 'Tagore is very generous in giving certificates. He has even given a certificate to a hair-oil company saying their product helps bald people grow their hair back.'

The ambassador smiled, 'We know that Tagore is a very famous poet but we don't know that he is such a generous man.'

Some other time I would have started collecting material for an article on 'Tagore in Germany' but my body was craving to go back to my bed.

After standing up I said, 'I don't have words to thank you enough for inviting me and offering your help, even in the middle of this crisis. It would be awfully nice if I get the scholarship, but it'll be fine too even if I don't. I shall never forget your kindness.'

The ambassador stood up as well. Shaking my hand warmly, he said, 'Don't worry, you'll get the scholarship.'

At the end of this encounter, a thought was stamped on my mind forever – this was an ambassador and so was Sir Francis Humphrys.

But that is enough. Bengalis tend to digress from the crux of the matter whenever they smell a sensitive subject.

My patient readers, I would like to ask for your forgiveness. What happened between the ambassador and I was something personal. I had serious doubts whether to narrate it in a travelogue.

After coming out of the German Legation I remembered that fourteen years ago when Afghanistan was a British protectorate, Amir Habibullah had put up Raja Mahendra in this building. Next to it was the tomb of Babur, Emperor of India. I had visited the tomb many times. It was not the time to visit it again, yet my legs led me in that direction.

It was a simple grave under the open sky, made with a few ordinary stone slabs. In India, the graves of ordinary clerks looked grander. His son Humayun's tomb was bigger than the Taj Mahal. The architecture left behind by his grandson and great-grandson Akbar and Jahangir far exceeded the dreams of Babur.

People who had read Babur's autobiography would feel a connection with him when they stood next to his grave. You would not get the same feeling while visiting the tombs of Humayun or Shah Jahan. Babur founded the Mughal empire; many other fighters also founded many dynasties, but there was no king who could match Babur's literary skills. As a writer Babur was close to the earth and that had been captured in every page of his writing. Standing next to the tomb I always felt I was visiting the grave of an ordinary man, possibly even a relative of mine.

One historian in our country compared the autobiography of Caesar with that of Babur and opined that the former was far better than the latter. In his opinion, Babur's autobiography was second grade literature. I had a different opinion but I would not want to bore readers by getting into that debate. My only submission was: both were literature, not historical writings. You did not have to be a historian to judge the literary value of these books. Readers could taste the literary flavour in their own way. It was a shame that Babur wrote in Jagatai Turk and Caesar in Latin, so it was not easy to read them in their original form. The only consolation was that the historians read them in translation too.

I turned around to look at the grave for the last time. It felt that Fakir Babur was praying for the last time in front of his tomb covered in a blanket of white snow. What was he praying for? Was he praying for the freedom of India, raped by the British?

Gurudeb had written this song for the Shivaji festival—

The immortal image on that throne of Death
That, with its risen temple,
Displays the Royal Jewel, will never ever
Its divine glow dissemble.
Finally today, have I recognised you, O King,
You are the great sovereign!
With your royal taxes in hand, stand before you
Your ten million Bengali children.

I first recited that; then by reading a verse from the Koran, I prayed for the departed soul and finally climbed down to the 'Baburshah' village.

I had heard that pilgrims did not die on their way to Mansarovar in spite of the most difficult trekking routes high in the Himalayas. They mostly died on their way back, even though by that time they were acclimatised to the high altitude and the freezing cold. They lost the will to walk because there was no longer anything to achieve. They were only going back to their daily drudgery, in their own homes and in the daily cycles of hope and despair. After such an immense achievement, it felt like a great fall – so they broke down at the smallest of obstacles. They then sank into the snow and could never get up. My legs had no strength, my back was breaking, my head was reeling. My fingers and toes were nearly frozen; my nose and earlobes were totally numb; I did not even have the strength to walk fast to keep my body warm. The road was deserted. After taking a turn I saw a group of uniformed soldiers coming from the other direction. I realised that they were Bacha's bandits – they had been promoted in rank by donning the uniforms discarded by Amanullah's soldiers. They had brand-new rifles slung on their backs and bullet belts on their waists. I had never seen such cruel and greedy faces anywhere outside of prisons. They had spent most of their lives outside public view, in the darkness of mountain caves. An unimaginable stink would envelop the surroundings if a herd of pigs trampled on piles of fresh pig-droppings. Likewise churned by the rebellion these bandits had spread like that stink right before my eyes.

They were not wearing overcoats. They could kill me only for that. Robbing and killing a lone pedestrian on a deserted street was nothing new to them.

I did not have the strength to run away, and there was no way out either. Above all, I was a village boy – we usually ran when facing a tiger, but we lost our nerve completely when we faced a wild pig. We fled in both situations in any direction.

When the bandits were only ten yards away, their leader ordered, 'Halt.' The other eight came to a dead halt. The leader said, 'Aim.' Immediately the barrels of eight rifles faced me.

I too halted where I stood, but I cannot remember properly what happened next.

I could not develop one single frame from the film of my memory. The shutter of my consciousness had closed completely so the super double-X film of my mind could not capture anything.

I had dreamed many times that the round holes of eight rifles were targeting me and I was facing them. So I could not say for sure if it actually happened or whether it was but a figment of my imagination.

I vaguely remember only one thing; however I would repeat that I could not confirm anything.

My right hand was inside the pocket of the overcoat holding the small pistol given by Abdur Rahman. For once I was tempted to kill at least one of them with it before dying. I thought, as I was about to die, I should at least earn some points so that I could enter heaven.

I later regretted that I did not try to kill one of them.

His subjects were the constant source of irritation for the 'mad' Emperor Mohammad Tughlagh and his subjects had the same feelings about him. After he died, Tughlagh's companion Ziauddin Biruni had said, 'Now the emperor is relieved of his subjects and the subjects of him.'

On that day if I killed one of them, some people in this world would have been relieved of me and I of them.

Suddenly I heard roars of laughter. '*Tarseed, tarseed*', they were saying (he's scared, he's scared, the man is scared stiff). They were laughing unanimously – some like a fox, some roared with rifle under armpit, some noisily, and some silently.

One of them said in a husky voice, 'By the name of Allah, it would be a total waste of eight bullets to kill this chicken.'

No need to give my dimensions – they had the right to call an average Bengali a chicken.

Whether chicken or cockerel, after being spared by the butchers, I wanted to run away as fast as possible. But feeling a strange churning in my stomach I started walking slowly.

I bumped into another group of bandits about a furlong away from my home; but I was not much worried as I saw there was a smartly dressed officer with them. When they came close, it seemed I knew the officer. Yes! He was my student just the other day. He was so stupid that I used to rebuke him almost every day.

After remembering that I visualised again the barrels of eight rifles. There was a lane to the right. I took a sharp turn into it like a kite out of control. Surely there was trouble for me if he wanted to take revenge – if not my life, some humiliation. Oh my murshid, why did I come to this land of enemies? Oh Moula Ali, I would sacrifice two—

I heard the quick steps of military boots behind me. Oh dear. My murshid, Moula Ali – all of them had deserted me. But even 'the worm turns'. I turned round. The young lad was shouting, 'Muallim Sahib, Muallim Sahib – sir, sir.' Coming close, he took my hands in the style of Abdur Rahman, kissed them again and again, asked my news and finally he scolded me, like an elder, for venturing out in the middle of this dangerous situation. I kept saying, 'Oh, oh, yes, yes, certainly, certainly, by God's grace, by God's grace, shame, shame' at right and wrong places in an attempt to recover from my fear.

I became bold after I had got over my initial fright. I asked, 'But my son, from where did you get the uniform?'

Inflating his chest like the Babur-Shahi mountain he answered, '*Cornail shudam*' (I've become a colonel).

My God. A colonel – overnight – at the age of nineteen! I got bolder. I asked again, 'So how far is the road to be a general?'

He answered seriously, '*Door nist*' (not far).

God was great – revolution indeed brought luck for some people. The newly promoted colonel explained, 'Amir Habibullah Khan is my third cousin four times removed.'

I did not remember what exactly the relation was but it was nothing closer. I felt proud, hurrah to my teaching, hurrah to my student, hurrah to this revolution, hurrah to this starvation. My student had become a colonel overnight.

I decided that I would send an article titled 'Achievement of an expatriate Bengali' to the *Probashi* magazine. If they could regularly publish the obituary of some gardener in the household of an established Bengali family from Allahabad, then my achievement should certainly merit publication.

I said, 'Son, allow me to go home now.'

In a military voice he said, 'I will escort you. The city is full of bandits.' He then glanced at his men. I had to accept – the table had turned – now he was the teacher and I the student.

After reaching home, he chatted with us for a bit, cursed Amanullah and lectured Maulana on military strategy. Before leaving, he entered Abdur Rahman's room. In the home of the guru the student normally went to the servant's room for a smoke. But Abdur Rahman would be in trouble as we had exhausted our stock of tobacco a long time ago. He also did not know how to pull the wool over the eyes of others – in spite of living with me for so long. But there was no surprise in that. Tagore's servant Banamali did not learn how to write poetry even after living with him for years.

Maulana said, 'I spent the whole morning in the British Legation and Bacha's foreign ministry, pleading like a beggar. Swearing on my beard I told them, "Haven't eaten anything but dry bread for two months. Won't even get that from the day after tomorrow." Told the British Legation, "Free me from the cages of Kabul." Told Bacha's foreign ministry, "Give us some rice to eat."' I said, 'Are the foreign ministry and the grocery the same institution? And did you only give them two options? Either free us or give us food? You could have given them the third one – kill us.' I was shivering in the freezing cold as if I had malaria. I would doze off every now and then. Sometimes it felt that I was in a free fall from the bed. Then I would stand straight stretching my legs. Sometimes I would shout, 'Abdur Rahman, Abdur Rahman.' But no one came. Sometimes I saw Abdur Rahman sitting there holding the bedpost, with his head hanging down; but I did not call him. I heard him muttering the few lines he knew from the Koran.

And there were nightmares; I was sitting in an aeroplane and Bacha's bandits were chasing after us with eight rifles to stop the plane, but the plane's engine was refusing to start. Then I heard the real sound of shouting and of rifles firing – robbery underway in the neighbourhood.

Then I saw mother frying hilsa fish.

Oh, ma!

It was getting dark. Why was Abdur Rahman not bringing the lamp? Oh, I had forgotten, there was no kerosene. What would we do with kerosene when the fuel of life – to hell with poetry.

But what was there before us? A big basket. Filled with flour, mutton, chicken, potato, onion and many other things. The young colonel was smiling naughtily, standing in front of it. Why was Abdur Rahman looking so pale? Was he scared wondering why I was not waking up? No, I was not sleeping; it was not a dream.

Abdur Rahman said, 'Sahib, colonel sahib has brought some gifts.'

How could one cope with so much excitement in one day?

Abdur Rahman said hurriedly, 'Don't blame me, Sahib, I didn't tell colonel sahib anything.'

The colonel said, 'Looking at his appearance I could make out what sir has gone through. But it's only God's wish that I bumped into you. How could I forget how much care you had for me?'

I said, 'What? I used to scold you most.'

The colonel's face lit up. 'Yes, sir. That was what I was saying. I see you remember it too. Why would you scold me so much if you didn't have deep care for me?' Then looking at Maulana, he said happily, 'You know what happened? Once sir was very angry with me and asked me to get a cane. The whole class was very surprised.

Normally the teachers asked the class monitor or the archrival of the student to fetch the cane. They normally got the toughest one. You know what I did? I thought that sir never caned anybody. It would be a sin to cheat him on his debut, so I brought him the hardest one.' Then, winking at Maulana, he asked, 'Do you know what sir did? After taking the cane in his hand he asked, "Why haven't you polished off the thorns on the cane?" The boys replied, "How else can he feel the pain?"'

Maulana said, 'You became a colonel because you got a caning that day.'

The colonel said sadly, 'No, sir didn't cane me, though I was ready for it. But I don't feel pain anyway.' Saying this he spread his palms out towards us.

He was the son of a peasant. Pushing the plough from an early age on the hard soils of Kohistan, had made his palms thick like the skin on the shoulder of a bullock. You could not distinguish between his nails and the skin. Except for one and a half, all other lines on his palms had vanished. There was no lifeline nor any head-line, and his heart-line had suddenly lost its way 'in the desert'. That was all. He was leading his life with only one and a half palm-lines – no Jupiter, Venus or Solomon's mound. The fingers – deformed like that of a leper – would not fall into any category of palmistry. It did not matter, because how many children from a bandit clan had become colonels, and how many of them had their palms read by Varahamihira[*] and Cheiro?

Abdur Rahman was sitting next to the basket looking down at his feet.

Maulana thanked the colonel and asked Abdur Rahman to take the basket to the kitchen. Abdur Rahman stood up with

[*] Famous Indian astrologer from the sixth century.

the basket but did not leave the room. Seeing no other way I told the student-turned-colonel, 'Please have dinner with us tonight.'

He said, 'You have to excuse me, sir. I've been ordered by the king to have dinner at the palace.'

Maulana asked, 'What does the king eat?'

The colonel said, 'Bread, cheese and raisins. Once in a while a handful of pulao. He says, "I won't have that food that converted Amanullah into a coward."' Then, with a naughty smile he said, 'But I don't listen to him. Amanullah's chef still cooks in the palace and I eat every dish he cooks.'

Before leaving, the colonel asked us not to worry about our daily provisions any longer.

Within ten minutes Abdur Rahman lit the fireplace with the wood brought by the colonel.

I do not have the ability to describe in words how my whole body, my flesh, bones, marrow and nerves were rejuvenated sitting in front of that fire. Every atom and nucleus of my body absorbed the heat from the fire in the same way that each pore of the dry cracked earth soaked up the first raindrops.

I realised why fire had been worshipped in the first verse of the Rigveda in the Aryan tradition in Indian civilisation, and in other traditional religions.

It was the same in the Semitic religions. Judaism, Christianity and Islam accepted that the only man who faced God was Moses or Musa. God appeared in front of him in the form of fire – 'tazallite'. Moses lost consciousness, and after waking up he saw that everything in front of him had been turned into ash.

The Greek king Prometheus and the king of the gods, Zeus, fought over fire. Human civilisation started with fire brought to earth by Prometheus. King Nal* was an expert in lighting fires. Was that why he fell foul of the Gods?

The Indian-Aryans, Greek-Aryans and the Iranian-Aryans or the Zoroastrians – all worshipped fire. Possibly they had come from cold climates; hence they knew the value of fire. But the Semitic land was hot, so why then did they respect fire? Was it because the people of the desert were so aware of the power of the almighty sun that in their faiths the creator of the universe appeared in the form of tazallite?

My body was pulsating with that warmth on one hand and on the other many such theories were coming out of my brain like steam. I started to form such a high opinion of my own erudition that I tried to pat my own back in appreciation but only succeeded in twisting my shoulder. I suddenly remembered that Shaitan, the Devil, Lucifer – all of them were made of fire; they were the kings of fire. Hell was all about fire – how could they live there if they were not made of it?

Alas, such a nice theory of mine was burnt to ashes after coming into contact with Shaitan.

Rose, nargis – nothing could compare with this. Only fools wrote poems about their fragrance. It was no match for the aroma of biryani-qorma-kebab, not even the sweet smell from the hair of your lady-love.

Opening my eyes I saw Abdur Rahman was laying out a banquet. Maulana was supervising unnecessarily and the two cats that had disappeared for two months were back in the dining room making a 'my dear', 'my dear' sound.

This dinner was the royal edition of what Abdur Rahman had cooked on our first night of acquaintance – like a special gift, for

---

* King from Hindu mythology.

a dear one, wrapped in silk. My heart filled with joy. Maulana roared, 'Zindabad Gazi Abdur Rahman Khan! – Long live, conqueror Abdur Rahman Khan!'

Raising my voice by one bar I said, '*Kamarat be shikanad, khudatora korsazad, be pundi, wabe tarqe*' (May you break your hip, may God blind you, may you blow up like a balloon and then burst).*

It seemed that Maulana was struck by lightning. He was a learned man, how would he know the meaning of such curses? But Abdur Rahman knew the meaning. Holding his hands as if lathering them with some invisible soap he said, 'Wash your hands, Sahib, I have hot water.'

What did he say? Hot water? Would I get the sweet touch of hot water after so long? It did not compare with heavy-breasted Vasantasena getting wet in the first rain and Charudatta's admiration for her. I said, 'Beradar Abdur Rahman, you framed this dinner scene in gold with this hot water.'

Abdur Rahman's joy had no limits. He did not respond to us, he only kept saying, '*Alhamdulillah*' – By God's grace.

I noticed that his hands had grown thinner and trembled while he moved the plates and the crockery.

Maulana warned me that I should chew every bite at least thirty-two times. But in reality he was gulping down food like the way the white people rushed to the refreshment room when the train stopped at stations. After parking some food in one corner of my stomach I said to Abdur Rahman, 'I'm ready to stay in Kabul for a bit longer if I get such food.' There could not have been a greater appreciation than this in such troubled times.

* See chapter 19.

But Maulana was the separated husband. His pain of separation from his wife escalated after he had eaten some food. He said, 'No,

> *Sangewata naaz takhte Suleiman beshtar*
> *Khareywata naaz gooley rehan behtar*
> *Yusuf kidar Misr pad shaheemee kard*
> *Mee guft gadabudney Canaan kushtar.'*

The stones of our country are more precious
Than King Solomon's royal hearth;[*]
Foreign flowers pale in comparison,
Our thorny bushes steal the heart.
Spoke King Yousuf, his royal highness,
Sitting atop the Egyptian throne,
'Alas, it's better to be a beggar
In Canaan,'[†] he moaned.

I consoled him,

> *'Yusufey gum ghashtey bazayad ba Canaan*
> *Gam ma khur.*
> *Kulba yeIhjan shawodruji gulistan*
> *Gam ma khur.'*

Moan not, O lost Yousuf,
You will return to Canaan soon,

[*] Biblical prophet and once ruler of Egypt, recognised both in the Bible (Judaic and Christian) as well as the Koran.
[†] A historically Semitic speaking region that corresponds roughly with today's Israel, the Palestinian territories, Lebanon, and some western parts of Jordan and Syria.

This dry and trodden desert again
Will, as a flower garden, bloom.

This jousting in verse did not last long. When swimming you
needed to catch your breath after the first stretch; likewise we too
paused for a bit before attacking the food again. Every dish was
vanishing fast – Abdur Rahman had been trained by me to serve
small quantities in the first round – but why was not he bringing
more? I could not wait any more. I commanded him, 'Bring
more.'

Abdur Rahman was silent. I said again, 'Bring more.' He said
everything was finished. Maulana and I had become desperate at
the taste of blood. I said angrily, 'You should be taught a good
lesson. Go, bring your portion.' Abdur Rahman would not budge.
He finally said that he had served everything and he would only
have bread and cheese himself.

I was mad by then. I abused him relentlessly, calling him a
lunatic, a fool, an elephant and many other names. Maulana was
a gentle soul, and even he expressed his displeasure in polished
Farsi words. Abdur Rahman listened to us patiently. He did not
smile but there was no sense of hurt on his face either. I became
angrier and said, 'I made a mistake by employing you as my servant. It was better to have dry bread and salt.' The more I rebuked
him, the angrier I got. Finally I told him, 'Fine, you cook a massive
feast for my wake after I die – and then feed everyone you come
across.'

Then Abdur Rahman said, looking at Maulana, 'Wait for a
moment or two, your stomach will fill very soon.'

Maulana's face too became red with anger. The fat padres gave
such advice to hungry villagers – in the name of 'heaven' or something like that. As Abdur Rahman's stomach was empty, Maulana

stopped short of cursing him, touching his beard. I said, 'So many people died from bullets in this rebellion, why didn't—'

By then Abdur Rahman had left the room. You called this gratitude? We were ready to give him the king's throne a while ago but now we were ready to buy him a ticket to hell.

But Abdur Rahman surely was an astrologer. In two minutes our hunger was gone. In five minutes it was the peaceful reign of Queen Victoria – totally calm. Then started the revolution. What churning and bloated feeling in the stomach. I was turning and tossing and sweating profusely. It was the same experience for Maulana. He finally said, 'We ate too much.'

It was killing us. We could now imagine what would have happened if we ate a little more. 'Oh Abdur Rahman, please come here, my son.'

After entering the room Abdur Rahman said, 'I have traditional digestive salt. Want some?'

Digestive salt from such a clever man would certainly calm the revolution. I said, 'Please, my dear, please give us some.' We felt better after taking the salt. I blessed Abdur Rahman by saying, 'Be a police officer, my boy.' I deliberately did not say, 'Be a king' as we had seen with our own eyes what a problem it was to be a king in Afghanistan.

There was no end to the excitement. A uniformed figure followed Abdur Rahman into the room. A messenger from the British Legation. I felt bitter at his sight. I asked Maulana, 'See what it's all about?'

One memo. The gist was that two seats had been allocated for Maulana and I the next day on the aeroplane that would leave at ten in the morning. Maulana collapsed on the sofa in joy. Our condition was such that we could not give the messenger any tip.

How did we get seats? As our 'right' or a 'favour' from Sir Francis – we could not resolve that debate. Abdur Rahman understood the meaning – he left the room silently. Maulana was overjoyed. As he had brought his wife to Kabul soon after the wedding, she did not get the chance to meet his family properly. His beard had started to grey through worrying about how she was getting on with his family in this advanced stage of pregnancy.

I was no less happy. My parents surely were spending time worrying about me. Father read every line of *The Statesman* – from the masthead to the printer's line. The British Legation used to receive some Indian papers by plane. Maulana once managed to get hold of one copy and we understood that the reporter's imagination had far exceeded the reality while reporting the revolution and the situation of Kabul. Everything had been concocted from Peshawar with a bottle by his side. My father would have camped permanently at the post office for my letters if he had read that report.

Maulana lay down on the sofa with his eyes closed. One talked little when dreaming of the happy future.

The crying and wailing did not stop. Once in a while we could hear the wailing of the deceased colonel's mother. Abdur Rahman said the old woman could not be consoled. He was her only son.

There was no difference between one mother and another. The hero's mother cried in the same way as a peasant's mother.

I was about to doze off when I saw Abdur Rahman was sitting next to the bed holding on to the bedpost.

I asked, '*Chee bacha*?' (What, my boy?)

Abdur Rahman said, 'Take me with you to your country.'

'Are you mad? Why do you want to go to a foreign land? Don't you have a family? What about your parents and your wife?' But he would not listen to any logic. 'Why will they take you on the plane? Besides, there's the strict order from Bacha that no Afghan is allowed to leave Afghanistan. If they take any Afghans, Bacha will decapitate every British diplomat in Kabul. Do you know how many people are ready to pay thousands of rupees to get a seat on that plane?'

He had lost all sense; he said, he would plead with all touching their feet and manage a seat, if I agreed.

What a hassle. I said, 'Call Maulana from the other room.' Abdur Rahman would not leave. Stubbornly he said, 'Who is he to me?'

Again repeated pleading. Did that mean that he had not served me properly? Or would my parents get angry if I took him with me? Who would shoot a rifle in the air at my shadeeyana – wedding celebration?

Abdur Rahman could never talk cogently about anything except for Panjshir and snow. Additionally, he had never asked for anything from me, no favour either. It would be impossible to collate what he was saying that day while trying to plead with me. Each of his hurtful words was making such a deep impression on me that I was finding it difficult to say anything. Besides, what could I say? The whole proposition was so absurd – how could one try to convince him with logical words? Could one kill a ghost with a pistol?

When eventually I fell silent with sadness, pain and exhaustion, Abdur Rahman thought he had nearly convinced me. He started talking with doubled energy – all gibberish. Losing his thread he was saying the same thing fifty times. He would serve my parents so well that they would not turn him away. It would have served no purpose that day had I told him that my mother did not turn away anybody from her doors – let alone a poor Afghan.

What bad luck. It was my misfortune that I had once told him the story of Tagore's *Kabuliwala* in its Farsi translation. Drawing the example from that story, he said that if little Mini could love an unknown Kabuli then why would my nephews and nieces not love him?

'Okay, all agreed. But how will you go?'

'I will arrange that.'

It was like a small child demanding the impossible from his mother. He would refuse to listen to anything, would not accept any reason.

Abdur Rahman never entered into any argument with me. Finally, finding no other way, I had to tell him, 'Listen Abdur Rahman, you know how painful it is for me to leave you. You should not aggravate it any more. This is my final order to you; you stay here as long as you can. At the first opportunity you will go back home – to Panjshir.'

Abdur Rahman was startled, he said, 'Then Sahib will never come back to Kabul?'

The reader should be kind enough not to ask what I said that day.

FORTY-TWO

When I awoke the next morning, the first person I thought of was Abdur Rahman. He entered the room instantly, carrying bread, omelette, cheese and tea. Normally he left the room but that day he stood there looking at the carpet. What trouble!

Maulana came to say, 'The note said we could only carry ten pounds of luggage with us. What should I take and what should I leave behind?'

I said, 'You won't ever get back what you will leave here. I've asked Abdur Rahman to go to Panjshir. There will be no one to guard the house. It will all be looted in no time.'

'Can't we keep it with someone?'

I said, 'Anticipating this situation, I had checked with a few friends. But in this anarchy where looting is the order of the day, no one will want to take responsibility for the belongings of others. Even if someone agrees, the chances of robbery in his own house will be very high. The robbers will know which house to go to when we move our things there.'

I explained it so easily to Maulana but the same question came to my mind when I looked around my room. What should I take and what to leave behind?

There were two volumes of the Russian dictionary. They came from Moscow via train to Tashkent, then by motor car to Amu

Darya. After crossing the river by boat, they traversed the whole of northern Afghanistan on a mule, negotiating the ups and downs of the Hindu Kush before reaching Kabul. Together, they weighed six pounds.

I was no writer, so I did not have any manuscript – I was luckier than Maulana in that respect – but I had brought all the notes from Tagore's lectures in Shantiniketan, on Shelley and Keats, hoping I might be able to do something with them during the winter months. They also did not weigh little.

So many other dictionaries, grammar books, a copy of Tagore's *Purabi*, a gift from Minu, Vinod's paintings, photos and two Bukhara carpets for a friend. Their weight was no less than that of three bodies.

Clothes? To keep up with the dereshi madness of Kabul there were so many tailcoats, smoking and morning suits. I did not have any attachment to any of them but if I got the chance to go to Germany, where would I get money to get new suits made?

I had nearly forgotten about the pair of Chinese vases. Lime-coloured, and if you touched them with your eyes closed, you thought you were touching a real lime.

So many little things. They had no value to others in this world but for me they were more precious than Aladdin's lamp.

Socrates' disciples once took him to the biggest shop in the city. The shop stocked the most expensive luxury goods, art objects from Egypt and Babylon, bundles of papyrus and alchemy implements – everything. Socrates could not believe his eyes as he looked at every object in the shop and touched them. The disciples were overjoyed – their teacher always preached a frugal existence and self-restraint because he had never seen such luxuries in life. They were keen to hear what he would say after this experience. Plato was quite uneasy seeing his guru's dazed look.

After scrutinising everything in the shop, Socrates said sadly, 'Alas. The world is full of so many interesting objects but I don't need any one of them.'

Standing in the middle of the room I realised that there was only one difference between Socrates and myself – I needed everything in that room. The difference was little, ticket number 53786 had won the derby race and my ticket number was 53785. What was the difference?

I was born into a Muslim family – at the end of my life I would go to Gobra* and not Nimtala† – only if I could manage to come out in one piece from the current crisis in Kabul. I knew that I would not take anything with me on that final journey. But was that a good reason to leave everything behind in Kabul? Getting used to possessing nothing by practising? Was that the ploy of God?

I will not prove my stupidity by telling the readers how I managed to make a bundle of ten pounds. And it was literally a bundle wrapped in an old dhoti – luggage was different, when you packed things in a suitcase – no point taking a five-pound-suitcase when I was allowed to carry only ten. If I did, I would then be left only with the suitcase.

I had put on layers of garments – not one. The officials had also advised us to cover ourselves well or else we could freeze in high altitudes. I remembered Abdur Rahman's description of Maulana's wife's feet being wrapped in straw, like a bottle of vinegar.

Maulana had started early with one of his Punjabi friends. Abdur Rahman had lit the fire in the room for the last time. I was sitting

* Biggest Muslim burial ground in Calcutta.
† One of the Hindu crematoriums in Calcutta.

on a chair and Abdur Rahman on the floor near my feet. I said, 'Abdur Rahman, I have thrown my temper at you many times and completely unjustly. Please forgive me.'

Abdur Rahman took my hands and placed them on his eyes. They were wet.

I said, 'Please, Abdur Rahman, not that. And listen, everything here is for you.'

My readers may look at me in disbelief yet I would still say that I saw this line in Abdur Rahman's eyes when he looked at me—

*Yena hongnamrita sang, kim hong tena kuryang?**

What shall I do with that by which I shall not become immortal? Out on the road now. Abdur Rahman was by my side carrying the bundle. I tried to talk to him a few times. I realised that he preferred to keep quiet.

We crossed the Russian embassy. I would never forget the Demidovs. I prayed for the spirit of Bolshov.

After crossing the Kabul river we took the road to the Arg Fort. Most of the shops were closed – yet I saw from a distance that the shop of the Punjabi was still open. He was standing on the porch. I asked, 'Won't you leave?' He indicated by shaking his head, 'No.' Making a farewell gesture, he entered the shop with his head down. I knew that they could not go away leaving their businesses, as all would be looted in no time. Yet his mind had been so numbed that he did not have the will to talk to me for two moments.

Twenty paces ahead was Dost Muhammad's house. It was evident that the house had been looted. But nobody would shed a tear for

---

* A line in Sanskrit from an ancient Indian tale. When the learned holy man Yagyabalka wanted to embark on the quest for enlightenment leaving behind all his worldly possessions for his wife Maitrayee, she had uttered that line to him.

that as he was like Socrates. Being totally engrossed in high theories the way Socrates was oblivious of the world, Dost Muhammad had also shunned all worldly possessions in search of aesthetics, the unusual, the grotesque. Nothing could tempt him. Patanjali[*] too had said the same. He advised that in order to stay away from temptation one should meditate on God and other holy men who had themselves conquered temptation, but finally he said '*Yatha vimata dhyadwa*' – Resist temptation with every way you like. So meditation was at the core, the content of the meditation was secondary. Dost Muhammad's meditation was for aesthetics.

The girl's school was to the left further down the road. A few weeks ago the colonel's wife had been crying out loud, thinking about the safety of her husband. Who knew if he was alive? The wailing of my neighbour's mother – the dead colonel, the cries of the colonel's wife and many such cries were floating in the air. But why? Some poet had said:

> For men must work
> And women must weep.

There was no debate, no logic, no sense of right or wrong – a woman's job was to pay the price for the stupidity of men by weeping. And it was strange that it was men – as poets – had expressed this pain. I had heard that poet-mothers had declared a war against wars with their tears five thousand years ago – on the mural scriptures of Babylon.

There was a small homestead next to the school building. The women dancers and singers who came from Lucknow in North

---

* Ancient Indian thinker between 200 and 150 BC; he compiled the *Yoga Sutras* or the aphorisms of yoga practices.

India for the wedding celebration of Amanullah's sister had been housed in this building. Some of us had gone there to look after them. They were overjoyed to talk in their own language in this foreign land. They knew that one could not get paan in Kabul, so they brought truckloads of it. They had shared it with us very generously. With that paan from Lucknow, zarda from Benaras and fine areca nut paste – my tongue had become so lucid that I impressed everyone by throwing classical Urdu in all directions.

Kabul had no tradition of classical music. They did not accept the Iranian school. The few Kabuli classical singers had been trained in the United Province[*] in India. So there was a fear that there would be only a few present in the soirees to appreciate the music. We had repeated requests to attend the concerts. We sat in the front row and showed our deep appreciation of the music by swaying our heads to the beat of the music.

When I returned home after I had had the last paan and spat out the red juice, Abdur Rahman nearly fainted. The red juice of the betel nut was unknown in Kabul but not tuberculosis.

We passed by the education ministry building. Dost Muhammad could not stand the minister, His Excellency Fayez Muhammad Khan. But I somehow liked him. A simple man and a gentle soul. His education was no less than that of others, but that was not enough to be the education minister. After becoming king, when Bacha was torturing the ministers to extract the hidden stash of cash, he gave him a reprieve saying, 'You can go, you never even took bribes.' It was possible to take bribes in the education ministry too. One could even make some extra bucks doing the job of counting waves – of course it had to be a government job.

---

[*] Now the state of Uttar Pradesh.

There was a personal reason for me to like the education minister. I would ask the reader's indulgence and narrate it here. The aeroplane could wait awhile.

People make progress in their careers either through their merit, or by the grace of God. If God helped the people with merit then there was no chance for fools in this world. Possibly I had God's mercy because the education minister took a special interest in me. Within a year he had increased my salary by one hundred rupees and promoted me to the highest position among all Indian teachers.

The Punjabi teachers were unhappy with that and told him in a deputation, 'Syed Mujtaba Ali's degree is from Shantiniketan and Shantiniketan is not a recognised university in India.'

True. But the minister apparently took the wind out of their sails – I heard so from someone. The minister had said, 'Your certificates carry the signatures of the governor of Punjab. In our small country we have no dearth of governors. But Agha Mujtaba Ali's certificate has been signed by *mashoor shayar* – the famous poet – Rabindranath Tagore. He has made the entire Orient proud in front of the world – *chasm roshan kaarde ast*.'

The minister wanted to bring Tagore to Kabul. But he feared that the poet may not be able to withstand the two hundred-mile journey by car. It would be a great loss to the world if the poet became incapacitated during that journey. Kabul wanted to see the poet but he did not want to be responsible for such a catastrophe. I used to tell him, 'No worries, the poet is six-foot-three. His body is strong and so are his bones.'

Taking the name of Allah he finally took the plunge. But that summer Amanullah went to Europe and in the winter Bacha arrived.

Enough.

To the left was Moin-us-Sultana's house, the tennis court slightly ahead. The tennis ball of fate was now in Moin-us-Sultana's hand. Kabul and Kandahar were playing with him.

There was the Maktab-e-Habibia. In their first attack Bacha's men had burned the tables, chairs, books and maps of this school. Who knew when the school would open again? I taught here. I skated on the frozen pond with the boys during winter. Under its trees I ate grapes sitting with the grape-vendors. I had heard so many theories from Mir Aslam in this school.

Kabul was like the eclipsed moon with hardly a pedestrian on the streets. The closed doors of the Habibia School reflected the state of Afghanistan. Afghanistan had closed its doors after shunning education, the rule of law and peace, a civilised existence and culture.

Leaving the city limits we came down upon the fields. The aerodrome was not very far from here. No sane man should feel sad to leave this dangerous and chaotic place. Possibly this was the reason the few people with whom I bonded here seemed like my closest relatives. Each one of them had occupied my heart. The very thought of leaving all of them seemed like someone was dividing my whole existence into two.

The plane arrived. They weighed our bundles ceremoniously. Some people looked struck by lightning when their bundles exceeded ten pounds. It was hard to imagine their emotions when asked to leave behind still more of their possessions. One broke down in tears.

At the aerodrome I got proof that people sometimes became blind when surrounded by plenty. Someone had included a mirror within that little allowance of luggage! I took a good look at the man. He did not look like the most handsome Apollo. It was not a lie that one took the broom with him while running out from a house on fire.

But my Abdur Rahman, what was that? You brought my tennis racquet? Abdur Rahman muttered something. I understood he had assumed that the racquet was my most valuable possession because I never allowed him to touch it. Abdur Rahman was like the drivers of our land – they believed that screws had to be tightened in such a way that they could never be loosened. After failing to make him understand the meaning of the world 'optimum' I had given him the strict order that he was not to touch my tennis press.

So Abdur Rahman thought that his master was going to take it home.

Sir Francis was there ahead of me. Since he was older than me, and also because he was facing me, I gave him the smallest of nods. He came forward and, extending his hand, he said, 'Good morning, I wish you a pleasant journey.'

I thanked him.

He said, 'I tried my best to help the Indians here. After going back, I hope you'll tell everyone how much I tried.'

I said, 'Sure I'll tell them everything.'

I could not make out if he was indeed that stupid or just a true diplomat.

In Afghanistan one said, when bidding farewell, '*Ba aman-e Khuda*' (Leaving you in God's protection). One who was not going would say, '*Ba Khuda sapurdamet*' (Giving you over to God's hands).

Abdur Rahman kissed my hands again and again. I told him, '*Ba aman-e Khuda*, Abdur Rahman,' like a hymn, Abdur Rahman kept repeating, '*Ba Khuda sapurdamet, Sahib, ba Khuda sapurdamet, Sahib.*'

I suddenly heard Sir Francis saying, 'He who carries his tennis racquet in this crisis, is a true sportsman.'

One official of the legation said, 'It was chucked out because it exceeded the ten pound limit.'

Sir Francis said, 'Put it back in.'

Without this gesture of generosity even the scavenger birds would not have touched the English.

Abdur Rahman was now shouting, '*Ba Khuda sapurdamet, Sahib, ba Khuda sapurdamet, Sahib*.' The propeller was making a loud noise.

Sitting inside the plane I could still hear Abdur Rahman's shouts. Abdur Rahman was scared of planes. So he was repeatedly saying that he was putting me in the hands of God.

The plane started to move. I heard his last word, '*Sapurdamet*.' In Kabul my first acquaintance with an Afghan happened through Abdur Rahman. The same Abdur Rahman bid me farewell on the last day.

In festivity, in celebration, in famine, in revolution and if I considered the last farewell as the funeral, then Abdur Rahman joined me at my funeral too. Abdur Rahman passed all the tests of friendship as coded by Chanakya. Who could I call a friend if not him?

Friend Abdur Rahman, God's mercy be upon you.

Maulana said, 'Look out of the window' and then he moved away to give me the window seat.

I saw white snow covering the horizon. Standing in the middle of the airfield was a figure who could only have been Abdur Rahman, bidding goodbye to me by waving the tail of his turban.

His turban was dirty, as we did not have any soap for such a long time. But I felt Abdur Rahman's turban was whiter than the snow and whitest of all was Abdur Rahman's heart.

Epilogue

Amanullah had to leave Afghanistan after he failed to regain his throne. The king of Italy offered him asylum. Moin-us-Sultana took refuge in Iran.

Nadir Shah was the general who fought the British for Amanullah during the war of independence. He was in France during the rebellion. He later returned to Peshawar. With financial assistance from the Indian traders and businessmen and through his valour, he became the king after taking over Kabul. Bacha was first bayoneted to death and then his body was strung from the gallows.

I gathered all this information from newspapers.

After returning home, I found out that our relative and a member of the Central Legislative Assembly, the late Maulvi Abdul Matin Choudhury, had thrown such a tantrum that the government had ordered (or requested) Sir Francis for my repatriation.

Soon after I left, the British Legation too was wound up and moved to India leaving behind many hapless Indians.

For showing this 'bravery' Sir Francis was showered with many honours, promoted and sent to Iraq.

Maulana Ziauddin took up a teaching job at Shantiniketan after returning home. He published many well-researched articles (one of the most significant publications was the translation of an ancient grammar in Braj language into Farsi) and many superlative translations of Gurudev's poems into Farsi.

Sadly he passed away at a young age. At his memorial at Shantiniketan, the eulogy read out by Gurudev, as the Chancellor, was published in the *Probashi* magazine. The transcript was included in the fourteenth volume of Tagore collections. With permission from Visva-Bharati University, I found it appropriate to include this poem entitled 'Maulana Ziauddin'—

> In your leisurely times you came
> And stood nearby, as I
> Used to greet you with 'Hey, there!'
> And 'Have a seat!' with a smile.
> One or two simple thoughts exchanged,
> Some homely queries placed—
> Our heartiest feelings we held within
> While jokes were interlaced.
> How deep they were and closely knit
> With love—our words unsaid;
> Now, when you're gone, I understand
> Forever, evermore!
> A trivial daily thought of yours
> which made you come and go,
> Losing such, can cause so much
> Of loss—today I know.
> Goods of accomplishments and
> Collected life-pursuits
> The ship you sailed with all-o'-it stacked
> Through mid-day breezy routes,
> Whatever it has, it's not of worth

So much that it can buy
In exchange your memories of

Your daily passing by—
Countless times, as I recall
I feel sheer disgust
Are they really valued somewhere,
Who are unknown to us?
Where could I find some words so simply
Sharp as well as knife,
Which can yield a matching pain
As this ignorance cites.
Someone's known as poet or warrior,
Someone's known as rich—
Someone's a friend to common man,
Someone's close to chief—
You may reply to your friends with grace
And kindness in return
It would always overweigh
The fame in life you earn.
As the lilies live and spread the joy
Of monsoon rains and rhyme
And they die their desired death
At their end of time—
Among the skies and blowing winds,
Also around ourselves
They spread the scent of bereavement
And there it still remains.

(*Nabajtak*)
Tamam Shud—The End

Acknowledgements

First of all I would like to thank the sons of Syed Mujtaba Ali, Syed Musharraf Ali and Syed Zaghlul Ali for giving the permission to publish this translation.

Ravi Singh did not hesitate to take it up after he read the manuscript. I will always be grateful to him. I wish him well in his new venture, Speaking Tiger.

I extend my heartiest gratitude to Nancy Hatch Dupree who very kindly wrote the wonderful preface in spite of her busy schedule of running the Afghanistan Centre in Kabul University and her own writings.

Jolyon Lesley, Shirazuddin Siddiqi, Marielle Morin, Ankita Khare, Ratna Mathur, Heela Najibullah and Thomas Wide helped me immensely by reading the early versions of the manuscript and giving me feedback. I am indebted to them.

I need to thank Sridarshini Chakraborty, Sudipto Chatterjee and Proshot Kalami for helping me with the translation of some of the poems and verses. Thanks to Tista Bagchi for translating a couple of lines in Sanskrit.

I am thankful to close friends like Waheed Mirza, Sam Miller, Behrouz Afagh, Hamid Ismailov and Jayalakshmi Chatterjee who encouraged me while I was working on the manuscript.

Special thanks to Mandira Sen for connecting me with Jerry Pinto who subsequently passed the manuscript onto Ravi. Thanks to Jerry too.

It was a most pleasant experience working with Renuka Chatterjee who edited the book and did a fine job.

It always feels good when your family gets involved in your work. I was really glad that my son Aarjan did the initial round of copy-editing with diligence soon after I finished the first draft of the manuscript.